P9-CML-895

Technologies for Education

BENEDICTINE UNIVERSITY LIBRARY
IN THE KINDLON HALL OF LEARNING
5700 COLLEGE ROAD
LISLE, IL 60532-0900

WITHDRAWN

Technologies for Education

A Practical Guide

Fourth Edition

Ann E. Barron, Gary W. Orwig,
Karen Ivers, and Nick Lilavois

2002

Libraries Unlimited
A Division of Greenwood Publishing Group, Inc.
Greenwood Village, Colorado

LB
1028.3
.B37
2001

Copyright © 2002 Libraries Unlimited
All Rights Reserved
Printed in the United States of America

No part of this publication may be reproduced, stored in a retrieval system, or transmitted, in any form or by any means, electronic, mechanical, photocopying, recording, or otherwise, without the prior written permission of the publisher.

LIBRARIES UNLIMITED
A Division of Greenwood Publishing Group, Inc.
7730 East Belleview Avenue, Suite A200
Greenwood Village, CO 80111
1-800-225-5800
www.lu.com

Library of Congress Cataloging-in-Publication Data

Technologies for education : a practical guide / Ann E. Barron ... [et al.].--4th ed.
    p. cm.
  Rev. ed. of: New technologies for education / Ann E. Barron, Gary W. Orwig. 3rd ed. 1997.
  Includes bibliographical references and index.
  ISBN 1-56308-779-0 (pbk.)
    1. Educational technology--United States. 2. Teaching--Aids and devices. I. Barron,
Ann E. II. Barron, Ann E. New technologies for education.

LB1028.3 .B37 2002
371.33--dc21
                                                            2001050746

CONTENTS

1
TEACHING WITH TECHNOLOGY

2
COMPUTER GRAPHICS

3
ADVANCED COMPUTER GRAPHICS
Animation, 3D Graphics, and Virtual Reality

4
DIGITAL AUDIO

5
DIGITAL VIDEO

6
LOCAL AREA NETWORKS

7
TELECOMMUNICATIONS

7
TELECOMMUNICATIONS
(*continued*)

8
DISTANCE LEARNING

9
ASSISTIVE TECHNOLOGIES IN THE CLASSROOM
Julie A. Barron and Christine M. Hackert

9
ASSISTIVE TECHNOLOGIES IN THE CLASSROOM
(*continued*)

PREFACE

Technologies for Education: A Practical Guide (fourth edition) offers an updated look at the technologies that are impacting education, including the web, wireless networks, desktop video production, virtual reality, and distance learning. Designed for educators who are interested in the instructional applications of technology, this book provides information about current technology standards for students and teachers, as well as research related to the effectiveness of technology in education. It also presents an overview of computer graphics, digital audio, digital video, local area networks, telecommunications, distance learning, and assistive technologies. Each chapter includes a scenario to illustrate implementation techniques, a list of educational applications related to the technology, detailed graphics, and generous glossaries and resources.

Technologies for Education is for all educators who are interested in bridging the technology gap. By *educators* we mean teachers, trainers, school library media specialists, and educational administrators. This book is intended as an introduction to educational technologies for those working in the teaching profession, as well as for those planning a career in education or training.

ORGANIZATION AND USE

Technologies for Education can be used as a resource book, a guide for in-service education, or a textbook. As a resource, this book contains a wealth of information. Each chapter begins with a "real-life" scenario that shows the implementation of technology in an educational setting. A list of topics provides an outline of the chapter's contents. Detailed graphics throughout the book provide configurations and illustrations of hardware, software, and the like. In addition, each chapter contains contact information for software and hardware vendors, up-to-date reference materials, and easy-to-understand glossaries. A detailed index for the entire book provides easy access to specific topics and information.

This book can also help in conjunction with preservice or in-service training for a wide variety of technologies. To facilitate workshops, each chapter was written to be independent of the others, although relevant topics are cross-referenced. Resources and terminology specific to each technology are provided at the end of each chapter and can be incorporated into teacher workshops.

As a textbook, *Technologies for Education* is appropriate for multimedia and technology courses at the undergraduate and graduate levels. Throughout the book, emphasis is placed on the educational applications of technology. In addition, the advantages and disadvantages for each technology are discussed to provide relevant examples for teacher training.

ACKNOWLEDGMENTS

Special thanks are extended to Nick Lilavois and Ted Newman for the graphics in this book. For additional information on Nick Lilavois, please see http://www.lilavois.com/nick/ and http://www.magentastudios.org.

1

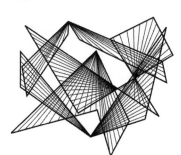

TEACHING
WITH
TECHNOLOGY

A Scenario

Elena and Phoebe sat anxiously at their computer while their teacher, Ms. Tassy, reminded them of the requirements for their assignment—a multimedia project about an animal of their choice. Ms. Tassy and the students had previously discussed the criteria and designed a rubric for the finished projects. They also viewed projects that had been made the previous year and stored on compact discs.

To begin the projects, the students compiled a list of reference sources and constructed storyboards and flowcharts. As the students worked, Ms. Tassy sat at her desk where she had access to all of the students' computers; through the network, she was able to monitor their work, provide individual assistance, and send specific instructions. As she monitored the students, Ms. Tassy noted that Toby and Natasha were scanning photographs of their household cats; Thompson and Samantha were videoconferencing with the city's zookeeper; Jewel and Leticia were capturing animal sounds from a CD-ROM; and Elena and Phoebe were conducting filtered Internet searches. Don, one of Ms. Tassy's homebound students, shared access to Zackary's computer workstation. They were working together to search the Internet and learn more about kangaroos for their project.

This was a typical day for Ms. Tassy's class. Her students were quite adept at using computers in the classroom for research, creativity, and communication. Many of the students also had cell phones—to keep in touch with their parents and access their e-mail. Although the phones allowed them to access the web, download homework, and complete interactive lessons, the children used them primarily to keep up with their friends. "The tools may change," Ms. Tassy thought, "but kids will be kids."

INTRODUCTION

Wireless networks, personal digital assistants (PDAs), and cell phones with Internet access—our social and professional lives are inundated with technology. In this chapter, we examine the trends of using technology in schools and outline the benefits that technology can offer education. Technology standards for students and teachers are also presented. Topics of the chapter include

- Trends in technology
- Benefits of technology in education
- Technology standards and professional development
- Suggestions for implementing technology in schools
- Resources for further information

TRENDS IN TECHNOLOGY

Technologies for Education: A Practical Guide investigates the advantages, disadvantages, and educational applications of several different technologies that fall within the domains of multimedia instruction and networks. *Multimedia instruction* can be loosely defined as educational programs integrating some, but not necessarily all, the following media in an interactive environment controlled by a computer: text, graphics, animation, sound, and video. Multimedia programs provide students opportunities to navigate, interact, create, and communicate. *Networks* consist of computers and other devices that are connected by cables, telephone systems, satellites, radio waves, or other means to supply enhanced communication and research capabilities.

Technology is evolving at a rapid pace, fueled by faster, smaller, more powerful, and less expensive components that are easier to use. Laptop computers with built-in DVD drives, modems, and wireless network capabilities are more powerful and less expensive than the mainframe computers of just a few years ago. The integration of television, telephone, and computer technologies is also changing the way we live. Telephone "operators" are often voice-recognition systems; through computers and the Internet, you can see and hear someone in another country; and, in some places, it is possible to touch the television screen to order a movie or interact with a computer program that is transmitted to your house via cable or satellite.

As cellular technology becomes more pervasive, phones are turning into personal digital assistants with access to e-mail, calendars, and other features. As Laura Lindhe of CNET (The Computer Network) predicted, "In the near future, your phone will be a multifunctional device—you'll be able to videoconference, play games, browse the web, and listen to music. In 10 years, the phone will be as small as a watch and you'll just use headphones to attach to it." ("Trends and Predictions," 1999, 75).

Although computers and other technologies have become basic tools in our society, it has been difficult for our educational system to keep pace with advances in multimedia and information access. Many of our schools have changed little, and many teachers continue to use the same strategy (lectures) and technique (writing on a large board) as educators in the 1920s.

Fortunately, some bright spots are on the horizon. Recent reports show that access to computers, the Internet, and other technologies is improving for schools. In the fall of 2000, approximately 98 percent of public schools had Internet access (U.S. Department of Education 2001). Seventy-seven percent of classrooms (including computer labs, school libraries, and media centers) had Internet access in 2000, compared to only 64 percent in 1999 (U.S. Department of Education 2001). The U.S. Department of Education also reports that about one in every seven students now has access to a multimedia computer or a computer with Internet access, compared to one in every thirteen students in 1999.

The government continues to show increased interest and commitment to national education standards, technology, and access for schools to the National Information Infrastructure (NII). For example, the Universal Service Fund for Schools and Libraries, most commonly known as the *E-rate*, was established by the Federal Communications Commission in 1996 to give all public and private schools and libraries access to affordable telecommunications and advanced technologies. The Federal government has also supplied billions of dollars to schools in the past few years through grant programs such as the Technology Literacy Challenge Funds, Technology Innovative Challenge Grants, Stars School Program, and the Preparing Tomorrow's Teachers to Use Technology Program (Web-Based Education Commission 2000).

State governments are showing their support as well. In California, Digital High School grants are available to schools serving students in grades 9–12. These grants are designed to help schools install and support technology, as well as provide staff training. Visit http://www.ed.gov/Technology/edgrants .html for more information on federal and state grants.

Education organizations, business leaders, and community members are also taking steps to ensure that our students have access to technology. For example, NetDay, a national volunteer effort to wire schools to the Internet, began in 1996. Since then, more than 500,000 volunteers have helped to wire more than 75,000 classrooms across the country (NetDay National Organization 2001). Visit http://www.netday.org to learn how to get your school involved. Thanks to this and other national, state, and local initiatives, technology is no longer seen as an "add-on" to education. It has become an integral and viable part of learning for today's students.

BENEFITS OF TECHNOLOGY IN EDUCATION

Information is becoming more accessible and transmittable. Important skills for students include the ability to use technology to access, analyze, filter, and organize multidimensional information sources; however, integrating technology into education can be challenging, frustrating, time-consuming, and expensive. A common question often surfaces: "Is it worth it?" Indeed, Brunner and McMillan (1994) stated that "if we had a nickel for every reporter who called us at the Center for Children and Technology to ask us if our research proves that technology raises test scores, we wouldn't have to apply for any more government grants" (22).

Archer (1998) notes that studies indicating that technology can improve student achievement are difficult to replicate because researchers are wary of presuming that the same results will exist in other classrooms where teachers might be less motivated or knowledgeable about computers. He reports that technology can have positive benefits, but they depend on how the technology is used. In some cases, computers seem to do more harm than good, highlighting the need for effective teacher preparation in the use of computers in instruction.

Reporters, parents, and teachers may be disappointed when they find that measuring the effectiveness of new technologies in education is often more complicated than giving standardized tests. Many of the multimedia programs are designed in an open-ended, constructivist format, and their assessment through multiple-choice tests does not supply adequate answers about their effectiveness. Also, many of the new networking technologies have not been fully analyzed. The number of variables in the integration of multimedia and educational networks complicates the research process; however, the following benefits have been published.

Instructional Effectiveness

One benefit of multimedia instruction can be an increase in student achievement. The *Report on the Effectiveness of Technology in Schools: 2000* detailed the results of several empirical research studies that found significant positive effects on student achievement (Sivin-Kachala and Bialo 2000). The research included findings in the areas of reading, writing, mathematics, science, and programming languages. The results of Liao's (1999) meta-analysis of hypermedia studies published between 1986 and 1998 also support the use of multimedia for increasing students' academic achievement. Schacter (1999) analyzed the five largest-scale studies of educational technology to date. In more than 700 empirical research studies, he found that students with access to at least one of the following showed positive gains in achievement on researcher-constructed, standardized, and national tests (9):

- Computer assisted instruction
- Integrated learning systems technology
- Simulations and software that teaches higher order thinking
- Collaborative networked technologies
- Design and programming technologies

Studies also show that at-risk students and students with special needs benefit from using interactive, multimedia software (Daley 1999; Pratt 1999). Bagui (1998) explains that "multimedia may make it easier for people to learn because of the parallels between multimedia and the 'natural' way people learn" (4).

Active Learning

Interactive technologies supply stimulating environments that encourage student involvement in the learning process. For example, instead of reading about Martin Luther King Jr. in a book, students can hear his speeches, witness his marches, and analyze documents about civil rights through multimedia. History can become more meaningful and relevant. In *Multimedia Projects for Education*, Ivers and Barron (1998) cite numerous studies that support the advantages of using multimedia to help students construct knowledge and work cooperatively.

Interactive technologies aid teachers with creating new learning environments. The International Society for Technology in Education (ISTE) notes, "[T]eachers must be prepared to empower students with the advantages technology can bring" (3). ISTE emphasizes the need to create learning environments that blend new strategies. These new learning environments are linked with strategies that promote student involvement and active learning in the educational process (see Table 1.1).

Table 1.1. Incorporating New Strategies

Traditional Learning Environments	New Learning Environments
Teacher-centered instruction	Student-centered learning
Single-sense stimulation	Multisensory stimulation
Single-path progression	Multipath progression
Single media	Multimedia
Isolated work	Collaborative work
Information delivery	Information exchange
Passive learning	Active/exploratory/inquiry-based learning
Factual, knowledge-based learning	Critical thinking and informed decision-making
Reactive response	Proactive/planned action
Isolated, artificial context	Authentic, real-world context

Apple Classrooms of Tomorrow (ACOT)—a long-term research project sponsored by Apple Computer, the National Science Foundation, and the National Alliance for Restructuring Education—revealed that students actively using technology benefited in many ways. For example, the students had a "higher degree of social awareness and self-confidence; they [were] more independent and [had] more positive attitudes about learning and themselves; they [were] able to experiment and problem solve with greater ease; they [saw] themselves as collaborators and experts; and they [had] a positive orientation about the future" (Apple Computer 1991, 3). Apple K–12 effectiveness reports continue to reveal that active learning through computers helps elementary students (of all ability levels) learn, increase their logical thinking and problem-solving skills, and show greater achievement on standardized tests (ACOT 1999).

Critical Thinking

The structure and use of technology can promote higher-level thinking skills (Barron and Ivers 1998; Ivers and Barron 1998; Jonassen 2000; Vockell and Van Deusen 1989). Some programs are designed to encourage problem-solving skills (examples include Adventures of Jasper Woodbury by Optical Data School Media; Dr. Brain series and Math for the Real World by Knowledge Adventure; The Factory Deluxe, Puzzle Tanks, How the West Was One + Three x Four, and The Hot Dog Stand by Sunburst Communications; and MicroWorlds Logo by Logo Computer Systems). Using technology such as hypermedia and telecommunications also affects thinking skills. For example, one of the most highly rated incentives for using telecommunications with students includes increasing students' inquiry and analytical skills (Honey and Henriquez 1993). These skills are imperative when teaching media literacy (Quesada and Summers 1998; Schrock 1998/99).

Individualization

Students learn and develop in different ways at varying rates. Technology offers students diversity, self-paced learning, and opportunities for individual growth and self-expression. It provides them with unique opportunities to apply skills and talents they might not otherwise be able to express and to interact with others in nonthreatening environments ("Turning Points 2000," 2000).

A dramatic shift from whole-class instruction to small-group and individual instruction has been documented with the integration of technology. When computers are introduced into the curriculum, teacher-led (lecture) activities decrease, and teachers are more likely to emphasize individualized and cooperative learning techniques. They also give students greater choice in their tasks, materials, and resources (Sivin-Kachala and Bialo 2000).

Motivation

Motivating students is a constant challenge. Technology can inspire students (and teachers) by making learning exciting and relevant. Researchers often find that when students are using technology, they are more successful, more motivated to learn, and have increased self-confidence and self-esteem (Sivin-Kachala and Bialo 2000; Wishart 2000). Liu, Macmillian, and Timmons (1998) note that students perceive using computers as having a positive effect on their learning. In the Apple Classrooms of Tomorrow study in Columbus, Ohio, the average rate of student absenteeism was cut nearly in half among the 216 students who took part in a technology-enriched environment (Dwyer 1994). In a statewide study by Barron, Hogarty, Kromrey, and Lenkway (1999), Florida schools that reported consistent, increased use of computers in instruction witnessed fewer conduct violations, such as theft, vandalism, fighting, and harassment.

Flexibility for Students with Special Needs

Technology offers many advantages for students with special needs. Modified presentation strategies have been effective for students with disabilities, and adaptive devices are available to supply alternate inputs and outputs for assistive needs (Milone 1997; Pratt 1999). Studies have found that students with special needs also perceive computer-based instruction as less threatening (Sivin-Kachala and Bialo 2000; "Turning Points 2000," 2000).

Technology enables students with disabilities to communicate with others and to express themselves in writing. Technologies such as voice recognition, text-to-speech synthesis, and adaptive hardware and software are providing means for all students to reach their potential. "More and more success stories are pouring in about how technology, combined with effective practice, can help students with disabilities overcome barriers to their success" (Zorfass, Corley, and Remz 1994, 62). The ABLEDATA database, sponsored by the National Institute on Disability and Rehabilitation Research (http://www.abledata.com), and the Alliance for Technology Access (http://www.ataccess.org/) provide extensive listings of assistive technology resources.

Cooperative Learning

Well-structured cooperative-learning activities can foster "the development of leadership abilities, a sense of teamwork, and improved self-esteem" (Strommen 1995, 27). By introducing technology into the educational environment, teachers can increase teacher-student interactions and promote learning that is more student-centered and cooperative ("Interactive Educational Systems Design,"

2000). Xin (1999) reports that students with and without disabilities perform better in cooperative learning groups that involve technology. Technology can be used to enhance and encourage cooperative learning in our schools through small groups using a single computer, network-based instructional programs (such as The Other Side by Tom Snyder Productions), or collaborative projects on the Internet. Cooperative groups are also recommended for developing multimedia projects (Ivers and Barron 1998).

Experts caution, however, that just because students are sharing a computer does not mean that cooperative learning is taking place. The success of cooperative groups depends on a group goal, individual and group accountability, and positive interdependence. David Dockterman of Tom Snyder Productions offers these guidelines for implementing cooperative-learning activities:

- Students should be cooperating, not just taking turns.

- The content of the collaboration should be about the content you want to teach.

- The software is structured to promote interaction (Dockterman 1995, 33).

Communication Skills

Communication skills can be enhanced by using technology in small groups and by integrating telecommunications into the curriculum. Research reviews show that networks can affect learning indirectly by providing unique opportunities for students to practice, demonstrate, and critique communication skills (Drumm and Groom 1999; Ingram, Hathorn, and Evans 2000; Reed 1996; Trollinger and Slavkin 1999). In addition, the Internet greatly extends the audience for student publishing (D'Ignazio 1997), as well as provides a stronger communication link between the home and school (Carter 1999).

Multisensory Delivery

One benefit of multimedia instruction is that it supplies information through multiple sensory channels, allowing students with various learning styles to assimilate and apply the knowledge (Holzberg 1994). Research in learning styles shows that some students learn better through specific modalities such as audio, visual, or kinesthetic (Doolan and Honigsfeld 2000; Shaughnessy 1998; Stahl 1999). In other words, one student may be an audio learner and benefit most when instruction is delivered through sound and narration; another student may be a visual learner and benefit most when information is conveyed through pictures and text.

Gardner (1999) identifies eight intelligences (linguistic, logical-mathematical, spatial, bodily-kinesthetic, musical, interpersonal, intrapersonal, and naturalist) noting that learners can develop each intelligence to an adequate level of competency, though they may appear stronger in some areas than in others. Using and developing multimedia applications provide students with a multimodal approach to learning, allowing them to develop and enhance specific intelligences.

Multicultural Education

Telecommunications make it possible to expand classroom "walls" and link students and teachers in national and international exchanges. These interactions enable students from vastly different backgrounds to build cultural bridges by looking at common problems from different perspectives. Students in distant countries such as Russia, Iceland, China, and the United States can communicate daily about lifestyles, politics, science, and global issues (Barron and Ivers 1998). The

Internet and other technologies provide second-language learners opportunities to engage in discussions, collaborative projects, and interactive activities that reinforce language acquisition (Burns 1996).

Although it is certainly possible for these students to exchange letters with regular mail service, feedback through computer networks is generally more meaningful because it is fast and the students can remain focused on the ideas, projects, and interchanges. In addition, the cost of communicating is minimal compared to international postal rates or telephone charges. "Indeed, never before could teams of students, thousands of miles apart, engage in a dialogue through which they jointly construct a model of their respective economics, cultural surroundings, or ecologies, and then collaboratively test its implications" (Salomon 1991, 43).

Technology is not the determining factor in effective education. The important issue is what is done with the technology; the instructional methods must be based on sound learning principles (Clark 1989). Evidence also shows that the teacher is a critical variable in the effectiveness of computers (Collis 1989; Hannafin 1999). In *Technology and the New Professional Teacher: Preparing for the 21st Century Classroom*, the National Council for Accreditation of Teacher Education states, "[c]lassroom teachers hold the key to the effective use of technology to improve learning. But if teachers don't understand how to employ technology effectively to promote student learning, the billions of dollars invested in educational technology initiatives will be wasted" (1997, 1). As technology advances, we must learn to use it wisely to motivate, instruct, and challenge students. Unfortunately, "the computer can be misused as easily as it can be powerfully applied" (Rockman 1992, 15).

TECHNOLOGY STANDARDS

To help educators and students better use technology for instruction, more state professional standards boards and accreditation agencies are establishing technology-related requirements for teacher licensure and certification (Dewert 1999). Also, professional organizations are taking steps to ensure both students and teachers meet designated technology outcomes. For example, the International Society for Technology in Education (ISTE) has developed national technology competencies for teachers and students. As a result, the National Council for Accreditation of Teacher Education (NCATE) and other leading educational organizations now require teachers to demonstrate technology competence *before* they can receive their preliminary teaching credential. The next sections discuss technology standards for teachers and students.

Standards for Teachers

Researchers continue to report that there is a tremendous lack of technological proficiency among educators, and that the need and desire for educational technology development is great (ISTE 1999; NCES 1999; OTA 1995; Willis, Thompson, and Sadera 1999). In response, the *National Educational Technology Standards for Teachers* (NETS), published by ISTE, lists standards and performance indicators for assessing teachers' ability to integrate technology into their classrooms (see Table 1.2). NCATE and other accreditation agencies refer to these standards.

Table 1.2. ISTE Technology Standards and Performance Indicators for Teachers

I. Technology Operations and Concepts *Teachers demonstrate a sound understanding of technology operations and concepts. Teachers:* A. demonstrate introductory knowledge, skills, and understanding of concepts related to technology (as described in the ISTE National Educational Technology Standards for Students). B. demonstrate continual growth in technology knowledge and skills to stay abreast of current and emerging technologies.	**II. Planning and Designing Learning Environments and Experiences** *Teachers plan and design effective learning environments and experiences supported by technology. Teachers:* A. design developmentally appropriate learning opportunities that apply technology-enhanced instructional strategies to support the diverse needs of learners. B. apply current research on teaching and learning with technology when planning learning environments and experiences. C. identify and locate technology resources and evaluate them for accuracy and suitability. D. plan for the management of technology resources within the context of learning activities. E. plan strategies to manage student learning in a technology-enhanced environment.
III. Teaching, Learning, and Curriculum *Teachers implement curriculum plans that include methods and strategies for applying technology to maximize student learning. Teachers:* A. facilitate technology-enhanced experiences that address content standards and student technology standards. B. use technology to support learner-centered strategies that address the diverse needs of students. C. apply technology to develop students' higher-order skills and creativity. D. manage student learning activities in a technology-enhanced environment.	**IV. Assessment and Evaluation** *Teachers apply technology to facilitate a variety of effective assessment and evaluation strategies. Teachers:* A. apply technology in assessing student learning of subject matter using a variety of assessment techniques. B. use technology resources to collect and analyze data, interpret results, and communicate findings to improve instructional practice and maximize student learning. C. apply multiple methods of evaluation to determine students' appropriate use of technology resources for learning, communication, and productivity.

(Table 1.2 continues on page 10.)

Table 1.2—*Continued*

V. Productivity and Professional Practice	VI. Social, Ethical, Legal, and Human Issues
Teachers use technology to enhance their productivity and professional practice. Teachers:	*Teachers understand the social, ethical, legal, and human issues surrounding the use of technology in PK–12 schools and apply that understanding in practice. Teachers:*
A. use technology resources to engage in ongoing professional development and lifelong learning.	A. model and teach legal and ethical practice related to technology use.
B. continually evaluate and reflect on professional practice to make informed decisions regarding the use of technology in support of student learning.	B. mapply technology resources to enable and empower learners with diverse backgrounds, characteristics, and abilities.
C. apply technology to increase productivity.	C. identify and use technology resources that affirm diversity.
D. use technology to communicate and collaborate with peers, parents, and the larger community in order to nurture student learning.	D. promote safe and healthy use of technology resources.
	E. facilitate equitable access to technology resources for all students.

To aid teacher preparation programs in the development of NETS-qualified candidates, ISTE created the Technology Performance Profiles for Teacher Preparation. These profiles suggest ways programs can incrementally examine how well candidates meet the standards. ISTE lists technology proficiencies for the following profiles:

1. General Preparation
   - receive experiences that teach them about the operation and hardware of a computer
   - learn how to use technology tools and information resources to increase productivity
   - use technology to locate, evaluate, and collect information from a variety of sources
   - other general uses of the computer

2. Professional Preparation
   - be able to identify the benefits of technology to maximize student learning and facilitate higher order thinking skills
   - identify, select, and use hardware and software technology resources specially designed for use by PK–12 students to meet specific teaching and learning objectives

3. Student Teaching/Internship

      • be able to identify, evaluate, and select specific technology resources available at the
        school site and district level to support a coherent lesson sequence

      • create and implement a well-organized plan to manage available technology resources,
        provide equitable access for all students, and enhance learning outcomes

      • design and facilitate learning experiences that use assistive technologies to meet the spe-
        cial physical needs of students

4. First-Year Teaching

      • engage in ongoing planning of lesson sequences that effectively integrate technology re-
        sources and are consistent with current best practices for integrating the learning of sub-
        ject matter and student technology standards (as defined in the ISTE National
        Educational Technology Standards for Students)

      • implement a variety of instructional technology strategies and grouping strategies (e.g.,
        whole group, collaborative, individualized, and learner centered) that include appropriate
        embedded assessment for meeting the diverse needs of learners

      • implement procedures consistent with district and school policies that protect the privacy
        and security of student data and information

Details of each of the performance profiles can be found at http://cnets.iste.org/index3.html.

Several states have developed their own educational technology standards for the teaching profession. For example, the California Commission on Teacher Credentialing (CCTC) has defined technology standards for preservice teachers and practicing teachers applying for Level 1 and Level 2
credential status (CCTC 2000). The California Technology Assistance Project (CTAP), a statewide organization supporting schools and districts in the implementation of technology, designed proficiency
profiles aligned with state requirements set by the CCTC to aid in the professional development process. Educators can self-assess their technology proficiency levels at http://ctap2.iassessment.org/.

International, national, and state organizations and agencies are taking steps to ensure that new
teachers are prepared to teach with today's technologies. In addition, agencies are helping administrators identify the needs of their schools. For example, an online School Technology and Readiness
(STaR) Chart, developed by the CEO Forum on Education and Technology, is a self-assessment tool designed to provide schools with the information they need to better integrate technology into their educational processes. It can be accessed at http://www.ceoforum.org/questions.cfm. Grants and other
resources are available to help with schools' technology needs, as well.

Standards for Students

In addition to *National Educational Technology Standards for Teachers*, ISTE has published *National Educational Technology Standards for Students* (2000). These standards provide technology
foundations for students as well as profiles for technology-literate students, including performance
indicators, curriculum examples, and scenarios. The technology foundation standards are divided
into six broad standards:

1. Basic operations and concepts

2. Social, ethical, and human issues

3. Technology productivity tools

4. Technology communication tools

5. Technology research tools

6. Technology problem-solving and decision-making tools

Performance indicators, curriculum examples, and scenarios are provided by categories: Grades PreK–2; Grades 3–5; Grades 6–8; and Grades 9–12. Scenarios provide sample lessons of how teachers can use technology to facilitate learning. The curriculum examples provide detailed lesson plans of how to integrate technology with the standards throughout the curriculum. Performance indicators for technology-literate students (ISTE 2000) are listed in Table 1.3, pages 13–14.

Technology has become an integral part of our society and world culture. It must become an integral part of the education system. Standards have been written for both teachers and students; we need to ensure that educators and learners are supported in their use of technology, now, and as the technology changes.

Table 1.3. ISTE Performance Indicators for Technology-Literate Students

Prior to completion of Grade 2 students will:	Prior to the completion of Grade 5 students will:
1. Use input devices and output devices to successfully operate computers, VCRs, audiotapes, and other technologies.	1. Use keyboards and other common input and output devices efficiently and effectively.
2. Use a variety of media and technology resources for directed and independent learning activities.	2. Discuss common uses of technology in daily life and the advantages and disadvantages those uses provide.
3. Communicate about technology using developmentally appropriate and accurate terminology.	3. Discuss basic issues related to responsible use of technology and information and describe personal consequences of inappropriate use.
4. Use developmentally appropriate multimedia resources to support learning.	4. Use general purpose productivity tools and peripherals to support personal productivity, remediate skill deficits, and facilitate learning throughout the curriculum.
5. Work cooperatively and collaboratively with peers, family members, and others when using technology in the classroom.	5. Use technology tools for individual and collaborative writing, communication, and publishing activities to create knowledge products for audiences inside and outside the classroom.
6. Demonstrate positive social and ethical behaviors when using technology.	
7. Practice responsible use of technology systems and software.	6. Use telecommunications efficiently and effectively to access remote information, communicate with others in support of direct and independent learning, and pursue personal interests.
8. Create developmentally appropriate multimedia products with support from teachers, family members, or student partners.	7. Use telecommunications and online resources to participate in collaborative problem-solving activities for the purpose of developing solutions or products for audiences inside and outside the classroom.
9. Use technology resources for problem solving, communication, and illustration of thoughts, ideas, and stories.	8. Use technology resources for problem solving, self-directed learning, and extended learning activities.
10. Gather information and communicate with others using telecommunications, with support for teachers, family members, or student partners.	9. Determine when technology is useful and select the appropriate tool(s) and technology resources to address a variety of tasks and problems.
	10. Evaluate the accuracy, relevance, appropriateness, comprehensiveness, and bias of electronic information sources.

(Table 1.3 continues on page 14.)

Table 1.3—*Continued*

Prior to the completion of Grade 8 students will:	Prior to completion of Grade 12 students will:
1. Apply strategies for identifying and solving routine hardware and software problems that occur during everyday use.	1. Identify capabilities and limitations of contemporary and emerging technology resources and assess the potential of these systems and services to address personal, lifelong learning, and workplace needs.
2. Demonstrate knowledge of current changes in information technologies and the effect those changes have on the workplace and society.	2. Make informed choices among technology systems, resources, and services.
3. Exhibit legal and ethical behaviors when using information and technology, and discuss consequences of misuse.	3. Analyze advantages and disadvantages of widespread use and reliance on technology in the workplace and in society as a whole.
4. Use content-specific tools, software, and simulations to support learning and research.	4. Demonstrate and advocate for legal and ethical behaviors among peers, family, and community regarding the use of technology and information.
5. Apply productivity/multimedia tools and peripherals to support personal productivity, group collaboration, and learning throughout the curriculum.	5. Use technology tools and resources for managing and communicating personal/ professional information.
6. Design, develop, publish, and present products using technology resources that demonstrate and communicate curriculum concepts to audiences inside and outside the classroom.	6. Evaluate technology-based options, including distance and distributed education, for lifelong learning.
7. Collaborate with peers, experts, and others using telecommunications and collaborative tools to investigate curriculum-related problems, issues, and information, and develop solutions or products for audiences inside and outside the classroom.	7. Routinely and efficiently use online information resources to meet needs for collaboration, research, publication, communication, and productivity.
8. Select and use appropriate tools and technology resources to accomplish a variety of tasks and solve problems.	8. Select and apply technology tools for research, information analysis, problem solving, and decision making in content learning.
9. Demonstrate an understanding of concepts underlying hardware, software, and connectivity, and of practical applications to learning and problem solving.	9. Investigate and apply expert systems, intelligent agents, and simulations in real-world situations.
10. Research and evaluate the accuracy, relevance, appropriateness, comprehensiveness, and bias of electronic information sources concerning real-world problems.	10. Collaborate with peers, experts, and others to contribute to a content-related knowledge base by using technology to compile, synthesize, produce, and disseminate information, models, and other creative works.

IMPLEMENTING TECHNOLOGY

Integrating technology into education is not easy. Although the price of software and hardware is decreasing, it is still difficult for schools to afford enough resources to meet the demands. Also, training for teachers is critical if we are to reap the benefits of technology in education. NCATE's Task Force on Technology and Teacher Education reports that to effectively use technology in the classroom will require new understandings, new approaches, and new forms of professional growth (NCATE 1997). This section offers some suggestions for implementing technology.

- Determine your instructional goals and objectives, then locate the technology to support them. In other words, choose the technology to fit your curriculum, not vice versa. Many times we become entranced with a new program or piece of hardware only to find that it does not come close to addressing the objectives. Technology, like other teaching tools, must be used only where appropriate. "Until classroom teachers are shown how new technologies can improve the way students learn and think in social studies, science and math class, they are unlikely to set up, take notice and make significant use of these new tools" (McKenzie 1999a, 2).

- Seek support from administrators. Talk to your administrators and keep them informed about your instructional goals and technology needs. "Even in difficult budget times, you can be confident that if you can directly link your requests for technology to the attainment of specific and highly valued student goals, you will get support from both administrators and community members" (Dyrli and Kinnaman 1994, 18).

- Form partnerships with local businesses and universities. Partnerships can provide donations of equipment, expertise, and time—all of which can be valuable additions to your quest to integrate technology in the classroom ("Donated computers in K–12 education," 1998).

- Acquire technology in increments. Hardware and software are changing so rapidly that they may be obsolete or outdated by the time you and the teachers in your school learn to use them (McKenzie 1999). Purchase technology in increments, learn to use it, absorb it into the curriculum, and then seek additional resources.

- Visit other schools and ask other educators for advice. One of the best ways to acquire ideas on the integration of technology into a classroom is to visit other schools. Most teachers are more than willing to share their successes and lessons learned in the classroom. Also, some states and districts have established model technology schools to test implementation techniques. Do not be afraid to ask questions of fellow teachers, other professionals, and students. Advances in technology are constant and overwhelming, and no one has all the answers.

- Provide in-service training sessions. To meet the training demand for emerging technologies, most districts, regions, and states offer in-service workshops and seminars for teachers. These activities are usually excellent avenues for learning about new developments. If possible, plan workshops that emphasize hands-on training, provide well-planned materials for future reference, include lesson-integration strategies, and promote interchanges with other teachers (Harris 1995).

- Supply training for teachers on the software and hardware available at their schools. One mistake that school districts make is to bring in outside experts, who arrive with their own hardware and software. Although it is helpful to see what others are doing, the training sessions should focus on the technology that the teachers will have available even after the expert leaves

(Siegel 1995). In addition, make sure the training is geared toward teachers' perceived needs and goals (Brand 1998).

- Provide follow-up support and coaching. Support for teachers after in-service training is essential (Office of Technology Assessment 1995). Schrum (1999) examines several models of professional development, noting that those with presentation of theory, clear demonstrations, practice with feedback, coaching, and ongoing follow-up are more likely to produce changes in how teachers use technology in their classrooms than traditional models of staff development. She describes traditional models as one-day seminars usually hosted by an expert or after-school workshops that focus on "hot" topics without follow-up, support, or direction. The support should include technical troubleshooting expertise, as well as pedagogical ideas for integrating technology into the curriculum (Tally 1995).

- Involve the students and capitalize on their expertise. It is not uncommon for some students to be more comfortable with new technologies than the teacher. This situation can be a real plus because the students' expertise can be tapped to train other students. Student involvement provides valuable assistance for the teacher and helps build students' self-esteem.

- Investigate public domain and shareware sources. Education money is tight, and most schools cannot afford all the software they need. Public domain software is available at no cost and may be freely copied. Shareware, however, is almost always copyrighted and should not be considered free. If you try a shareware program and intend to use it, send the registration fee to the author of the program. This payment serves as the license to continue using the program, and you will receive information about updates.

- Investigate technical support and documentation. Access to quality documentation and technical support is invaluable for any buyer of hardware or software. Be sure the vendors are reputable and have a history of reliable service. A toll-free number and web address are especially important for the integration of technologies purchased from a distant source.

- Subscribe to magazines and journals. There is a wealth of periodicals focusing on technology in education. These publications are a great means for keeping up with the latest developments and releases. In addition, research, integration ideas, and product reviews are provided. A list of periodicals is included in the resources at the end of this chapter, along with contact information. Many of the publications are available at little or no cost to qualified professionals.

- Monitor the use of technology. Unfortunately, technology can provide easy access to materials that are not appropriate for students. Check with your school district about filtering Internet sites, and monitor student use of chat rooms and e-mail.

- Balance high tech with high touch. The integration of technologies will not replace classroom teachers because technology cannot provide a teacher's compassion or ability to analyze an individual student's learning needs. Instead, teachers can use technology as another tool for imparting knowledge. Human beings—teachers—remain the essential factor for providing high touch in an increasingly high-tech world (Kinnaman 1994).

- Be flexible and ready for change. We must accept that we cannot force technology to fit neatly into our traditional paradigms. For technology to foster collaboration, cross-discipline explorations, and complex problem solving, we may have to adjust our school schedules. Likewise, the evaluation of technology-based projects requires a new look at the assessment of student and teacher performance (Barnett 2000; Sun 2000).

SUMMARY

Technology continues to shrink in size and grow in power, as it touches more aspects of our daily lives. The integration of technology into school curricula is no longer a luxury; it is a means to survival in a future that will be driven and supported by technology. "Traditional educational practices no longer provide students with all the necessary skills for economic survival in today's workplace" (ISTE 2000, 5). We must be prepared to use technology to learn, teach, collaborate, communicate, and compete.

Integrating new technologies is not a cure-all for education, but indicators show that new technologies can help in restructuring our classrooms with activities that promote collaboration and supply effective tools for interpretive skills, information management, and open inquiry. Technology also provides an excellent avenue for student motivation, exploration, and instruction in a multisensory, diverse world. Technology, however, is only a tool. The challenge rests with educators to effectively integrate it into appropriate places throughout the curriculum.

TECHNOLOGY JOURNALS AND MAGAZINES

American Journal of Distance Education
http://www.ed.psu.edu/acsde/ajde/jour.asp

AV Video Multimedia Producer
http://www.avvideo.com/Htm/homeset.htm

Computers in the Schools
http://www.haworthpressinc.com/

Educational Technology
http://www.bookstoread.com/etp/default.htm

Educational Technology Research and Development (ETR&D)
http://www.aect.org

Educational Technology Review
http://www.aace.org/pubs/etr/

EMedia
http://www.emedialive.com/

Instruction Delivery Systems
http://www.salt.org

Journal of Computers in Math and Science Teaching
http://www.aace.org/pubs/jcmst/

Information Technology in Childhood Education Annual
http://www.aace.org/pubs/child/

Journal of Computing in Higher Education
http://jchesite.org/

Journal of Computing in Teacher Education
Http://www.iste.org/jcte/index.html

Journal of Educational Computing Research
http://baywood.com

Journal of Educational Multimedia and Hypermedia
http://www.aace.org/pubs/jemh/default.htm

Journal of Educational Technology Systems
http://baywood.com

Journal of Interactive Instruction Development
http://www.salt.org

Journal of Research on Technology in Education
http://www.iste.org/jrte/

Journal of Technology and Teacher Education
http://www.aace.org/pubs/jtate/

Learning and Leading with Technology
http://www.iste.org/L&L/index.html

Library Hi Tech Journal
http://www.lib.msu.edu/hi-tech/

Media & Methods
http://www.media-methods.com

MultiMedia Schools
http://www.infotoday.com/MMSchools/

Online
http://www.onlineinc.com

Online Learning Magazine
http://www.onlinelearningmag.com/

Syllabus
http://www.syllabus.com

Technology and Learning
    http://www.techlearning.com

TechTrends
    http://www.aect.org

T.H.E. Journal
    http://www.thejournal.com

Wired
    http://www.wired.com

RECOMMENDED READING

Baker, E. L. 1999. Technology: How do we know it works? [Online]. Available: http://www.ed.gov/Technology/TechConf/1999/whitepapers/paper5.html. (Accessed January 3, 2002)

Barksdale, J. M. 1996. New teachers: Why schools of education are still sending you staff you'll have to train in technology. *Electronic Learning* 15(5): 38–45.

Conte, C. 1997. The learning connection: Schools in the information age [Online]. Available: http://www.benton.org/Library/Schools/. (Accessed January 3, 2002)

Goldman, S., K. Cole, and C. Syer. 1999. The technology/content dilemma [Online]. Available: http://www.ed.gov/Technology/TechConf/1999/whitepapers/paper4.html. (Accessed January 3, 2002)

Heinecke, W. F., L. Blasi, N. Milman, and L. Washington. 1999. New directions in the evaluation of the effectiveness of educational technology [Online]. Available: http://www.ed.gov/Technology/TechConf/1999/whitepapers/paper8.html. (Accessed January 3, 2002)

Honey, M., K. M. Culp, and F. Carrigg. 1999. Perspectives on technology and education research: Lessons from the past and present [Online]. Available: http://www.ed.gov/Technology/TechConf/1999/whitepapers/paper1.html. (Accessed January 3, 2002)

Kosakowski, J. 1998. The benefits of information technology. ERIC Digest (August) [Online]. Available: http://ericir.syr.edu/ithome/digests/edoir9804.html. (Accessed January 3, 2002)

O'Neil, J. 1995. Technology and schools: A conversation with Chris Dede. *Educational Leadership* 53(2): 6–11.

REFERENCES

Apple Classrooms of Tomorrow. 1999. *Apple K–12 Effectiveness Reports* [Online]. Available: http://www.apple.com/education/k12/leadership/effect.html. (Accessed January 3, 2002)

Apple Computer. 1991. *Apple Classrooms of Tomorrow: Philosophy and Structure and What's Happening Where.* ERIC Document Reproduction Service No. ED340349.

Archer, J. 1998. The link to higher scores. *Education Week on the Web (Special Issue: Technology Counts '98)* (October) [Online]. Available: http://www.edweek.org/sreports/tc98/ets/ets-n.htm. (Accessed January 3, 2002)

Bagui, S. 1998. Reasons for increased learning using multimedia. *Journal of Educational Multimedia and Hypermedia* 7(1): 3–18.

Barnett, H. 2000. Assessing the effects of technology in a standards-driven world. *Learning and Leading with Technology* 27(7): 28–31, 63.

Barron, A. E., and K. S. Ivers. 1998. *The Internet and Instruction: Ideas and Activities*, 2d ed. Englewood, CO: Libraries Unlimited.

Barron, A. E., K. Hogarty, J. D. Kromrey, and P. Lenkway. 1999. An examination of the relationships between student conduct and the number of computers per student in Florida schools. *Journal of Research on Computing in Education* 32(1): 98–107.

Brand, G. A. 1998. What research says: Training teachers for using technology. *Journal of Staff Development* 19(1), 10–13.

Brunner, C., and K. McMillan. 1994. Beyond test scores. *Electronic Learning* 14(1): 22–23.

Burns, D. 1996. Technology in the ESL classroom. *Technology and Learning* 16(6): 50–52.

California Commission on Teacher Credentialing (CCTC). 2000. Effective use of computer-based technology in the classroom [Online]. Available: http://134.186.81.70/ceap/ceap.html. (Accessed January 3, 2002)

Carter, K. 1999. Making the home/school connection with corporate help. *Technology and Learning* 20(3): 26–34.

Clark, R. E. 1989. Current progress and future directions for research in instructional technology. *Educational Technology Research and Development* 37(1): 57–66.

Collis, B. 1989. *Using information technology to create new educational situations*. ERIC Document Reproduction Service No. ED310793.

Daley, P. 1999. Turning the tide. *Instructor* (May/June): 23–26.

Dewert, M. H. 1999. The times they are a-changin': A look at technology-related requirements for teacher licensure and certification. *Journal of Computing in Teacher Education* 15(2): 4–6.

D'Ignazio, F. 1997. Young authors at home on the web. *Multimedia schools* 4(3): 22–28.

Dockterman, D. 1995. Yes, but is it cooperative? *Electronic Learning* 14(4): 33.

Donated computers in K–12 education. 1998. *Learning and Leading with Technology* 25(5): 52–56.

Doolan, L. S., and A. Honigsfeld. 2000. Illuminating the new standards with learning styles: Striking the perfect match. *Clearing House* 73(5): 274–78.

Drumm, J. E., and F. M. Groom. 1999. Teaching information skills to disadvantaged children. *Computers in Libraries* 19(4): 48–51.

Dwyer, D. 1994. Apple classrooms of tomorrow: What we've learned. *Educational Leadership* 51(7): 4–10.

Dyrli, O. E., and D. E. Kinnaman. 1994. Gaining access to technology: First step in making a difference for your students. *Technology and Learning* 14(4): 16–20.

Gardner, H. 1999. *Intelligence Reframed: Multiple Intelligences for the 21st Century*. New York: Basic Books.

Hannafin, R. D. 1999. Can teacher attitudes about learning be changed? *Journal of Computing in Teacher Education* 15(2): 7–13.

Harris, J. 1995. Teaching teachers to use telecomputing tools. *ERIC Review* 4(1): 2–4.

Holzberg, C. S. 1994. The new multimedia: What researchers say about multimedia. *Electronic Learning* 13(8): 55–62.

Honey, M., and A. Henriquez. 1993. *Telecommunications and K–12 Educators: Findings from a National Survey*. New York: Center for Technology in Education, Bank Street College of Education.

Ingram, A. L., L. G. Hathorn, and A. Evans. 2000. Beyond chat on the Internet. *Computers & Education* 35(1): 21–35.

Interactive Educational Systems Design. 2000. *Report on the Effectiveness of Technology in Schools*. Washington, DC: Software Publishers Association.

International Society for Technology in Education (ISTE). 2000. *National Educational Technology Standards for Students*. Eugene, OR: ISTE.

International Society for Technology in Education (ISTE). 2000. *National Educational Technology Standards for Teachers*. Eugene, OR: ISTE.

International Society for Technology in Education (ISTE). 1999. *Will New Teachers Be Prepared to Teach in a Digital Age?* Santa Monica, CA: Milken Exchange on Educational Technology.

Ivers, K. S., and A. E. Barron. 1998. *Multimedia Projects in Education: Designing, Producing, and Assessing*. Englewood, CO: Libraries Unlimited.

Jonassen, D. H. 2000. *Computers As Mindtools for Schools*, 2d ed. Upper Saddle River, NJ: Prentice Hall.

Kinnaman, D. E. 1994. Remember the human element in your technology planning. *Technology and Learning* 14(5): 62.

Knowledge Adventure [Online]. Available: http://www.knowledgeadventure.com/. (Accessed January 17, 2002)

Liao, Y. C. 1999. Effects of hypermedia on students' achievement: A meta-analysis. *Journal of Educational Multimedia and Hypermedia* 8(3): 255–77.

Liu, X., R. Macmillian, and V. Timmons. (1998). Assessing the impact of computer integration on students. *Journal of Research on Computing in Education* 31(2): 189–203.

Logo Computer Systems [Online]. Available: http://www.microworlds.com/index.html. (Accessed January 17, 2002)

McKenzie, J. 1999. Strategic deployment of hardware to maximize readiness, staff use, and student achievement. *From Now On: The Educational Technology Journal* 8(8) [Online]. Available: http://www.fno.org/may99/strategic.html. (Accessed January 17, 2002)

———. 1999a. *How Teachers Learn Technology Best*. Bellingham, WA: FNO Press.

Milone, M. N. 1997. Technology for everyone: Assistive devices for students with special needs. *Technology and Learning* 17(5): 44.

National Council for Accreditation for Teacher Education (NCATE). 1997. *Technology and the New Professional Teacher: Preparing for the 21st Century Classroom* [Online]. Available: http://www.ncate.org/accred/projects/tech/tech-21.htm. (Accessed January 17, 2002)

NetDay National Organization. 2001. About NetDay [Online]. Available: http://www.netday.org/about.htm. (Accessed January 17, 2002)

Office of Technology Assessment (OTA). 1995. *Teachers and technology: Making the connection* (OTA-HER-616). Washington, DC: U.S. Government Printing Office.

Optical Data School Media [Online]. Available: http://www.opticaldata.com/main.html. (Accessed January 17, 2002)

Pratt, B. 1999. Making it work. *Learning and Leading with Technology* 26(8): 28–31.

Quesada, A., and S. L. Summers. 1998. Literacy in the cyberage: Teaching kids to be media savvy. *Technology and Learning* 18(5): 30–36.

Reed, W. M. 1996. Assessing the impact of computer-based writing instruction. *Journal of Research on Computing in Education* 28(4): 418–37.

Rockman, S. 1992. *Learning from technologies: A perspective on the research literature.* U.S. Office of Technology Assessment, ERIC Document Reproduction Service No. ED361499.

Salomon, G. 1991. Learning: New conceptions, new opportunities. *Educational Technology* 31(6): 41–44.

Schacter, J. 1999. The impact of educational technology on student achievement: What the most current research has to say. *Milken Exchange on Educational Technology* [Online]. Available: http://web.mff.org/publications /publications.taf?page=161. (Accessed January 2, 2002)

Schrock, K. 1998/1999. The ABCs of web site evaluation. *Classroom Connect* (December/January): 4–6.

Schrum, L. 1999. Technology professional development for teachers. *Educational Technology Research and Development* 47(4): 83–90.

Shaughnessy, M. F. 1998. An interview with Rita Dunn about learning styles. *Clearing House* 71(3): 141–45.

Siegel, J. 1995. The state of teacher training. *Electronic Learning* 14(8): 43–53.

Sivin-Kachala, J., and E. R. Bialo. 2000. *Report on the effectiveness of technology in schools*, 7th ed. Washington, DC: Software and Information Industry Association.

Stahl, S. A. 1999. Different strokes for different folks? A critique of learning styles. *American Educator* 23(3): 27–31.

Strommen, E. 1995. Cooperative learning: Technology may be the Trojan horse that brings collaboration into the classroom. *Electronic Learning* 14(4): 24–35.

Sun, J. 2000. How do we know it's working? *Learning and Leading with Technology* 27(7): 32–35.

Sunburst Communications [Online]. Available: http://www.sunburst.com/. (Accessed January 17, 2002)

Tally, B. 1995. Developmental training: Understanding the ways teachers learn. *Electronic Learning* 14(8): 14–15.

Tom Snyder Productions [Online]. Available: http://www.teachtsp.com/. (Accessed January 17, 2001)

Trends and predictions. 1999. *Technology and Learning* 20(5): 75–78.

Trollinger, G., and R. Slavkin. 1999. Purposeful e-mail as stage 3 technology: IEP goals online. *Teaching Exceptional Children* 32(1): 10–15.

Turning points 2000. 2000. *Technology and Learning* 21(5): 16–22.

U.S. Department of Education, Office of Educational Research and Improvement. 2001. *Internet Access in Public Schools and Classrooms: 1994–2000.* NCES 2001-071. Washington, DC: U.S. Government Printing Office.

Vockell, E., and R. M. Van Deusen. 1989. *The Computer and Higher-Order Thinking Skills.* Watsonville, CA: Mitchell.

Web-Based Education Commission. 2000. *The Power of the Internet for Learning: Moving from Promise to Practice* [Online]. Washington, DC: U. S. Department of Education. Available: http://www.webcommission.org. (Accessed January 3, 2002)

Willis, J., A. Thompson, and W. Sadera. 1999. Research on technology and teacher education: Current status and future directions. *Educational Technology Research and Development* 47(4): 29–45.

Wishart, J. 2000. Students' and teachers' perceptions of motivation and learning through the use in schools of multimedia encyclopedias on CD-ROMs. *Journal of Multimedia and Hypermedia* 9(4): 333–47.

Xin, J.F. 1999. Computer-assisted cooperative learning in integrated classrooms for students with and without disabilities. *Information Technology in Childhood Education Annual*: 61–78.

Zorfass, J., P. Corley, and A. Remz. 1994. Helping students with disabilities become writers. *Educational Leadership* 51(7): 62–66.

2

COMPUTER GRAPHICS

A Scenario

Thuy, Ronni, and Jasmine worked diligently to complete their project-based web site. They had finished the research for their topic, developed storyboards for the web pages and created the graphics and animations. However, merging it all into a meaningful and effective presentation was taking more time than they had anticipated. They found that some of their graphics took forever to download; several of the colors looked different on other computers; and their fonts did not always display as they had planned. Could it be that their WYSIWYG web page program was not so WYSIWYG after all? Perhaps creating a web page was not as easy as it had looked. Or, maybe, they had stumbled upon something that the teacher had covered in an earlier class, while they were away playing softball for the district championship.

When they approached Mrs. Wang about the difficulties they were encountering, her face lit up and she smiled, "Good observations! I'm glad you are asking for help. Yes, these are things we covered in an earlier class—I believe you were out winning the championship! Now, let me share with you how to be 'champion' webmasters!" With that, Mrs. Wang introduced the students to web-safe palettes, compression, graphic and font formats, and other information that would help them in creating their web pages and multimedia projects.

INTRODUCTION

Multimedia programs rely heavily on graphics. For example, web pages usually include photographs, cartoon images, or fancy bullets; presentations often contain charts and graphs. Newsletters, pamphlets, and other documents incorporate graphics as well. Whether you and your students are using HTML, HyperStudio, Microsoft Word, PageMaker, or any other program, graphics will be an important ingredient.

Why are graphics so important? Graphics illustrate ideas and concepts, show relationships among data, depict procedures, motivate and direct learners, and supply cues and other feedback to aid learning. When designing and using graphics, it is important to consider the purpose of the graphic information before creating or capturing the images.

Computer graphics come in all shapes, sizes, colors, and formats. They can be created in specialized programs, like Adobe PhotoShop, or in application programs, such as Microsoft Word or AppleWorks. Graphics can also be scanned, shot with a digital camera, downloaded from the web, or purchased in a clip art collection. In this chapter, you will learn some of the concepts behind the art of computer graphics. An overview of computer graphics is provided, including the following topics:

- Screen and Image Resolution
- Bitmaps vs. Objects
- Color Depth
- Compression
- Graphic File Formats
- Fonts
- Scanning Images
- Digital Cameras

All of the links, full-color versions of the graphics, and resources referred to in this chapter are accessible at http://www.magentastudios.org/.

OVERVIEW OF COMPUTER GRAPHICS

Have your students ever asked you why their computer pictures looked different on two different computers—why they filled the screen on one and were only partially visible on another? Did they ever want to know why they couldn't click on a portion of their image (like a circle) and move it or change its color? These issues are all related to an image's resolution and format.

Resolution

Computer screens and computer images are similar to graph paper—they are measured horizontally and vertically in small squares, called *pixels* (for picture elements). The number of pixels you have for your screen (or for your image) is called your screen resolution (or your image resolution). The resolution of the screen is expressed as the number of pixels wide by the number of pixels tall. Older computer screens had 640 pixels across and 480 pixels down, which is 640 x 480 = 307,200 pixels total.

Now, most computer screens have even more possibilities, like 800 x 600, 1024 x 768, 1280 x 1024, or 1600 x 1200. The more pixels you have, the higher the resolution, and the sharper the image.

Most computer displays have the same standard 4:3 aspect ratio as television—meaning that the height is exactly three quarters of the width. You will notice that most of the settings for monitor resolution values have that same 4:3 aspect ratio. (Note: To view the resolution options on your computer, you can access the Display Settings in Window's Control Panel or the Monitor Settings on a Macintosh.)

Your computer display must be set to a specific resolution; however, any image you show on that monitor will have its own resolution, independent of the display. That means that if your image is shown on a higher resolution monitor, it will appear smaller. For example, Picture A in Figure 2.1 was created as 700 pixels wide by 700 pixels tall and, therefore, it would fill only a part of the screen if it

700 pixels x 700 pixels

Picture A, as if it were shown on a 1024 x 768 computer display.

(It is smaller than the screen, so it does not fill the screen.)

Picture A, as if it were shown on a 640 x 480 computer display.

(It is wider and taller than the screen. The display chops off the image at the bottom. The user may have to scroll to see it all.)

Picture A, as if it were shown on a 800 x 600 computer display.

(It is narrower than the screen, yet taller. The display chops it off on the bottom. The user may have to scroll to see it all.)

Figure 2.1. Image and screen resolutions.

was displayed on a monitor set to 1024 x 768. Someone showing it on a display that is set to 640 x 480, however, would be able to see only part of the image, and would have to scroll to see the rest. Likewise, if that same image were shown on an 800 x 600 display, it would look narrower, yet taller than the screen. In general, when files will be shared between computers or displayed on the web, it is best to stick to a 640 x 480 resolution for a more consistent screen format and faster downloading.

Bitmapped Images

In computer graphics, there are two main categories of images—bitmaps and objects. Bitmaps are also known as paintings, while object-oriented images can be called drawings or vectors. Each category has unique properties, advantages, and disadvantages.

To visualize bitmaps, think of a piece of graph paper (or a grid of little colored lights, like the LiteBrite toy). When you are "painting" a bitmapped image, all you are doing is filling in each individual pixel or group of pixels with a solid color (see Figure 2.2).

Figure 2.2. Bitmapped images.

With bitmapped images, the pixels retain their "independence." In other words, the pixels may be arranged to look like a rectangle, but when you zoom in, you can see that the rectangle is made up of individual pixels. If you want to move the bitmapped rectangle, you have to select the pixels that compose the rectangle (usually with a lasso), and move those pixels. This is because no actual rectangle exists, just a bunch of pixels. When you move the pixels, an "empty" area will be left where the pixels were (see Figure 2.3).

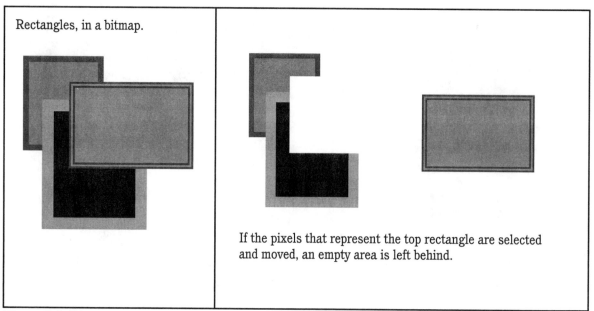

Figure 2.3. Bitmapped rectangles.

Painting programs, also known as bitmap editors, can simulate traditional painting techniques such as airbrush, oils, and watercolors, allowing you to blend, smooth, and otherwise treat the image as paint. You can also do a lot of things that you can't do with traditional painting techniques. For instance, you can mix many media such as oils, charcoals, and photographs that you can't mix without a computer. The most popular bitmap editing program for professional graphics production is Adobe PhotoShop. Less expensive bitmap editors include Microsoft Paint (free with Windows) and ColorIt (Macintosh only). Many applications, such as HyperStudio, have image editors built right into the program.

Object-Oriented Images

The other category of graphic images (object-oriented drawings) is very different from bitmaps. They work more like a collage (or the toy, Colorforms). When you draw an object (for example, a circle), the computer knows it as a circle and will always treat it as a circle. Standard draw objects are limited to simple geometric shapes such as lines, rectangles, ovals, and polygons, but modern programs use special curved lines called *splines* to make objects of any possible shape. Plus, after the object is created, it can always be squashed, stretched, rotated, flipped, or skewed.

If you draw one object on top of another, the objects underneath do not change, they just get layered. It is possible to select an object and bring it on top, push it back, or move it around, without impacting anything else on the screen (see Figure 2.4). Any object can be selected at any time, and you can change its attributes, such as line thickness, line color, line style, and so forth. If the object is a closed figure, you can also determine the color and pattern that fill the enclosed region.

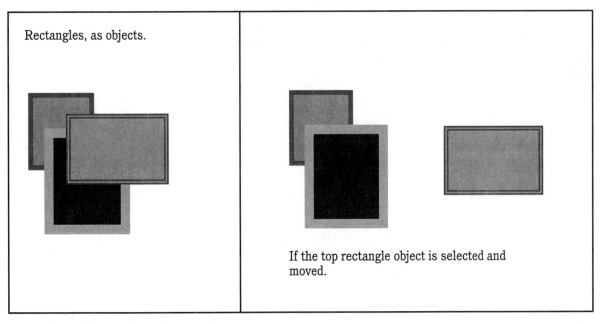

Rectangles, as objects.

If the top rectangle object is selected and moved.

Figure 2.4. Object-oriented rectangles.

Adobe Illustrator, CorelDraw, and ClarisDraw are popular programs for creating and editing object-oriented graphics. The "drawing" tools in PowerPoint, Word, and other applications can also create and edit object-oriented graphics.

One of the main differences between bitmaps and object-oriented drawings is that bitmaps are resolution dependent, while object-oriented drawings are resolution independent. That means that if you create a bitmapped image at a certain size, it should be viewed at that size. Enlarging it would make it look awful—all of the pixels would be stretched, and the image would look very pixilated (blocky). Object-oriented drawings can be enlarged to any size, and they will always look smooth, because they will adjust to the resolution of the screen.

COLOR

Have you or your students ever wondered why a scanned image wouldn't fit on a floppy disk? Have you ever gotten frustrated waiting for a graphic to display from the Internet? A major factor in the size of an image file is the number of colors the image contains. Representing colors on computers involves pixels and the bits that compose them. A bit is the smallest piece of information a computer can handle— it is a number value, limited to either 1 or 0. Remember that your computer images are represented by colored pixels arranged in rows and columns. Computers don't actually understand the concept of "pixels," but they do understand bits, so those pixels need to be represented by bits in the computer.

If each pixel's color were defined by a single bit, then each pixel could be either 0 or 1. Since 0 and 1 are numbers, not colors, we need to take each of those two numbers (the two possible pixel states) and assign colors to them (such as black and white). Then, we need to decide which color should be which number. Different computers handled that decision differently—most early Macintosh graphics programs used 0 (off) to mean white, and 1(on) to mean black. Windows graphics programs were the opposite—0 (off) was black, and 1(on) was white. The reason was not that arbitrary—they were aiming for different graphics markets. The Macintosh was aiming for the print graphics world, and a blank (off) piece of paper is white, and ink (on) that paper is black. The PC was aiming for on-screen graphics, and a monitor or TV that is off is black, and a lit pixel is white.

When a bitmapped image is represented by only one bit for each pixel, it is a called a one bit per pixel bitmap. We have now successfully turned numbers into pictures. Black and white images are fine if you are going for a film noir theme, but what about raspberry? Or mauve? Fortunately, we are not limited to black and white images, or defining a pixel's color with a single bit. By adding more bits to each pixel, we can define more colors. For example, 16.7 million colors are possible with 24 bits per pixel.

Color Depth

The more colors a computer image contains, the more numbers (bits) it must use to represent each pixel of the image. The more bits that you have per pixel, the more file space the image will consume. In other words, a black and white image will generally be much smaller (in file size) than the same image presented in multiple colors (see Table 2.1). For example, if an image is 640 x 480, with 24 bits per pixel, then its file size will be a little more than 921,000 bytes, or about one megabyte. There are eight bits in each byte, so the formula is: 640 x 480 x 24/8. At this size, only one image would fit on a diskette! *Color depth* is a term that is used to refer to the number of colors in a computer graphic. Table 2.1 displays the settings of the most common color depths for computers.

Table 2.1. Color Depths

Color Depth	Number of Colors	File size for 640 x 480 image	Setting on PC	Setting on Mac
1-bit	2 (black/white)	38.4K	N/A	N/A
4-bit	16	153.6K	N/A	N/A
8-bit	256	307.0K	256 Color	256 Color
16-bit	65,536	614.4K	High Color (16-bit)	Thousands of colors
24-bit	16.7 million	921.0K	True Color (24-bit)	Millions of colors

Although an image saved with 24-bit color may look much better than an image saved with 8-bit color, the file size will also be much larger (three times as large). File sizes are especially critical for web-based graphics: the larger the file size, the longer it takes for a user to download it. Hence, when you and your students are designing web pages, consider various modem speeds and ensure your graphics download in a timely fashion.

Reducing Color Depth

When most graphic artists create their work, they use high-end computer workstations with high resolution, 24-bit color displays. However, if the images they create need to be transferred on the Internet or viewed on systems with lower quality displays (such as ones with only 256 colors), the artist may decide to reduce the number of colors used in the images. This color reduction will decrease the quality of the images, but it will also shrink the file sizes. (Note: If the artist did not reduce the number of colors used, the image would still display on a low-quality screen, but the computer would substitute colors for those it could not display. That is why, if you view web pages with your monitor set to 256 colors, some of the graphics might look atrocious.)

When a graphic is saved with 256 colors (or converted to 256 colors), you can select a color palette. This palette tells the computer which 256 colors it should use (out of the 16.7 million possibilities). Netscape Navigator and Microsoft Internet Explorer have a master palette—a list of colors—that contains 216 colors that are considered "safe" to use on the Internet. These colors will always appear as intended, and any other color requested will be made to match one of those 216 colors. A full-color chart of the colors of the web-safe palette is located at http://www.magentastudios.org/. To get the best possible results in the 256-color mode, be sure you and your students design web graphics with the web-safe palette in mind. Any other colors you use might not appear as intended.

Dithering and Halftoning

To minimize the "damage" caused by reducing the number of colors, the missing colors can be simulated with certain dot patterns. These dot patterns are known as *dithering* or *halftoning*. While both dithering and halftoning use dots, they each use the dots differently. Halftoning always uses the same number of dots per area of the image, but the dots change in size to represent amounts of color. Dithering uses dots that are always the same size, but varies the number of dots in an area.

Halftoning is usually used for print graphics, while dithering is generally used for on-screen graphics. Take a look at any of the color photos in your newspaper with a magnifying glass, and you will see they are not as colorful as you thought; they are just printed with tiny cyan, magenta, and yellow dots arranged with a halftone to create the illusion of other colors. Figure 2.5 provides examples of halftoning and dithering patterns on a simple strip that varies in value from dark to light.

10 line per inch halftone.

16 line per inch halftone.

32 line per inch halftone.

Bayer patterned dither.

Error diffusion dither.

Figure 2.5. Halftoning and dithering patterns.

As illustrated in Figure 2.5, there are two different techniques for dithering—*Bayer patterned dither* and *error diffusion dither*. With Bayer dithered images, the pixels are arranged in precise chessboard patterns, while error diffusion arranges the pixels pseudo-randomly in the images. Figures 2.6, 2.7, and 2.8 provide examples of images created with halftone, a Bayer patterned dither, and an error diffusion dither. In general, a diffusion dither looks much better than a patterned one for most images.

COMPRESSION

As discussed, bitmapped images can contain a lot of data. In addition to decreasing the file size of the image by reducing the color depth or resolution, the file size can also be reduced by compressing the image. Compression reduces the size of a file by eliminating redundant information, without reducing the color depth or resolution. Graphics are compressed so that similar pixels can be referred to collectively instead of individually. For example, let's look at the American flag—how can we describe it? In an "uncompressed" way, we would have to describe each part of the image individually, not collectively: A blue field with a white star, and another white star, and another white star, and another white star . . . This becomes a long, redundant description.

Figure 2.6. Halftone image.

Figure 2.7. Bayer patterned dither.

Figure 2.8. Error diffusion dither.

A "compressed" description would be: The American flag has 13 alternating red and white horizontal stripes (rectangles) and a field of blue in the upper left corner with 50 white stars. By referring to similar things in groups, the description is more compact, so it takes up less room and results in a smaller file size.

There are two different ways to compress bitmapped images: *lossless* and *lossy*. Lossless means every pixel in the image is retained after compression. In other words, the picture will look the same after it was compressed as before, and compression does not cause the image to lose any quality. GIF files (a popular format for images used on the web) are compressed using the lossless technique.

The lossy compression method removes what it feels are unnecessary details in order to make the file smaller. Lossy compression causes the image to lose detail, but at standard magnifications, the loss is not noticeable. What makes lossy compression so beneficial is that the compressed file sizes can be very small. Small file sizes are very important for transmitting large quantities of data across the Internet, or for trying to fit thousands of graphics on a hard drive.

JPEG (another popular web format) is the most commonly used lossy compression method. Figures 2.9 and 2.10, contain two copies of the same picture. Figure 2.9 is uncompressed and Figure 2.10 uses JPEG compression. Notice how some details were lost in the compression, replaced by large, dirty-looking rectangular areas. Notice also the difference in file sizes between the two files. Because of the decreased quality of a compressed file, you should avoid editing compressed JPEG files. Always save your original version uncompressed and treat the compressed JPEG files as output files, not as working files.

Figure 2.9. Uncompressed picture.
File size is 3,165 Kilobytes.

Figure 2.10. Highly JPEG compressed picture.
File size is 37 Kilobytes.

GRAPHIC FILE FORMATS

A file format is the structure of how the image's resolution, palette, compression, color, and other characteristics are stored in the file. If a program cannot understand the file's format, it will not be able to display the image; therefore, it is important to choose a format that is compatible with the your programs. In Microsoft Windows, you can normally distinguish one file format from another by the *file extension*—the last three letters of the filename (e.g., "picture.gif" has a file extension of gif). Table 2.2 lists the most common graphics file formats in use.

It is important to note that the file extension shows only how you can distinguish between file formats; it is not the file format itself. Merely changing the extension on a file does not change the file's contents anymore than changing the label on a can of peas will turn it into applesauce. Instead, to change a file from one format to another, you must use an image editor or a conversion program, such as Adobe PhotoShop or GraphicConverter (available at http://www.lemkesoft.de/us_index.html).

Table 2.2. Graphic File Formats

File Extension	Full Name	Type	Comments
BMP	Microsoft Bitmap	Bitmap	This is the standard bitmap format for Microsoft Windows.
PIC, PCT, PICT	Macintosh PICTure format	Bitmap and simple objects	This is the standard bitmap format for Macintosh.
GIF	Graphics Interchange Format	Bitmap	This format is now the standard for 8-bit Internet graphics. It can only display 256 colors.
JPG, JPEG	Joint Photographic Experts Group	Bitmap	This format was created as the standard for 24-bit Internet graphics.
PNG	Portable Network Graphics	Bitmap	This is the new Internet graphics format designed to replace GIF.
TIF, TIFF	Tagged Image File Format	Bitmap	This format is the standard for print-related bitmap graphics.
PSD	PhotoShop Document	Bitmap	This is the file format used by Adobe PhotoShop. It is just used for editing purposes, not for presentation or output.
PS, EPS	PostScript and Encapsulated PostScript	Object oriented	This is a pure PostScript language file, and it has become a standard for creating printed documents.
PDF	Portable Document Format	Object oriented	This is a full document format based on PostScript, and it has become the standard for creating paperless documents—including those delivered on the web and eBooks.
WMF	Windows MetaFile	Object oriented	This is a common vector graphics format in Microsoft Windows.

Graphic Formats for the Web

Two of the most common graphic formats on the web are GIF and JPEG. When you or your students create an image and save it (or convert it), you will need to decide which of these two formats to use. Although both formats can produce relatively small file sizes (important for transmitting over the Internet), there are major differences between the formats.

One differentiating factor in the formats is the number of colors. Images saved in the GIF format can only have a maximum of 256 colors. This makes GIF an ideal choice for graphs and charts and simple line-type drawings. On the other hand, JPEG images can have up to 16.7 million colors; therefore, JPEG is the best format for saving photographs and images that have subtle color changes. For example, a picture of your principal should be formatted in JPEG because it will look best with multiple colors, and the lossy compression will not be noticeable. On the other hand, a bar chart will display best in the GIF format because it only needs a few colors, and there are large areas with solid blocks of color.

Figure 2.11 displays two images, each saved in both JPEG and GIF. Note that the butterfly, with many, subtle colors, looks great in JPEG, but appears pixilated and dithered in GIF. On the contrary, the cow, which is a black and white drawing, looks best in GIF, with sharp and clean lines.

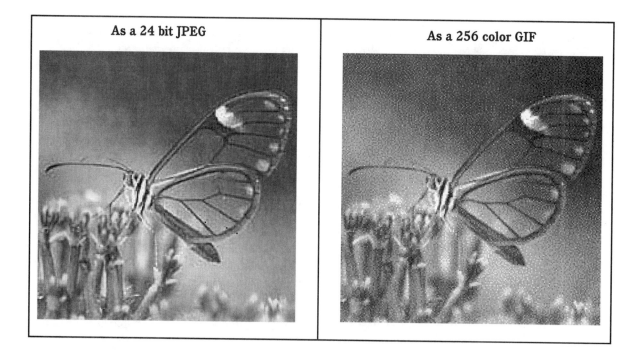

As a 24 bit JPEG

As a 256 color GIF

(Figure 2.11 continues.)

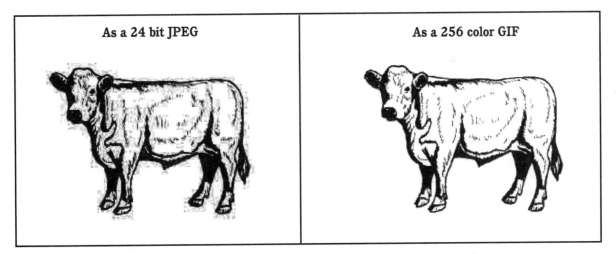

Figure 2.11. JPEG and GIF files.

Advantages of the GIF format are that you can make a color transparent or animate the files. (Animation of GIF files is covered in detail in Chapter 3.) Table 2.3 summarizes the advantages and appropriate applications for GIF and JPEG formats.

Table 2.3. Advantages and Uses of GIF and JPEG on the Web

Format	Advantages	Appropriate Uses
GIF	Lossless compression Allows transparency Allows animation	Line drawings Text Images with solid areas Images with sharp edges
JPEG	Offers high compression rates Supports 24-bit color	Photographs Continuous tone graphics

PNG (Portable Network Graphics) is another graphic file that is used on the web. Similar to GIF, it uses a lossless compression scheme, and similar to JPEG, it allows millions of colors. It seems like the best of both worlds; unfortunately, it has been slow to gain in popularity, since older browsers could not deal with the format. It is supported by Netscape Communicator 4.0 and higher and Microsoft Internet Explorer 4.0 and higher, so it is likely that we will see more of this format being implemented in the future.

FONTS

Although we often don't realize it, fonts used for text on computers are also graphics. In fact, each font (such as Arial or Courier) consists of special graphics files that contain the shapes of all of the letters of the alphabet, numbers, punctuation, symbols, and so on. This explains why the text in a HyperStudio stack or on a web page may look great on one computer, but terrible on another. If the specified font is not available on a computer, a different one will be substituted—sometimes with disastrous results.

Fonts have many different file formats, but two of them are the most widely used by far: *TrueType* and *Adobe Type 1*. Both TrueType and Adobe Type 1 formats describe the shape of each letter as *Bezier curves*—special curved lines that can be adjusted to any shape (see Figure 2.12). Because they use curves, the fonts can be of any size and always print smooth, from 1 point to 1,000 points (a point is 1/72 of an inch).

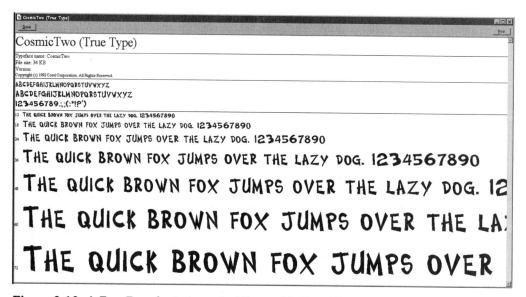

Figure 2.12. A TrueType font shown in Microsoft's Font Viewer.

TrueType fonts are handled natively by the Windows and Macintosh operating systems, however, in order to use the Adobe Type 1 fonts, the program Adobe Type Manager must be installed. Once a TrueType or Adobe Type 1 font is installed on your computer, any program on your computer can use it. However, if you create a document using a specific font, and then open the document on a computer that does not have that font installed, the computer will not display or print the text properly. It may substitute a similar font, or it will use a default font. This is because the fonts are part of the operating system and do not generally travel with individual documents.

Some TrueType fonts can be embedded into documents, meaning that the font will travel with the document and can only be used with that specific document. For example, if you create a PowerPoint presentation, and want to ensure that the fancy bullets and text that you selected will be displayed on the computer at a different school, you should embed the fonts into the presentation. There are millions of fonts available, created by thousands of different companies and individuals. Prices for fonts vary from free shareware fonts to $500 for a single font. A large library of fonts comes with CorelDraw and some other graphics packages.

OpenType was introduced as a joint venture between Apple, Microsoft, and Adobe, which as a single font file format that works on both Macintosh computers and Microsoft Windows-based computers, can contain either TrueType or Adobe Type I font data and can be handled natively by the operating systems. It will eventually replace both TrueType and Adobe Type I as the single font format.

Typefaces

Fonts are placed into many categories according to the typeface and style of their designs. Here are some of the basic styles:

- *Serif.* Serif fonts have small points called "serifs" that cap the ends of most strokes. The most common serif font is Times Roman.

This is an example of a serif font.

- *Sans serif.* Sans serif fonts have no points capping the strokes. *Sans* means "without." The most common sans serif font is called Helvetica; in Microsoft Windows it is called Arial.

This is an example of a sans serif font.

- *Script.* Script fonts try to mimic handwriting. Some look like unconnected print writing, while others look like they have connecting cursive characters.

This is an example of an unconnected script font.

This is an example of a connected script font.

- *Novelty.* Novelty fonts are wild and wacky fonts that have nothing in common other than that they are not designed for large amounts of text. Novelty fonts are used for a few words or Logos.

THIS IS AN EXAMPLE OF A NOVELTY FONT.

- *Special purpose.* Special purpose fonts fill a specific need, for example, the numbers used on the bottom of bank checks.

This is an example of a special purpose font used for Character Recognition Systems.

One design rule should be followed when using fonts: Don't use too many fonts in a single image or on a single page. One or two fonts is usually recommended. Use one typeface for the text body (normally a serif font), and one typeface for the headlines or captions (normally a sans serif font).

Font Attributes

By changing a font's attributes, its appearance can be varied without changing the font itself. Font attributes include style, kerning, and leading.

Styles are very common attributes that are used to describe the weight, structure, and form of the text. Examples include:

- Bold   **This is an example of a bolded sans serif font.**

- Italics   *This is an example of an italicized sans serif font.*

- Underline   <u>This is an example of an underlined sans serif font</u>.

- Condensed   This is an example of a condensed sans serif font.

- Expanded   **This is an example of an expanded sans serif font.**

Kerning is a term used to describe the spacing between characters. Normally, characters have a predetermined spacing, but sometimes letter areas have to overlap. For example, an upper case letter "A" followed by an upper case letter "V" would often have to be pushed together to simulate standard letter spacing. You can see this example in the word "AVIATOR." If it is not properly kerned, the letter "A" and the letter "V" look farther apart then the other letters in the word. If they are kerned, the top of the "V" will overlap the bottom of the "A." Kerning is a feature that is available in most desktop publishing programs, such as PageMaker. It allows you more control over the precise location of each font. For example, when students are creating a newspaper layout, kerning may be necessary.

Leading is a term used to describe the spacing between lines of text. Typically, lines of text have about one to two points of leading. When there is no leading between lines of text (e.g., a lower case "g" on the upper line would touch an upper case "T" on the lower line), the text is called "set solid." Leading, or line spacing, is available in word processing and desktop publishing programs.

Most fonts only contain 256 characters, which are all of the letters, numbers, and punctuation marks used in English and the other western European languages. This Western super alphabet is called Latin-1 because it supports all of the languages that evolved from Latin. In addition, there is a single standardized set of characters to write in most of the languages of the world. This standard is called Unicode, which defines a single global alphabet containing 65,535 characters. It is becoming the standard on the Internet and for computers in general. For more information about Unicode, visit http://www.unicode.org/.

Scanning Images

Creating graphics from scratch can be a time-consuming process that requires specific, artistic skills. When the time or ability are not available, numerous sources of preexisting artwork can be used royalty free. This is called clip art. In the past, clip art looked rather dull and uninviting, but now many, avant-garde clip-art libraries are available on the web or CD-ROM. Clip art can be either bitmapped or object-oriented. Make sure you buy it in a file format your software can read and use.

If you have a photograph, drawing, or other image that you would like to use as a graphic, you can scan it into a computer. Scanning is the process of placing a print, slide, drawing, object, photograph, or document on a device called a scanner, which then makes a bitmap image out of it (see Figure 2.13). When you scan an image, the result is always a bitmap.

Of the many decisions to make when you are scanning an image, the most crucial two are setting the size and the image resolution. These two settings are related, and your decisions will vary based upon the output you plan for the image (whether it will be displayed on a computer or printed on paper).

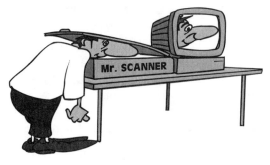

Figure 2.13. Scanning an "object."

Printers can print a much higher resolution than monitors can display. A good comparison is that most laser printers can output from 600 to 1200 dpi (dots per inch), whereas, most computer screens can only display from 60 to 120 ppi (pixels per inch). Note that although dpi and ppi are often used interchangeably, dpi should be used to refer to printer resolution, and ppi refers to image resolution.

Therefore, if you are scanning a picture for the school web page or a PowerPoint presentation, you would want to set the scanner for 60–120 ppi at 100 percent (a common setting is 100 ppi at 100 percent). These settings will ensure that the picture is the same size on the screen as it is in your hands. Since 100 pixels on a screen is approximately one inch, the settings in Figure 2.14 will result in an image that is about 3 by 2 inches, with a size of 60K.

If you wanted a smaller image (let's say 1.5 by 1 inch), you could change the scale to 50 percent as illustrated in Figure 2.15. Note that the result of this scan will be an image that is about 1.5 inches wide and 1 inch tall, with a file size of 16K. Reducing the scale by 50 percent reduced the file size to almost 25 percent. That's because both dimensions of the image were decreased (width and height), reducing the resolution and number of required pixels by one quarter.

Figure 2.14. Scanning settings for 100 percent and 100 ppi.

Figure 2.15. Scanning settings for 50 percent and 100 ppi.

If you need the image to be larger than it is in real life, then you need more pixels. To get more pixels, don't stretch the image in an image processing program—just set the ppi higher, and you will get a larger, onscreen image. For example, the duck in Picture A of Figure 2.16 was scanned at 350 ppi. It looks much sharper than the duck of the same size in Picture B that was scanned at 35 ppi and then stretched. Realize, however, that the difference in the resolution will be much more noticeable if the ducks are printed on a high quality printer than if they are displayed on a computer screen (which can only display 60–120 ppi).

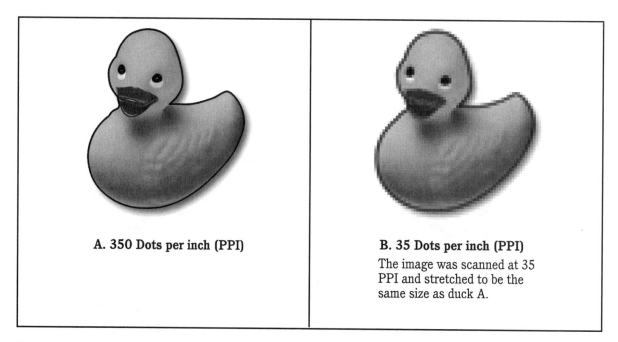

A. 350 Dots per inch (PPI)

B. 35 Dots per inch (PPI)
The image was scanned at 35 PPI and stretched to be the same size as duck A.

Figure 2.16. Scanning resolutions.

If you want a high-quality scan for printing or archival purposes, select 300 (or more) ppi for the resolution at 100 percent scale. Be prepared, however, for large file sizes and pictures that will not "fit" on your computer screen.

If you scan a document or poster that contains text, the entire page will become a bitmapped image (and you won't be able to edit the text). However, most scanners provide software known as OCR (optical character recognition). With the OCR software installed, you can scan letters and numbers, and the software will recognize them as text. You will then be able to edit the text with any word processor!

DIGITAL CAMERAS

Scanners are great if you have a photograph to copy, but what if you still need to take the picture? The best solution may be to use a digital camera. With digital cameras, you do not have to buy film, pay for processing, or wait for the pictures to be developed. Also, since they are already in digital form, they can be downloaded directly into a computer. Things to consider when purchasing and using a digital camera include resolution, compression, and storage media.

Resolution

Digital cameras are sold based on the number of *megapixels* (millions of pixels) they can record for each image. The more pixels, the higher the resolutions. With higher resolutions, you can print larger sizes of high-quality photos. However, just like scanners, the higher resolution settings are designed for printing, not for displaying on the computer. For example, a 3.34 megapixel digital camera can capture an image with 2048 x 1536 pixels, and it can print in sizes greater than 13 x 10 inches. That's great if you plan to print large, high-quality pictures. However, if you will be using the digital camera to capture images for a web page, and your computer is set to a resolution of 800 x 600, you'll only be able to display 480,000 pixels (less than half a megapixel) at a time. Common resolutions are illustrated in Table 2.4.

Table 2.4. Digital Camera Resolutions

Megapixels	Screen Size (pixels)	Print Size (300 dpi)	Print Size (150 dpi)
1.3 megapixels	1280 x 960	4.25 x 3.2 inches	8.53 x 6.4 inches
2.1 megapixels	1600 x 1200	5.33 x 4 inches	10.66 x 8 inches
3.34 megapixels	2048 x 1536	6.83 x 5.12 inches	13.65 x 10.24 inches
5 megapixels	2560 x 1920	8.5 x 6.4 inches	17 x 12.8 inches

As you can see, even the 1.3 megapixel cameras are fine for capturing computer images (most schools are using monitors with less than 1280 x 960 resolution). However, if you want to print some of the images, you might want to consider a camera with higher resolution. In most cases, the price difference is not great between the cameras, and different image resolution modes can be selected whenever you record a picture (high for printing; low for displaying on a computer).

Compression

Two factors influence the file size of an image captured with a digital camera. The first is the resolution of the image (higher resolution images result in larger file sizes). The second is the amount of compression used to store the file. An uncompressed image shot at 2048 x 1536 with 24 bits of color would be almost 10 megabytes in size.

To reduce the file size so that more images can be stored in the camera, use compression. Most often, JPEG compression is used, which decreases the file size, while retaining as much image quality as possible. For example, Kodak cameras offer the selection of Good, Better, or Best picture quality. Each quality level uses different amounts of JPEG compression and results in different file sizes. For photos that require lots of detail, you would use *Best*; for pictures that will be posted on the web, you would use Good. Remember, JPEG compression is lossy—that means that once it is compressed, you can't "go back" to the original, uncompressed image.

Memory Media

Digital cameras don't use film; instead, a CCD (charge-coupled device) in the camera "sees" the image through the lens when the shutter is open. The light collected by the CCD is then converted into digital data, and the data is stored on the camera's memory media. As digital cameras have evolved, several options for memory media have come about—unfortunately, nearly all are incompatible with each other.

Currently, five major types of removable memory (memory media) exist—Smart Media, Compact Flash, Stick memory, CD-R, and diskettes. The first three generally provide 16–64MB of storage (although it can be increased to over 128MB). Built-in CD-Rs (compact disc recordables) are becoming popular because they can store up to 650MB. Floppy disks are convenient, but they can store only 1.44 MB, which is appropriate for a few lower resolution images.

As an example of the storage capacity, a 3-megapixel camera with a 16MB memory card will be able to store about 20 high resolution images with low compression (high quality), while a 1-megapixel camera using the same 16MB card would be able to store three times that many since it has fewer pixels and less information in each image file.

Unless you are planning to take a lot of pictures at remote sites, there is no need to purchase great amounts of additional memory. After you transfer the images to a computer, you can use the same memory over and over again. Nearly all digital cameras also provide a small LCD screen that allows you to view the image as soon as you take it. If you are not happy with the photo, you can simply delete it and free up space for another one.

Transferring Images from the Camera to the Computer

When you are finished taking pictures (or your memory media is full), you will want to transfer the photos to your computer. You have two main options for transferring the pictures—you can connect the camera directly to a computer through the serial, USB, or FireWire port, or you can use a card reader that is attached to the computer. (Note: If you are using floppy disks or CDs, you would simply transfer the files as you would any other data.)

Newer computers have a USB or FireWire port, which are faster for transferring images than a serial port. The transfer process consists of installing download software on the computer (it is provided with the camera), and connecting the cable from the camera to the computer. After the photos are transferred to the computer, you can clear the memory media and take additional pictures.

The other option for transferring images is to purchase a card reader or memory reader. This is a small device that must be compatible with the type of memory you are using. After connecting the reader to the computer and installing the software, you can use it to transfer photos from the memory media. This approach is useful if you take numerous pictures at a remote site, and have several memory sticks or memory cards.

Once an image is transferred from the camera to the computer, you can use image processing software to crop it or change it any way you want. Most cameras come with image editing software.

If you want to display the photos on a television monitor instead of a computer, you can connect the analog output on the camera to the television through an RCA (video) cable.

SUMMARY

Graphics come in many forms, shapes, and sizes. Besides conveying concepts and other information, graphics can be used to motivate and direct learners, as well as to personalize and improve their presentations.

Computer graphics can be created in an image editing program, purchased as clip art, scanned into a computer, or captured with a digital camera. With a basic understanding of how images are created, displayed, and saved, you will be able to answer students' questions and help them produce images that communicate knowledge and information through better presentations, web pages, and documents.

GLOSSARY

4-bit color. A graphic setting that can contain up to 16 different colors for each pixel.

8-bit color. A graphic setting that can contain up to 256 different colors for each pixel

16-bit color. A graphic setting that can contain up to 65,536 different colors for each pixel.

24-bit. A graphic setting that can contain up to 16.7 million different colors for each pixel. It is often referred to as true color.

adaptive palette. When an adaptive palette is created, the 256 most commonly used colors in a 24-bit color image are selected and used to convert that image to a 256 color image.

Adobe Type 1. A popular format for fonts (object-oriented). The program Adobe Type Manager must be installed on the computer before these fonts can be used.

aspect ratio. The relationship between the width and height of an image. For example, if an image has a 4 by 3 aspect ratio (written as 4:3) that means if you divide the width by 4, then take that number and multiply it by 3, you will have the height. The resolutions of 640 x 480, 800 x 600, 1024 x 768 and 1600 x 1200 all have a 4:3 aspect ratio.

Bayer patterned dither. A dithering technique in which the pixels are arranged in precise chessboard patterns.

Bezier curve. Special curved lines that can be bent to any shape by moving points that change its curvature. Used for fonts and other graphic images.

binary. Mathematical system used internally by a computer. It consists of only two numerals: 0 and 1. Each place value is in multiples of two.

bit. The smallest piece of information a computer can handle. A bit is a single 0 or 1 value. Eight bits working together is a byte.

bit depth. The total number of bits needed to make each pixel of an image. Common bit depths are 8 bits per pixel (256 colors) and 24 bits per pixel (16.7 million colors). See color depth.

bitmapped graphic. A computer graphic image composed of a grid of pixels, which are in turn represented by bits.

browser safe colors. The 216 colors that do not shift between platforms, operating systems, or most browsers.

byte. Eight bits working together. A single byte can have any value from 0 to 255.

color depth. The maximum number of colors an image can have because of the number of bits per pixel that are available. Common color depths are 256 colors (8 bits per pixel) and 16.7 million (24 bits per pixel). See bit depth.

compression. Technique used to store files with fewer bits; therefore, less disk storage space is required.

digital camera. A camera that records images in true digital form. The images are usually saved on the camera (or a memory card) and then downloaded to a computer.

dithering. The positioning of different colored pixels within an image that uses a 256-color palette. Dithering is used to simulate a color that does not exist in that particular palette.

dpi (dots per inch). Refers to printing resolution of an image. Most printers can print 300–1200 dpi.

error diffusion dither. A dithering technique that arranges the pixels pseudo-randomly in the images.

file extension. A portion of a filename, separated from the primary filename by a period. It contains information about the image's resolution, palette, compression, color, and other characteristics.

font. Special graphics files that contain the shapes of all of the letters of the alphabet.

font style. Common attributes used to describe the weight, structure, and form of a font.

GIF (graphic interchange format). File format for web graphics that allows for 256 colors. It uses a lossless compression and is best used for line art and graphics with solid areas of colors. GIFs also support interlacing, transparency, and animation. GIF89a is another name for transparent or animated GIFs.

halftoning. A way to simulate additional colors and values by varying the size of gridded dots used to compose the image.

interlacing (GIF). Allows a GIF to load quickly at a low resolution and then gradually display a higher resolution.

JPEG (Joint Photographic Experts Group). A file format for web graphics that allows for millions of colors. JPEG images use a lossy compression, and they are best used for continuous tone photographs and gradients.

kerning. A term used to describe the spacing between characters.

leading. A term used to describe the spacing between lines of text.

lossless compression. Graphic compression technique (such as GIF) that preserves all image qualities and information from the original file.

lossy compression. Graphic compression technique (such as JPEG) that sacrifices some image quality for greater compression ratios.

megapixels. A term used to define the image resolution of digital cameras. A megapixel is one million pixels. Digital cameras range from one to five megapixels in resolution.

memory media. Methods used to store images inside a digital camera, until they are transferred to a computer. Current options include: Smart Media, Compact Flash, Stick memory, CD-R, and floppy diskettes.

object-oriented drawings. Graphics that are composed of separate geometric objects that can be layered one atop the other to create images. Also known as vector drawings or simply drawings.

OCR (optical character recognition). Software that enables a scanner to recognize individual letters. Text that is scanned with OCR software can be imported and manipulated by a word processing program.

palette. Total number of colors that can be used in an image at one time. The size of the palette is the color depth of the image.

pixel. Pixel stands for "picture element." It is a small square of a single color. It is the smallest element of a bitmapped image or a computer screen. Many pixels arranged in a grid create a bitmapped image, and the total number of pixels' width and height is the image's resolution.

PNG (Portable Network Graphics). PNG is a lossless format that supports interlacing and transparency.

Postscript. A page description language, invented by Adobe, and is one of that company's core technologies. It is a language used to describe object-oriented graphics, bitmaps, and text to postscript-compatible devices, such as printers. It is also the basis of Adobe Illustrator drawings and Adobe Acrobat documents.

ppi (pixels per inch). Refers to image resolution. Most monitors can display 60–120 ppi.

primary colors. The primary colors are the three colors that when combined compose all other colors. Red, green, and blue are the primary colors used in computer graphics. Magenta, yellow, and cyan are the primary colors used in printing.

resolution. The total number of pixels that compose an image. For on-screen graphics, resolution is normally expressed as the number of pixels wide times the number of pixels tall, such as 1280 x 1024. For print graphics, resolution is normally expressed as the inches wide and tall, and the number of dots per inch, such as 8 x 10 at 600dpi.

RGB color model. Red, green, and blue are the three primary colors of light. RGB is additive color, meaning if you mixed the colors together, you would get white. RGB is the color setting you want to use for anything that will be seen on a computer monitor.

sans serif. Sans serif fonts have no points capping the strokes. "Sans" means "without." The most common sans serif font is called Helvetica; in Microsoft Windows it is called Arial.

scanner. A hardware peripheral that takes a "picture" of an item and transfers the image to a computer.

serif. Serif fonts have small points called "serifs" that cap the ends of most strokes. The most common serif font is Times Roman.

true color. True color occurs when each pixel is defined by 24 bits. True color can display 16.7 million different colors for each pixel.

Truetype. A standard for representing fonts in an object-oriented form that can be easily scaled to any desired size.

Unicode. A standard for representing letters and symbols for many different written languages. The standard English letters are a subset of Unicode.

vector drawings. Graphics that are composed of separate geometric objects that can be layered one atop the other to create images. Also known as object-oriented drawings or simply drawings.

web-safe palette. A computer palette that contains 216 colors that are considered "safe" to use on the Internet. The colors will appear the same in both Netscape and Internet Explorer, without dithering.

RESOURCES

Image Processing and Bitmap Editing Programs

URL	Product Name	Description
http://www.adobe.com/products/photoshop/ http://www.planetphotoshop.com/ http://desktoppublishing.com/photoshop.html	Adobe Photoshop	The leading bitmap editing application. It is almost infinitely extendable by using plug-ins, which are small third-party components that add features to PhotoShop.
http://www.corel.com/	Corel PhotoPaint	An image processing program that is bundled with the CorelDraw suite.
http://www.corel.com/	Corel Painter	The leading "realistic" painting program—for simulating oil paints, watercolors, charcoal, etc.
http://www.jasc.com/	PaintShop Pro	A popular, inexpensive image processing program—perfect when you don't want an application as expensive as Photoshop.
http://www.gimp.org	GIMP	Open source freeware image editing application. The most widely used on Linux platform.
http://www.microfrontier.com/	ColorIt and Enhance	Two Macintosh-only image editing programs.

See also: http://directory.google.com/Top/Computers/Software/Graphics/Image_Editing/

Object-Oriented Drawing Programs

URL	Product Name	Description
http://www.adobe.com/ products/illustrator/	Adobe Illustrator	The first object-oriented postscript drawing program, from the company that invented postscript.
http://www.macromedia.com /software/freehand/	Macromedia Freehand	The second popular postscript drawing program—integrates well with Macromedia Flash for web graphics development.
http://www.corel.com/	CorelDraw	Feature-rich postscript drawing program with many unique tools and effects.
http://www.xara.com/ products/xarax/	Xara X	An advanced, inexpensive Windows-only vector drawing program that simulates artistic effects usually limited to bitmap editing applications.

See also: http://directory.google.com/Top/Computers/Software/Graphics/Vector_Based/

3

ADVANCED
COMPUTER GRAPHICS
Animation, 3D Graphics, and Virtual Reality

A Scenario

Tracy finished dinner and went to her desk, tired after a long day of classes and basketball practice. Her bed looked inviting, but she knew she needed to study for the American history quiz. The focus of the quiz was the Civil War, in particular Florida's role in the battle. Tracy was not overly excited about the Civil War, or history in general. However, her teacher had mentioned a Florida history web site that sounded really interesting.

Before Tracy realized it, three hours had passed. She was almost mesmerized by the information she found on the web. The web site had original letters written by slaves during the war, movies of Civil War reenactments, animations showing troop movements, and, best of all, virtual reality (VR) tours of many of Florida's Civil War forts.

When she accessed the VR movie of Fort Jefferson (located on a small island off the southern tip of Florida), Tracy felt like she was actually on the island. She could easily visualize the way the fort had looked 150 years ago, when it was one of the few Union forts located in the South. Using her mouse, she was able to see the entire panoramic view of the fort, and could even zoom in to see close-up shots of the cell where Dr. Samuel Mudd had been imprisoned. "Wow!" Tracy thought, "Maybe history can be interesting after all!"

INTRODUCTION

After students have mastered the basics of creating and editing computer graphics, they will probably become intrigued with advanced graphic techniques. For example, animations, such as a ball bouncing or a bird flying, are relatively common features on web pages and in HyperStudio stacks. Simple 3D graphics can be created in PowerPoint or Excel, and inexpensive programs are available for more complex figures. In addition, armed with a camera and a software program, students can create virtual reality tours of their classrooms or schools. This chapter provides an introduction to the following topics:

- Bitmapped (frame-based) animations

- Object-oriented (path-based) animations

- 3D graphics techniques

- Panoramic virtual reality

- Object-based virtual reality

Note: Color illustrations, links, more detailed information, and examples can be found at http://www.magentastudios.org/.

ANIMATION

Animations encompass a wide-variety of media—from inexpensive flipbooks to complex movies, such as Disney's *Toy Story*. All animations consist of a series of images (with minor changes from one to the next) that are shown in rapid succession and "fool" the eye into seeing motion. This same technique is used in television or filmstrips, which consist of individual frames, played in rapid sequence. Rapidly showing a sequence of still images causes an illusion of motion, which is called *persistence of vision*.

The optimal speed for the appearance of smooth motion in an animation is 30 frames per second (fps). American TV and VHS video both adhere to the standard 30 fps (known as NTSC video). Considering that there are 60 seconds in each minute, to create a 30 fps animation (of one minute duration), you would have to create 1,800 individual images! Luckily, you can make animations with slower frame rates that will still be acceptable. However, if the playback speed is below about 10 fps, your eye sees the separate frames and loses the illusion of motion. When preparing an animation for the web, remember that the frame rate will also impact the file size—a 30 fps animation sequence would be about three times the file size of a 10 fps animation, and would take three times as long for a user to download.

Animations fall into the same two main categories as other two-dimensional graphics: bitmaps and object-oriented (see Chapter 2). Bitmapped animation systems show one bitmapped image rapidly after another to simulate motion, while object-oriented animation systems take objects (including small bitmaps) and move them along linear or curved paths.

Bitmapped (Frame-Based) Animation

Bitmapped animations consist of individual images that are displayed in rapid sequence. For example, in Figure 3.1, each figure would be an individual image. If these eight images were then displayed in rapid succession, it would appear as if the man was walking. Creating a bitmapped animation, therefore, means drawing several individual images—or, more commonly, beginning with one image and then modifying it a little for each new frame.

Figure 3.1. Bitmapped animation.

One of the most popular formats for creating animations in educational settings is GIF animation. The GIF format was originally created by CompuServe to allow for a lossless compression of images on the Internet. Although it was not originally designed for animations, a variation (known as GIF89) is now the most common animation format being used on the web. Nearly all of the small, animated figures you see on the web (such as a bouncing ball or a dancing rabbit) are GIF animations.

Several, free software programs are available that you and your students can use to create GIF animations. The two most popular are GIF Construction Set (for Windows) and GIF Builder (for Macintosh). To create a GIF animation, you can use almost any graphics program to produce a series of still images that have slight alterations from one image to the next. Then, you import these images into a program such as GIF Construction Set and set the play time so that each image will display a split second before the next one appears (see Figure 3.2, page 52). HyperStudio offers a similar method for creating bitmapped animations (referred to as Cel Animations).

Adobe Photoshop, the professional image processing program, comes integrated with Adobe ImageReady. ImageReady is an application for preparing graphics for the web—including creating GIF animations out of Photoshop layers. With simple, bitmapped animation programs, you have to draw each frame of the animation sequence, which can be a time-consuming process. With more advanced programs, you draw only certain major frames called *keyframes,* and the program calculates the other frames called the *in-betweens*. If your program does not calculate the in-betweens for you, it might at least provide *onion skins*—the ability to see previous frames and trace over them like tracing paper on a lightbox. With onion skins, it is easier to create the small changes from one frame to the next.

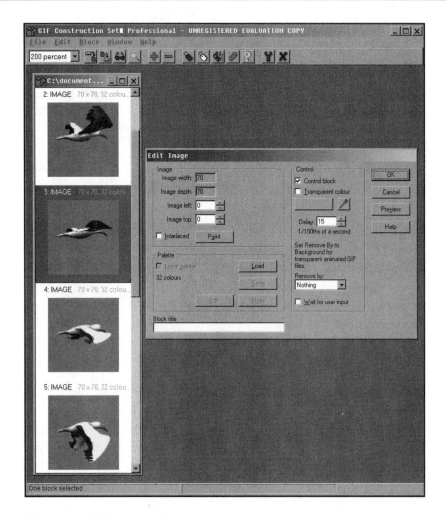

Figure 3.2. GIF construction set.

Object-Oriented (Path-Based) Animation

Simple object-oriented animations (also referred to as path-based animations) involve moving an object on a screen that has a constant background; for example, an airplane may fly across the screen or a ball may bounce through the scene. To create an object-oriented animation, you generally create the background first, then select an object or image and define a path. For example, in HyperStudio, you would create a background, then select "Add a Graphic Object" from the *Objects* menu, define an object, and select "Play Animation" from the *Actions* menu. You then define the path (by dragging the object with your mouse) and specify the options in the *Animation* dialog box (see Figure 3.3). Additional options can be set in the *Path Options* dialog box (see Figure 3.4).

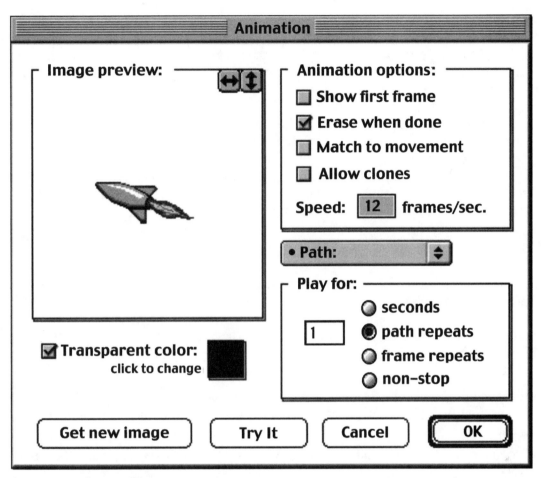

Figure 3.3. HyperStudio Animation dialog box.

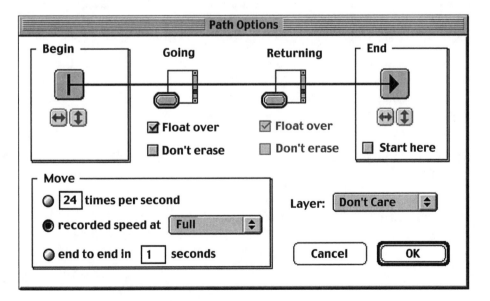

Figure 3.4. HyperStudio Path Options dialog box.

Another popular animation program is Flash by Macromedia. This program has become popular for creating animations for the web because it uses object-oriented graphics, which are often much smaller than the bitmapped graphics. Another advantage of object-oriented graphics over bitmaps is the ability to zoom in toward an object, while retaining a sharp image. Flash also offers many sophisticated options, such as keyframes and in-betweens. You can draw a character on frame one, go to frame 10, grab its left arm and raise it. The software will then calculate the arm's motion for frames 2 through 9. You can also incorporate sounds with Flash animations.

In addition to Flash, Macromedia produces another object-oriented 2D animation package, called Macromedia Director. In Director, you can take objects, such as circles, squares, or small bitmapped images, and move them along paths across the screen. You can find more information on both Flash and Director at http://www.macromedia.com/. Note: Most object-oriented animation programs can also output animations in the bitmapped formats.

Animation Guidelines

Creating animations can be a lot of fun, but it can also be very time-consuming. The following guidelines can help ensure that your students' animations are appropriate and effective.

- Make sure the animation has a purpose. Effective animations can be used to illustrate concepts that are difficult to convey in words or still pictures. However, inappropriate animations can be distracting.

- Start with a plan. Prior to working with the software programs, it is beneficial for the students to map out their plan on paper or storyboards. Even rough sketches can save valuable time later.

- Be conscious of file sizes. Animations are great on the web; however, the file sizes must be very small. This may mean using fewer colors, making the physical size smaller, or limiting the number of frames per second.

- Test the animations on different computer systems. The speed of an animation may vary based on the connection speed and the speed of the computer. An animation may work great when a student creates it, but become a real "dud" over the Internet or on a slower computer.

- Beware of plug-ins. Some older web browsers require plug-ins to play animations. Flash requires a plug-in for browsers other than Internet Explorer; however, it is by far the most ubiquitous plug-in there is, and it is safe to assume most people will have it. With Internet Explorer, you don't have to worry about most of the popular plug-ins—it can download them automatically when they are needed.

- Design carefully. If you try to create the illusion of movement in a small part of the frame (for example, only a hand moves on a person), the animation will look much smoother, even at low frame rates.

- Keep the animation sequences short, or allow an option to interrupt the animation and proceed with the program. If the animation is created in Flash or as a video file, include buttons for the viewer to be able to pause, resume, and replay the animation.

- Avoid animations that loop infinitely—they can be distracting when the viewer is attempting to read the text on the page. If it must loop, limit it to two or three times, and have only one animation per page.

3D GRAPHICS

All of the graphics types discussed so far (both bitmaps and objects) are 2D graphics—meaning as you work on them in your graphics programs, you are only dealing with flat things layered together on a flat surface. If 2D graphics are like painting and drawing in the real world, then 3D graphics are like sculpting. Three-dimensional computer graphics provide a way to create objects, characters, and scenes inside a computer that are more than just flat images—as you work on them, they have actual depth. The distinction between 2D and 3D graphics is not what the end result looks like. For example, some 2D graphics can look very realistic and deep, while 3D graphics can be designed to have a flat look. The differences between the two types are the tools used by the artist and the techniques used to create the images with those tools.

3D graphics are very popular in movies, commercials, games, and other forms of entertainment, as well as having almost unlimited applications within an educational environment. Creating three-dimensional graphics and animations can be a complicated and creative process that involves many steps, and sometimes many different software applications. The steps can be broken down into these categories: modeling, attributes, lights and cameras, animation, and rendering.

Modeling

The first step is modeling. This is where you build (within the computer) the objects that will be the characters, sets, props, or scenery. Modeling systems use various methods for constructing 3D objects. At the high end are programs such as Discreet 3DS MAX and Silicon Graphics Maya that allow a lot of flexibility in the models and how they are created (see Figure 3.5). At the low end, simple 3D objects can be created in programs such as Microsoft PowerPoint and Word (see Figure 3.6). The Microsoft Office products are limited to a single type of 3D object called an *extrusion*—meaning they are simple flat shapes that have been given depth. Squares become cubes, circles become cylinders, but there are no spheres, cones, teapots, or dolphins. Actual 3D graphics applications can create any shape you can imagine.

Figure 3.5. Complex 3D model created in Discreet 3DS MAX.

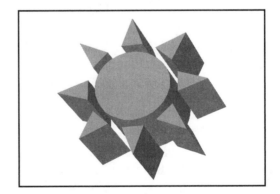

Figure 3.6. 3D graphic created in Microsoft Word by taking a flat drawing of a sun and giving it depth.

Polygonal modeling means the image or sculpture is composed of flat triangles or other polygons, connected together to form surfaces of objects. Think of this as small pieces of stiff cardboard attached edge to edge to construct something. A sphere, for example, would not be completely smooth. It would have a faceted appearance, like a cut gemstone or Disney World's EPCOT ball in Orlando, Florida. The more triangles, the smaller they are, and the greater their distance from the camera or your eye, the smoother the appearance of the surface. Polygonal modelers are the most common modeling systems on the market because they are simpler mathematically and faster to calculate than the other methods.

Because creating 3D models requires a great deal of time and talent, it often helps to purchase 3D models. The polygonal file format (DXF) is the industry standard for exchanging models between different applications and for 3D clip art libraries of prebuilt models.

Attributes

After your model is created or purchased, you move on to the next step, which is applying *attributes*. Here, you decide which materials to use to compose the objects. In traditional arts, a sculptor first chooses a block of marble, wood, or metal and then creates the sculpture from it. In computer graphics, the process is reversed—you create a sculpture, then decide what it will look like. Objects in 3D graphics applications can be any color; they can be reflective, transparent, or opaque; they can be rough or smooth, shiny or dull (see Figure 3.6). They can have images, patterns, and textures, or even animation sequences or video clips applied to their surfaces (see Figure 3.7). Models can be made to mimic most objects that exist in the real world, and many that do not.

Figure 3.7. Attributes applied to spheres.

Lights and Cameras

You have created the models and applied their paint and texture. Next, you will want to place your *lights* and *cameras* in the scene, just like for studio photography. There are many kinds of lights, such as directional spotlights, omnidirectional lights, ambient light, constant light, linear light, quadratic light, area lights, and so forth. Each light creates different effects and a different look (see Figure 3.8). The nature of the lighting is key to establishing the mood and realistic appearance of a 3D scene, as important as the modeling and the attributes. In high-end programs, the cameras can be set as wide angle, telephoto, or anywhere in-between, just like cameras in the real world. Some cameras even have filters and options to modify the image as it is being shot.

Figure 3.8. The same model and attributes, with three different lighting conditions. The first one appears flat and cartoon-like; the middle one has proper shading creating a look of depth; and the third has a high contrast look.

Animation

The fourth step is animation. This is usually done by a process called *keyframing*, which means the objects are placed at the extremes of their motion, and the computer calculates all of the frames in-between. For example, let's say you want a ball to start at the top of the screen on the first frame, hit a table on the thirtieth frame, bounce high by the fortieth, and hit the floor on the sixtieth. To do this, you need to position the ball only on those four frames, not on all 60 frames in the sequence, like in traditional hand-drawn or stop-motion animation (see Figure 3.9).

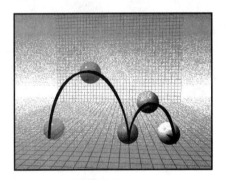

Figure 3.9. Animating a ball.

Cameras and lights can animate, and in many programs attributes can, too, so they become more or less transparent, change color, go from marble to wood texture, or whatever. Objects can move, rotate, squash, and stretch or even morph. *Morphing* means one object can change shape to look like another object. In addition to keyframing, many high-end animation programs use processes called inverse kinematics and physical modeling. These processes allow objects to move on their own according to natural laws such as force, gravity, flocking, wind, and collision. With these systems, you could create a virtual pool table, strike the cue ball with your virtual cue, and the other balls would all animate as necessary when struck. *Skeletal animation* is a process whereby you can animate structures (bones) that control the shape of a surface (skin) according to predefined relationships between them (muscles). Animation systems are becoming so advanced that you can cause objects to react to the actions of other objects or even according to personality profiles and behavior rules, without moving them directly.

Rendering

Your models are built and they have their attributes. You have set lights and cameras in the scene, and animated everything that needs to move. *Rendering* is the final step. The computer handles this, but it is usually the most time-consuming part. The computer reads the information the animator provided about the models (including the attributes, movements, lights, and cameras) and calculates the appearance of every frame. The time it takes to calculate a frame depends on the speed of the computer and the rendering method. Common rendering methods are: Wireframe, Flat shading, Gouraud, Phong, Raytracing and Radiosity. The more realistic rendering methods are the most time-consuming.

Wireframe simply draws lines around the edges of the surfaces of an object (see Figure 3.10). In most programs, this is the display mode you see when you are working on the model. You would use this rendering mode to do quick animation tests. It is the fastest to calculate and the least realistic, because it ignores the lights and does not use an object's attributes.

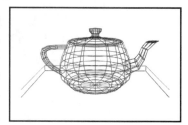

Figure 3.10. Wireframe.

Figure 3.11. Flat shading.

Flat shading is fast and not very realistic. It works by calculating a color for each polygon face (see Figure 3.11). Each surface is given a solid flat color and any attempts at attributes, such as transparency or patterns, are pitiful at best. This method is used for simulators, games, and other real-time applications, because the images can be calculated very quickly. In some 3D modeling programs, the models are rendered flat-shaded instead of wireframe as you work on them. Most computer games use flat shading.

Gouraud improves on flat shading by smoothing out edges between polygons (see Figure 3.12). It calculates the color for each vertex, then blends them across the surface of the polygons. On most modern computers, this is fast enough for real-time display.

Figure 3.12. Gouraud.

Figure 3.13. Phong shading.

Phong shading is much more realistic, and can handle nearly any kind of attributes, yet it is more time-consuming than flat shading (see Figure 3.13). Although wireframe calculates each polygon edge, flat shading calculates each polygon face, and Gouraud calculates each polygon vertex, Phong works by calculating colors for every pixel of an image. Phong and its related methods, such as Blinn, Straus, and others (named after the people who invented them) are the highest quality rendering methods used by many of the more budget-conscious animation products available on Macs and PCs.

Raytracing is an even more realistic method, because it approximates the actual physical properties of light as it bounces off objects toward the camera (see Figure 3.14). It literally "traces" the path of each beam of light from the light source to the objects in the scene. Only raytracing can create truly realistic transparent and reflective objects and cast real shadows. Raytracing is incredibly time-consuming because it requires that the computer perform a great deal of calculations per image pixel. Because of the calculations involved, it is usually performed on larger multiprocessor UNIX computers and Windows 2000 or Windows XP workstations, such as from Silicon Graphics, yet there are raytracers available on the smaller computers as well.

Figure 3.14. Raytracing.

Figure 3.15. Radiosity.

Some people feel that raytracing is too realistic—more realistic than reality. Raytracing creates a clean, sharp, quality look that screams "this was done on a computer." *Radiosity* is a rendering process that, when combined with raytracing, creates even more accurate lighting conditions by creating images that are not as sharp and crisp as raytracing (see Figure 3.15). In the real world, many surfaces in an interior environment are not lit directly by a light source at all, and are visible only by light reflected off other surfaces. For example, sunlight filtering through a window will cast a bright square of illumination onto the floor, which then bounces onto the walls and furniture within the room. Also, a surface illuminated indirectly may appear to be a different color than it would appear if lit directly, since color from one surface can "spill" or "bleed" onto another, particularly if bright colors are placed next to more subdued hues. Also, as you might suspect, because it is one of the highest quality rendering methods, radiosity is even more time-consuming to calculate. The simplest scenes can take hours to create.

HARDWARE AND SOFTWARE
FOR 3D GRAPHICS

Although creating simple 3D figures in PowerPoint could be your initial step into 3D graphics, you may soon find that you want to obtain an actual 3D graphics program. While software for high-end 3D graphics production could cost more than $10,000, it is possible to gain exposure to this exciting field for much less. Most 3D software for Windows and Macintosh computers ranges from $300 to $12,000. Some 3D programs are even free (see Table 3.1).

Table 3.1. Software for 3D Graphics

Company	Product	Platforms	Description	Price*	URL
Silicon Graphics	Alias| Wavefront Maya	Windows NT/2000 Pro, IRIX, Red Hat Linux, and Mac OS X	High end and expensive. Used for games and feature films.	$7,500+	http://www .aliaswavefront.com/
Avid	SoftImage	IRIX and Windows NT	Expensive popular high-end software.	$7,995–$11,995	http://www.avid .com/
Discreet	3DS MAX	Windows 98/NT	Midrange price and popular. Widely used in game development.	$3,495	http://www.discreet .com/
NewTek	LightWave	Windows NT, Macintosh and Mac OS X	Midrange price. Used in TV and film.	$2,495	http://www.newtek .com/
Caligari	Truespace	Windows 98/NT	Inexpensive entry-level software. Easy to use yet powerful.	$299	http://www.caligari .com/
Hash	Animation Master	Windows 98/NT and Macintosh	Inexpensive entry-level software. Easy to use yet powerful.	$299	http://www.hash .com/

No company. Open-source freeware.	POV-Ray (Persistence of Vision Raytracer)	All platforms. It runs in a text-mode command line.	Freeware high-quality Raytracing engine.	Free	http://www.povray.org/
Soft-Tronics	Moray	Windows 95/98/NT	Shareware Modeler for POV-Ray.	Donation	http://www.stmuc.com/moray

*Prices are as of the time of this writing. See the web sites of each product for current pricing information.

Most 3D animation software programs for Microsoft Windows-based PCs prefer that you run Windows 2000 or XP, although many will run on Windows 98 and Windows ME. At least 128MB of RAM would be the minimum to operate most 3D graphics programs, with 512MB being a good level for practical use. However, the more RAM, the better.

To create 3D animation on a Macintosh, you should use a Macintosh G3 or G4, though some of the programs will run on an iMac or even an older PowerMac. The higher-end Macintosh graphics applications are designed for OS X. Memory requirements would be about the same as for the PC. The Macintosh supports a large variety of 3D graphics programs, many of which focus on multimedia production.

VIRTUAL REALITY

Virtual reality (VR) is one of those overly hyped buzz phrases that you hear used to describe things ranging from the capabilities of StarTrek's Holodeck to the 3D movies (with 3D glasses) from the 1950s. For our purposes, we define it much narrower: Virtual reality means navigable computer graphic simulations or environments. Its applications are designed to simulate a place, so that you, as a user, can explore that place. With the addition of Artificial Intelligence, that virtual place can be populated with virtual people, animals, and other critters that react to each other and to you.

With many VR applications, you can do more than just look at objects in a scene—you can open doors, go up or down stairs, pick up objects, open boxes, and interact with a computer graphic world as fully as if you were there. For a complete VR experience, you need special input and output devices. One of these, VR goggles, uses the rotation and angle of your head to show you the proper view of your synthetic surroundings. Data input gloves and wearable, whole body suits let you manipulate the objects in front of you.

High-end VR with head displays, data gloves, and sensors are too expensive and complex to be feasible for most schools. There are, however, ways to create VR that you simply view on the screen and control with a mouse—something far more feasible, economical, and effective for education.

VR technologies, like 2D graphics and animation, can be divided into the same two primary categories—bitmapped and object-oriented, or more precisely, image-based VR and object-based VR. Each has its advantages and disadvantages, depending on the situation.

Image-Based Virtual Reality

Several years ago, Apple Computer Corporation developed a virtual reality technology called QuickTime VR. It is an extension to QuickTime, their popular digital video format. This technique allows you to create a virtual world out of a single, flat *panoramic* image or to rotate an object.

Panoramic VR

Panoramic VR is similar to being tied to a swivel chair in the middle of an environment—you can look up and down, left and right, even turn all the way around. What you cannot do is get up and walk from place to place, or grab things in the scene and manipulate them. This is because image-based VR works by taking a single panoramic bitmap and "wrapping" it around you, like it was painted on the inside surface of a giant sphere or a cylinder that you sit inside (see Figure 3.16).

Figure 3.16. Panoramic VR.

The process of photographing the scenes is simple. You need a camera with a wide-angle lens and a tripod. You place the camera on the tripod, but position the camera so it can rotate on the focal point of the lens. Take a shot, then rotate the camera a few degrees—making sure the new view overlaps the old shot a sufficient amount. Continue shooting and rotating until you have a series of pictures that represent a full 360 degrees around the tripod (see Figure 3.17).

Figure 3.17. Series of photographs for VR panorama.

Next, scan the photographs into the computer (or download them from a digital camera). If you look at the photos next to each other, they do not blend smoothly like a panorama. That's where the stitching program (such as QuickTime VR Authoring Studio or MGI Soft PhotoVista) comes in. The stitching program bends each image, overlaps the matching parts, and stitches the images together (see Figure 3.18). Note that the straight lines (like the sidewalk) appear as curved.

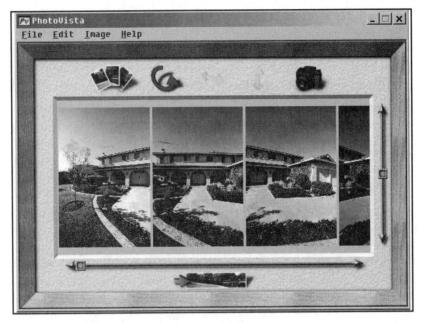

Figure 3.18. Stitching program overlaps photographs.

A panorama VR player (such as QuickTime) can correct the distortion by unbending the part of the image it displays. Viewing this image through a VR player creates an illusion of "looking" around the scene in all directions. Figure 3.19 illustrates the same panoramic image, as seen through the QuickTime Player. Use the mouse button or the keyboard to "move" left or right or to zoom in and out of the image.

Figure 3.19. The panorama through the QuickTime viewer.

The wider the angle of your camera's lens, the fewer shots you need to take. That means the stitching program has to do less distortion and your panorama quality will be greater. Or, you can use a panoramic camera that creates a single panoramic image directly on film. With this approach, you can take a single 360-degree panorama in one shot. Panoramas don't even have to be created photographically—they can be made from worlds built in a 3D-modeling program. In this case, simply rotate the virtual camera in the program the same way you would rotate the real camera for photos.

VR panoramas can also support the creation of hot-spot areas. For example, you could click on a doorknob in a panoramic image and a new image would be displayed, as if you walked into the next room. Imagine your students creating panoramas of several classrooms at your school and then linking them together with hot spots!

Object Movies

In addition to the panoramas, there is another form of image-based VR called *object movies*. With panoramas *you* "rotate" to see the environment you are in; with object movies you stay still as you rotate an object in front of you. Like panoramas, VR objects also support hot spots for linking to other objects or media, and you can zoom into or out from a given view.

The process for photographing an object movie is a bit more involved than photographing a panorama. While panoramic VR is created from a single bitmapped image, an object movie needs many images of an object, seen from every possible angle. For a small object, you place it on a turntable in front of a camera on a tripod. Rotate it bit by bit and photograph it every few degrees, until it has spun a full 360 degrees. Then the camera is moved higher or lower, to get a different elevation perspective (see Figure 3.20).

Figure 3.20. Photographing an object movie.

The object is photographed again in a full 360-degree sequence. Repeat this process for each desired elevation. The pictures are then imported into a computer program, sorted into rows and columns, and compiled into an object movie file. The result is a movie of an object that can be manipulated or "spun" for viewing on all sides (see Figure 3.21).

Figure 3.21. Four different views of an object movie featuring Pietá by Käthe Kollwitz. Used with permission from the Teacher's Guide to the Holocaust web site.

Apple invented these VR technologies for the Macintosh platform, but several other software products are on the market that use similar techniques for development on Windows computers. The price ranges between them are immense—companies like IPIX charge "annual subscriptions" starting at $6,000, but MGI Soft PhotoVista offers a one-time software cost of $49.95 (see Table 3.2). Each of these programs has their own development tools, and most can playback either through the QuickTime 5.0 plug-in or with their own browser plug-ins. Some of the programs are compatible with each other; some are not.

Table 3.2. Software for Virtual Reality

Company	Product	Description/Comments	URL
Apple	QuickTime VR Authoring Studio	Develop on Macintosh only, best choice if you use Macintosh.	http://www.apple.com/quicktime/qtvr/authoringstudio/
IPIX	IPIX	Software, camera kits, and service. VERY expensive.	http://www.ipix.com/
MGI Soft	PhotoVista and Reality Studio	Inexpensive, good quality, open standards.	http://www.mgisoft.com/
IMove	IMove	Panoramic full-motion video.	http://www.imoveinc.com/

Object-Based Virtual Reality

Object-based virtual reality is the "true" type of virtual reality. It consists of geometric shapes created with 3D modeling programs to create a virtual environment. Object-based VR differs from image-based VR in that the objects are fully three-dimensional, not just 2D bitmapped images. With object-based VR, users are not confined to a single point rotation; they can fully explore a virtual world or object. It is possible to walk up or down stairs, go down a turning hallway, and enter the next room. Figure 3.22 illustrates an object-based VR web site, created by NASA, that allows you to move around the space station and manipulate objects. Object-based VR is, therefore, much better for many interactive games and immersive environments.

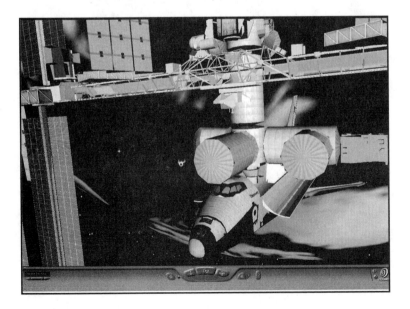

Figure 3.22. NASA's VRML model of the Space Shuttle docked at the International Space Station.
Available at: http://spaceflight.nasa.gov/gallery/vrml/station/iss_20k_jem.wrl.

Though object-based virtual reality is extremely popular with computer games, it has been slow to take off on the Internet. The standard that was established for object-based virtual reality on the Internet was VRML (Virtual Reality Modeling Language). VRML is not just a file format; it is an actual language for describing the objects you see, not unlike HTML is a language describing the text and graphics on a web page. Though a single company (Open Inventor) created VRML, it became an open standard. A multicompany governing body, called the Web3D consortium (http://www.web3d.org/), keeps up VRML's standards. The consortium is developing the next-generation 3D modeling language called X3D.

Because VRML is a programming language similar to C and Java, VRML worlds can also be programmed directly without using third-party software. (The intricacies of the language are beyond the scope of this book.) However, you don't have to type in complicated programming commands to make VRML worlds because many 3D modeling programs allow you to make VRML scenes easily. VRML can be developed in traditional 3D modeling and animation software, like the ones listed in the 3D graphics section.

Once the VRML code is created, any 3D viewer that handles VRML can read and view it. To view VRML in a web browser, you need a browser plug-in, such as the Cosmo Player (http://www.cai.com /cosmo/). The VRML files store dimensions and texture commands and transmit this information to the plug-in, which then handles rendering and manipulation. Since the plug-in is responsible for the rendering and screen updates, a VRML world can look very different from one computer to another.

To keep the file sizes small enough to transfer efficiently over the web, the objects are generally created with a minimum of bitmapped textures, and those textures are low resolution. The complexity of the geometry is also kept to a minimum to increase the playback speed. Users who are accustomed to viewing high-quality 3D interactive games on CD-ROM may be disappointed with the low level of detail included in most VRML objects and scenes.

Besides VRML, there are other competing object-based VR technologies, such as Cycore's Cult3D (http://www.cult3d.com/), Viewpoint's MetaStream (http://www.viewpoint.com/), and Adobe's Atmosphere (http://www.adobe.com/products/atmosphere/main.html). These use highly optimized, proprietary binary file formats, unlike VRML and X3D, which are language specifications. Take a look at their examples—they seem better and are more realistic than VRML, and are growing in popularity while VRML use is on the decline.

There are some VR programs that create *VR scenes*—integrated VR worlds that combine panoramic VR, object movies, and object-oriented VR in a single virtual environment. For example, you could create a scene with a panoramic VR backdrop, a building made in VRML, and assorted people and objects made as object movies. MGI Soft Reality Studio is a scene creation program for the Windows platform and QuickTime VR Authoring Studio from Apple is one for the Macintosh.

SUMMARY

Through desktop applications of animations, 3D modeling, and virtual reality, students can explore, imagine, and create. Advanced computer graphics give students the chance to display their understanding and knowledge in much more complex terms.

These technologies are cost-effective, fairly easy to learn, and provide an interesting, motivating interface for students. However, after the hardware decisions are made and the software has been bought, the most important components to producing quality 3D graphics, animations, and virtual reality scenes (even on low-end systems) are imagination and skill.

GLOSSARY

2D graphics. Images that you work with in graphics programs, in which you are only dealing with flat things layered together on a flat surface.

3D graphics. Images that have actual depth, as well as height and width. Three-dimensional computer graphics provide a way to create objects, characters, and scenes inside a computer that are more than just flat images.

AI (Artificial Intelligence). Computer simulations of an individual's decision-making processes, designed to create the illusion of intelligence.

bitmapped animations. Animations created by displaying several bitmapped images in rapid succession.

Cel animations. Term used by HyperStudio for frame-based animation.

CSG (Constructive Solid Geometry). A 3D modeling method where one combines 3D primitives in order to create more complex shapes. The 3D primitives are the cube, sphere, cone, cylinder and torus.

DXF. A file format for precision object-oriented 2D and 3D graphics.

extrusion. A simple 3D object created by taking a 2D shape and giving it thickness, or extending it along a path. A cylinder is a extrusion of a circle.

flat shading. A rendering method for 3D graphics where flat colors are calculated for each individual polygon.

fps (frames per second). The number of video frames (or animation frames) that are displayed each second.

GIF animation. A variation of the GIF file format (known as GIF89) that supports bitmapped animations. The most popular animation format on the web.

GIF89. See GIF animation.

Gouraud. A rendering method for 3D graphics where colors are calculated for each vertex or corner of each polygon, and then blended across the face of each polygon.

in-betweens. With more advanced programs, you draw only certain major frames called keyframes, and the program calculates the other frames called the in-betweens.

keyframes. Frames of an animation that contain the objects placed at the extremes of their motion.

metaballs. Special spheres used in 3D modeling systems that change their shape to soften their edges and fill seams when they are combined together.

modeling. The process of building 3D objects. Modeling is done with a 3D modeling program.

morphing. When one object changes shape (usually in a rather slow process) to look like another object.

NTSC video. The U.S. standard for motion video of 525 horizontal lines per frame at 30 frames per second.

object movies. An interactive VR movie file that represents a single object floating in space. The user can then "grab" that object and rotate it to view it from all sides.

object-oriented animations. Animations created by moving an object or objects on a screen that has a constant background.

onion skins. The ability that some animation programs have to display previous frames and trace over them like tracing paper.

panorama. A single image that represents an environment as seen by turning 360 degrees around a single point.

particle systems. Used in 3D graphics to create objects that have no definable edge, such as flames, clouds, waterfalls, etc.

path animations. Animations created by moving an object or objects on a screen that has a constant background.

persistence of vision. This illusion of motion caused by rapidly showing a sequence of still images.

Phong shading. A rendering method for 3D graphics where colors are calculated for each pixel of the image being rendered.

polygon. A multisided geometric shape. In 3D graphics, the polygon used is the triangle—polygonal models are created by attaching many small flat triangles edge-to-edge to form shapes.

polygonal modeling. A 3D modeling method where complex shapes are created out of small triangles attached edge-to-edge. It is the most commonly used modeling process.

radiosity. A rendering method for 3D graphics that extends raytracing, not by following each beam of light, but by tracking how the light reflects off of objects and bleeds color on to surrounding objects.

raytracing. A rendering method for 3D graphics that approximates the actual physical properties of light as it bounces off objects toward the camera. It literally "traces" the path of each beam of light from the light source to the objects in the scene.

rendering. When a 3D image or animation is calculated by the computer to create the final bitmapped images or movie files.

rotation. A simple 3D object created by taking a 2D shape and rotating it along an axis. Both a torus and a sphere are two possible rotations of a circle, depending on where the axis is placed.

spline. Splines are special, curved lines, which are used to create 2D and 3D object-oriented graphics.

voxels. Tiny cubes arranged in 3D grids to compose larger organic shapes.

VR (Virtual Reality). Navigable computer graphic simulations of environments.

VRML (Virtual Reality Modeling Language). A programming language used to define 3D objects for use on the Internet, based on the C programming language syntax.

wireframe. A rendering method for 3D graphics, in which only the outlines of polygons or splines are drawn.

X3D. A markup language used to define 3D objects for use on the Internet, based on the XML markup language syntax.

4

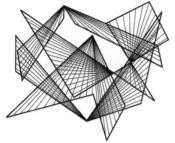

DIGITAL AUDIO

A Scenario

Ariel, Adam, and Joshua were working as editors of the yearbook. The paper version was ready to go to press; however, for the first time, they decided they would also create a web site with some of the pictures on it. They'd already finished scanning the pictures, and now they wanted to add an audiovisual introduction.

Ms. Mills, the faculty advisor, suggested they use a few of the photographs of the students and school activities to make a slide show. She also suggested they create it in a streaming format so users would not have to wait for a long download.

The students began by putting the text and photographs for the slide show together in PowerPoint. After they were satisfied with the results, they saved the slide show as a series of JPG images. The command, "Save As...JPG" resulted in a folder with an individual image for each slide, each with a consecutive number.

Next they selected all of the JPGs and dragged them into the timeline of the Real SlideShow program (a free download from Real Networks). After that, it was easy—just click on an image, click the record button to add audio, preview the audio, and save. At first it was difficult to get it to "sound" the way they wanted it, but they could record over and over on the same slide until they liked it.

When they were finished with the last slide, they previewed the entire presentation and saved it as a slide show. The final step was to "send" it to a web server. For this, they called in Mr. Yamacuchi, the school's webmaster. He put in the passwords and URLs, and now they could link their production from the school's web site.

That night Joshua decided to test the online version of the project from his home (with his mother's 28.8 modem). He was really surprised at the quality of the audio and the fact that it was able to start playing almost immediately after he clicked on the file. He already had ideas for a similar slideshow with music for the Art Club!

INTRODUCTION

The human voice and music are two powerful forms of information, communication, and education. As audio technologies evolve on computers, we are witnessing additional uses for home, business, and school. For example, students in Florida can easily talk to students in Russia via the Internet; web browsers can "read" a web site to visually-impaired students, and your class can listen to a live presidential address through a computer. You might even have a vocal password to a computer network that is programmed to respond only to a specific voice (by a unique audio imprint). These, and other advances, have been possible with the growth of digital audio technologies. In this chapter, we examine digital formats for recording, storing, and playing audio on a computer. This chapter includes:

- An overview of digital audio
- Procedures for digitizing audio
- Educational applications for digital audio
- Compact disc-audio technology
- Text-to-speech synthesis
- Voice recognition
- MIDI technology
- Audio on the Internet

OVERVIEW OF DIGITAL AUDIO

Sound, in its natural form, is best described as variations in air pressure, caused by vibrations. For example, if you hit a drum or a tuning fork, it will vibrate, causing variations in the air pressure around it to reach your ear. For many years, the recording and storage of sound took place with an analog technique—the pressure waves were converted to electrical pulses and stored on tapes, records, films, and so forth. With the advent of microcomputers, techniques have been refined to store sounds on computer disks in digital form (as numeric values). Note that in Figure 4.1, an analog signal from a microphone is converted to a digital signal (using an A/C converter on a digital audio chip) for storage in the computer. When the sound is played, it is converted back into an analog signal and sent to the speakers.

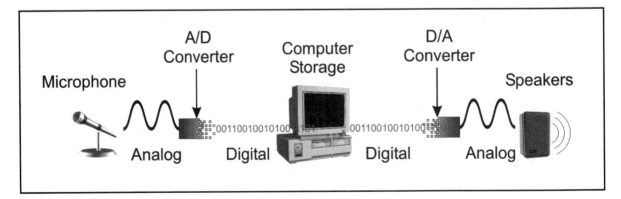

Figure 4.1. Conversion process for audio.

The conversion from analog to digital and back to analog takes place through a digital audio chip in a computer. Like Macintosh computers, most PCs now have on-board audio chips that convert the sounds to and from digital form (or sound cards, such as SoundBlaster, can be added separately). As shown in Figure 4.2, the digital audio cards have a number of inputs and outputs for audio.

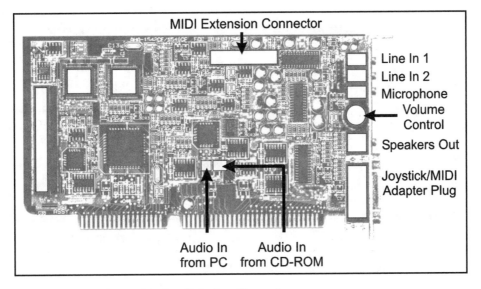

Figure 4.2. Configuration for digital audio card.

A software program is required to set the parameters for the audio and select the right file format. Most computers come with simple audio recording programs already installed. More sophisticated programs, with advanced editing options, can be downloaded as shareware or purchased. After the audio files have been digitized, they can be controlled by a computer program, retrieved, and played instantly. With minimal hardware and software, teachers and students can record their own voices or sounds and incorporate them into multimedia projects or web pages.

One of the major advantages of digital audio over analog audio is the ability to make "perfect" copies. In other words, each time you make a copy of an audiotape, the quality decreases and the amount of noise (usually in the form of a hiss) increases. By contrast, you can copy a digital CD thousands of times, and the first copy will be as crisp and clear as the last. Another advantage is that a digital form of audio makes file transfers over networks, such as the Internet, feasible.

There are, however, some disadvantages of digital audio. For instance, digital audio files tend to be quite large. For example, a one-minute segment of a song recorded at CD-audio quality would require more than 8 megabytes of storage space. That means only about eight seconds would fit on a floppy disk. Luckily, several variables (such as sampling rates, resolution, and number of channels) can be manipulated to create smaller files, while maintaining quality sound.

Sampling Rates

Bringing sound into the digital domain of computer bits and bytes requires a sampling process. At small but discrete time intervals, the computer takes a "snapshot" of the level of the waveform. The result is a digital, stairstep-type representation of sound rather than a continuous analog waveform (see

Figure 4.3). This process is called *sampling*, and the number of samples taken each second is referred to as the *sampling rate*—the more samples, the better the sound. For example, audio sampled 44,000 times per second (44 kilohertz or kHz) will provide better quality than audio sampled 22,000 times per second (22kHz).

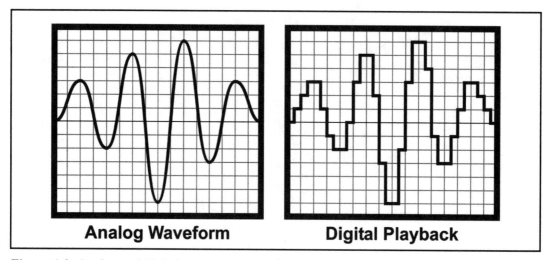

Analog Waveform   **Digital Playback**

Figure 4.3. Analog and digital representation of sound.

A major decision when recording digital audio files is which sampling rate to use. Most digital audio recording programs supply at least three choices, usually between 11kHz and 44.1kHz. The selection of a sampling rate is based primarily on two factors: the quality of sound needed and the disk storage space available. The two factors are interrelated because the higher the quality, the more disk space required, and vice versa. For example a file saved at 44kHz will be twice as large as a file saved at 22kHz.

For most educational applications, a sampling rate of 11kHz is sufficient, especially if it involves voices rather than music. If storage space is at a real premium, even 5–8kHz will provide intelligible narration. When recording music, higher quality, and, therefore, higher sampling rates are recommended (usually 22kHz or 44kHz).

Resolution

Another variable with digital audio is the resolution (usually 8-bit or 16-bit). The number of bits of resolution used to record an audio file shows the accuracy with which the digital sample is stored. With 8-bit resolution, there are 256 possible values; with 16-bit sound, there are 65,536 possible values, providing more exact measurement and playback of the sound. If you are recording with a 16-bit card, you have the option to record with 8-bit or 16-bit resolution. Remember that the 16-bit resolution might sound better, but it will also require twice as much storage space.

Number of Channels

You can record audio in either stereo or mono. With stereo, two separate channels are recorded, resulting in twice the file size. If you need high-quality music or special sound effects, stereo is appropriate; otherwise, you can stick to mono.

To see how these factors (sampling rate, resolution, and channels) impact the file size, review Table 4.1. Note that CD-quality audio is always recorded at 44.1kHz.

Table 4.1. Approximate File Sizes for One Minute of Audio

	44.1kHz	22.05kHz	11.025kHz
16-bit stereo	8.47MB	4.23MB	2.12MB
16-bit mono	4.23MB	2.12MB	1.06MB
8-bit stereo	4.23MB	2.12MB	1.06MB
8-bit mono	2.12MB	1.06MB	0.53MB

Digital Audio File Formats

When you record and save audio files, several different formats can be used. Selecting the appropriate format is very important because different programs and platforms accept only specific formats. If you have an audio file in the wrong format, you can use a conversion program, such as SoundEdit, to transfer from one format to another. The following formats are common options in recording software:

- *WAV*. The WAV format is the default standard for Windows-based computers. All PC programs can recognize and play this format, and many Macintosh programs can also play the files.

- *AIFF*. The AIFF format is the default standard for Macintosh computers. All Macintosh programs can recognize and play this format, and most PC programs can also play the files.

- *AU*. AU is a UNIX format that was once very popular on the Internet. The quality is low, and it is not used very much any more on Macintosh or PC platforms.

- *MP3*. MP3 stands for Moving Picture Experts Group, Audio Layer III. It is a compression format that can decrease the size of an audio file, but maintain a high quality sound. Although MP3 files can be compressed at different rate, the standard is about a 10:1 ratio. This enables a three-minute song to be stored on less than 4 MB of disk space. See MP3.com for MP3 players and available files.

- *RA or RM*. RealAudio or RealMedia files can be used to stream audio over the Internet. These files are generally created with products from RealNetworks.

- *ASF (Active Streaming Format)*. ASF is Microsoft's format for streaming media. It works very well with Windows Media Player.

- *QT or MOV*. Although QuickTime was originally designed for digital video, it can be used for a combination of audio and video or for audio-only files. See page 107 for more information about QuickTime, ASF, and Real.

- *SWA*. Shockwave Audio is a file format used by Macromedia (the company that produces Authorware, Director, and Flash) to stream audio on the Internet.

RECORDING DIGITAL AUDIO

Recording digital audio is a relatively simple procedure. The basic steps include:

- Plug a microphone, tape player, or other source into an audio input port on a computer.
- Start the software program that controls the audio port.
- Select the quality level (sampling rate, bits-of-resolution, and mono/stereo).
- Choose *record* on the menu of the digitizing software program.
- Speak into the microphone, or play another audio source.
- Test the recording with the *play* command. If it is acceptable, select a file format, and save the file to the computer.

Several factors, however, should be considered to ensure the best quality recording. The first device in the recording chain of events is often the microphone. It therefore defines the maximum quality that can be achieved for the rest of the recording process. Remember that all microphones are not created equal, and the ones that are provided with a basic computer system are not generally of very high quality. It may be worthwhile to contact an audiovisual company and investigate the purchase of one or two quality microphones.

Another issue that affects recording quality is the amount of environmental noise that is captured. For example, a computer fan makes a lot of noise, and, if you're not careful, this noise will also be recorded. Solutions include using a sound-absorbing blanket over the computer, moving the computer as far away as possible, and moving the mic closer to the source of the audio. Other noise-generating items, such as air conditioners and heating systems, must also be considered.

If you have a class of 30 students, and they are all recording audio for individual projects, you would probably want them to use settings that would result in small audio files. However, if they are recording a file that will be edited and placed on the CD version of the school yearbook, you should advise them to capture the file with CD quality settings (44.1kHz, 16-bit, stereo). That way, they can experiment with the file, and change the settings until they are pleased with the file size and quality, but do not have to continually rerecord the audio.

Finally, consider the quality of the speakers that are used to play the audio files. Again, the speakers provided with or in computer systems are not generally the highest quality. To achieve adequate volume for the audio, external speakers are generally required. Contact a professional to locate the best speakers that you can afford, especially for school presentations and so forth.

Editing Sounds

Digital sounds recorded with computers can be edited like text in a word processor. With the right software program, sounds can be selected, cut, copied, pasted, and mixed with other sounds. Figure 4.4 shows the editing window for the digitized phrase *Technologies for Education*. The center portion (*for*) has been selected and can now be cut, copied, or deleted. In other words, if you wanted to place the middle of the phrase at the beginning, you would cut it and click at the beginning to paste the segment. Audio editing is a powerful tool that allows you to rearrange sounds or cut out parts you do not need.

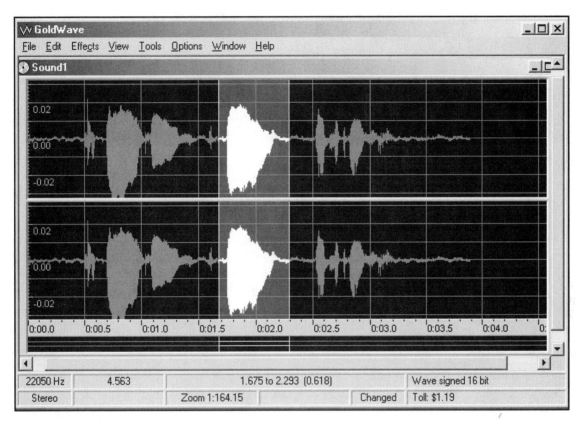

Figure 4.4. Editing sound in GoldWave.

Sounds can also be "mixed." This means that two different sounds can be combined into one. For example, a student may want to narrate a story while background music is playing. If both files are recorded separately, an audio editing program (such as GoldWave) can be used to mix the two files together.

EDUCATIONAL APPLICATIONS FOR DIGITAL AUDIO

Now that digital audio is feasible, teachers are discovering many ways to incorporate it into instruction. For example, it is easy for students to record audio segments and merge them into word processing or PowerPoint files and multimedia programs. Audio is an integral part of nearly all educational software programs, and it has had a major impact on the teaching and composition of music. With a computer and a software program, students can learn to read, edit, compose, and record music with applications such as Music Ace and Making Music.

Educational applications for digital audio include the following categories (note that programs listed in this section are listed in the Resources section of this chapter):

- *Computer-based slide shows and presentations.* Computers have become effective presentation tools for teachers, administrators, and students. With the addition of audio, the equivalent of a slide-tape show is possible. Multimedia presentation programs such as PowerPoint by Microsoft have features for easy incorporation of audio files. As noted in the scenario at the beginning of this chapter, the presentation can also be streamed over the web.

- *Custom hypermedia programs.* Audio makes programs come alive and can be used to enhance instruction—especially for nonreaders and students with poor vision. The audio is under computer control and can be accessed instantly. Programs such as HyperStudio provide easy interfaces for digitizing and playing audio.

- *Audio feedback.* Some commercial programs allow learners to record their own voices and then compare their recordings to the correct pronunciation in the digital file. Examples of programs with audio feedback include English Express by Knowledge Adventures and Learn Spanish Your Way by Encyclopaedia Britannica Educational Corporation. This is an ideal way to learn and practice another language.

- *Audio notes.* Many word processors, spreadsheets, and e-mail systems allow the users to add sound notations. With applications such as this, students or teachers can produce papers or messages that "talk" or provide a spoken glossary.

- *Speech therapy.* Programs such as SpeechViewer III by IBM can be used by speech and language pathologists to help people with speech impairments. Speech-therapy programs digitize and analyze verbal characteristics such as pitch, loudness, and intonation. They also provide exercises on pronunciation, pitch, and speech timing.

- *Audio Imprints.* As schools become more networked, students are often expected to remember and use several different passwords. Audio imprint technology can recognize a unique voice with a very high level of security, providing secure access to networks or facilities.

Advantages of Digital Audio

- *Random access.* Digital audio can be retrieved and played almost instantly. In most systems the user accesses the audio simply by entering a *play* command followed by the name of the file.

- *Ease of editing.* Audio files are stored with a file name, just like other computer files. Therefore, audio files can be deleted or replaced simply by using file command utilities. Sound-editing programs enable users to cut and paste sounds to edit narration. The process is as easy as using a word processor.

- *Cost.* Moderate-cost, good-quality digital audio cards for Windows computers are generally preinstalled at the factory. Macintosh computers have built-in audio record-and-play capabilities. Most software is inexpensive or free.

Disadvantages of Digital Audio

- *Large storage requirements.* Audio files need a tremendous amount of disk storage space.

- *Wide variety of audio file formats.* Numerous audio formats exist—both for playing audio files and streaming audio. This range of formats can cause frustration because of their incompatibility across platforms or programs.

COMPACT DISC-AUDIO

Compact disc-audio (CD-Audio) is the popular consumer format that can store up to 74 minutes of high-quality music on a compact disc. CD-Audio was developed in 1982. The standard sampling rate for CD-Audio is 44.1kHz—providing high-quality sound.

CD-Audio discs can be played on CD-Audio players (such as the one in your car) or on CD-ROM players (such as the one in your computer). If the discs are played in a CD-ROM, the computer can access a specific song by specifying the time code. For example, if you want to create a multimedia program with HyperStudio that plays a particular section of Beethoven's Fifth Symphony, you would specify the time code—in minutes, seconds, and frames—at which to start playing and the time code at which to stop.

It is also possible to record your own CD-Audio. If you have a CD-R or CD-RW device (designed to record compact discs), there may be a setting in the software that will record music in the CD-Audio format, making it compatible with your car stereo. Be careful of copyright issues, however, when copying commercial music.

Advantages of CD-Audio

- *Quality.* CD-Audio is recorded at 44.1kHz, providing top-quality sound.

- *Durability.* CD-Audio is recorded on durable compact discs that are read with a laser beam. The discs do not wear out and are impervious to minor scratches.

- *Ease of access.* The audio is stored by time code—minutes, seconds, frames—on the discs. Most hypermedia and authoring programs can easily access the audio for interactive control.

Disadvantages of CD-Audio

- *Read only.* Audio that is stored on a compact disc cannot be changed or revised (unless you record it onto a writeable disc).

- *Limited to 74 minutes.* The CD-Audio standard specifies that the audio be recorded at 44.1kHz. With "traditional" CDs, this limits the amount of audio on each disc to 74 minutes. With DVD, this limit can be increased by up to 17 times.

- *Requires CD-ROM player.* To play CD-Audio with a computer, a CD-ROM or DVD player must be connected.

TEXT-TO-SPEECH SYNTHESIS

Do you ever get tired of reading a computer screen, and wish that someone would read the text to you? Do you have a student who is visually impaired and has difficulty reading web pages? A solution to both of these issues is a *text-to-speech synthesizer*, also referred to as voice synthesis or screen reader. With this approach, language is defined as a fixed set of sounds, and computer algorithms translate text into "spoken" output without any recording process.

Text-to-speech sound is ideal for "talking" word processors that can "read" anything that is typed into the computer, children's online storybooks that can read the stories, and talking web browsers. The potential vocabulary is unlimited: Any word or group of letters can be spoken by the synthesizer. It simply applies its phonetic rules to pronounce the word.

The disadvantage of the text-to-speech synthesis method is a slightly unnatural and mechanical sound. For instance, problems arise with words such as *live* that do not follow consistent rules of pronunciation. Some computer synthesizers cannot accurately differentiate between the use of *live* in these two sentences: *I live in Florida* and *We are using live bait.* Although voice synthesizers have improved a great deal, the robotic sounds produced can still be a problem in educational settings, where realistic speech is important for teaching pronunciation and language.

Nevertheless, text-to-speech synthesizers have many applications. The best-quality and most expensive units are found in business. They can be used to read computer documents over telephone lines. For example, an executive might place a telephone call to the office computer to retrieve his or her e-mail messages. A text-to-speech synthesizer can answer the telephone and "read" the documents to the executive.

Some commercial multimedia products incorporate text-to-speech synthesis, and you can create programs with text-to-speech capability. For example, HyperStudio has a synthesizer (called Blabber-Mouth) that can be used when developing HyperStudio stacks.

A recent application of this technology is talking web browsers, such as WeMedia for PCs and iCab for Macintosh. These browsers are designed to help people with low vision use the Internet more easily. They can "speak" all of the text on a web page or vocalize selected areas.

Advantages of Text-to-Speech Synthesis

- *Unlimited vocabulary.* The potential vocabulary of text-to-speech synthesis is unlimited: Any word or group of letters can be "spoken" by the synthesizer. The computer simply applies the phonetic rules to pronounce the word.

- *Very little RAM or storage space needed.* Because text-to-speech synthesis works with a set number of rules to produce sounds, little computer memory is required. In addition, the technology needed is already built-into most audio cards and computers.

Disadvantages of Text-to-Speech Synthesis

- *Robotic sound.* A major disadvantage of text-to-speech synthesis is the unnatural sound. Synthesizers do not have natural voice inflections, and the words sound mechanical.

- *Phonetic pronunciations.* Another limitation is that the pronunciations are strictly phonetic, and, unfortunately, the English language does not always follow the rules of phonics.

VOICE RECOGNITION

Voice recognition (also referred to as speech recognition) is the opposite of text-to-speech synthesis. With voice recognition, computers can interpret spoken words or phrases and convert them into text (or respond in some other way). It is used primarily for dictation, interface, and security.

As a dictation device, voice recognition is valuable for doctors and others who like to dictate their records and for people who do not have the use of their hands. Voice recognition/dictation software is incorporated into educational software. For example, the Tell Me More and Tell Me More Kids series by Auralog use speech recognition as the primary tool for foreign language education.

Voice recognition is also used as an interface and control system for computers. For example, you could say "save, close, exit" to leave a word-processing file without touching the keyboard or mouse. In addition, it is being used by the telephone companies and others to automate voice mail systems. We are now familiar with telephone options such as "press or say three."

As a security device, voice recognition uses biometric technology to restrict access to a PC, a network, or voicemail, based on unique voice patterns. Most biometric applications require you to say specific words (such as your name). The software then analyzes characteristics of your voice (such as cadence, pitch, and tone) and matches them to your voiceprint that is stored in a database. VoiceCheck, Speak N Set, and ID Key are commercial products from Veritel Corporation that use voice verification for access to computers, web sites, buildings, and so on.

Voice recognition technology is relatively new. The first software-only voice recognition system was produced by Dragon Systems in 1994. It provided discrete speech, meaning that you had to pause after each word. In 1996, IBM introduced the first continuous speech recognition software, which allowed you to talk more naturally. Since then, NaturallySpeaking (from L&H Dragon) and ViaVoice (from IBM) have remained the leaders in this technology, and voice recognition has become much more affordable to a wide range of users.

When selecting a voice recognition system, there are several factors to consider, including the following:

- *Size of vocabulary*. Look for a vocabulary of at least 150,000 words, plus the ability to add new words with a text file.

- *Compatibility with software programs*. Make sure it can interface directly with your common applications, such as Microsoft Word or AppleWorks.

- *Short enrollment period*. When you buy a voice recognition system, you usually have to train it to recognize your accent. This training period is referred to as the enrollment period and should ideally be less than 15 minutes.

- *Accuracy*. Similar to OCR software, voice recognition systems are not perfect. With a good system, you can expect an accuracy rate of about 95 percent.

- *Natural language*. Systems with "natural" language allow simple phrases, such as "insert here" rather than more complicated commands.

- *Price*. Expect to pay between $100 and $2,500 for a voice recognition system.

- *Speech feedback*. It is helpful if the system can read the text back to you for editing purposes.

The most natural way to communicate with another person is by spoken words. With a computer, we have been forced to "communicate" by typing on a keyboard. As voice recognition systems continue to mature, you can expect to see more natural communications options in business, medical fields, and education.

MUSICAL INSTRUMENT DIGITAL INTERFACE (MIDI)

One of the most compact and flexible methods used to store and transfer music is MIDI (Musical Instrument Digital Interface). MIDI does not record the actual sounds; instead, it stores the instructions needed to tell the computer (and any connected MIDI devices) which instrument sound to use, which note to play, how loud it should be played, and so on. Similar to sheet music, MIDI files provide the instructions on how to reproduce the music. The computer then interprets the MIDI instructions and produces the music using the sounds that are embedded in the sound card or sound module. MIDI files are much smaller than digital audio files (such as WAV) because only the instructions are recorded, not the sounds.

MIDI technology does not have a long history. In 1983, musicians and manufacturers got together and agreed on a hardware standard for musical instruments. The agreement led to the development of the MIDI specification. Since then, many electronic instruments have been manufactured to conform to the MIDI standard, making it possible for musical signals to be easily communicated among all synthesizers.

A *synthesizer* is a musical instrument or device that generates sound electronically. Synthesizers can produce the sounds of many different things—from bells and guitars to drums and electric pianos. Synthesizers have existed in various forms since the 1940s, but, before MIDI, they spoke different "languages" and could not communicate with one another to play, sequence, or mix music.

The configuration for the MIDI includes MIDI software, a MIDI-equipped audio card or interface box, cables, speakers, and one or more MIDI instruments. (See Figure 4.5.) Piano keyboards and other electronic instruments that contain synthesizers can be used to input the musical information to the computer software and to output the recorded songs.

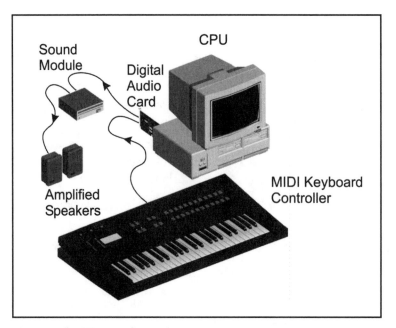

Figure 4.5. MIDI configuration.

An advantage of MIDI technology is that it can produce complex music. For example, it can play the sounds for stringed instruments, woodwinds, brass, and percussion simultaneously. Each of the instruments is stored in a separate channel, allowing you to use software and edit individual instruments without affecting the rest of the composition. For example, if you were teaching musical concepts, you could isolate different instruments or parts of a melody for the students to analyze. Figure 4.6 shows the information box of a MIDI file being played through QuickTime. Note that you can delete or change any of the indicated instruments.

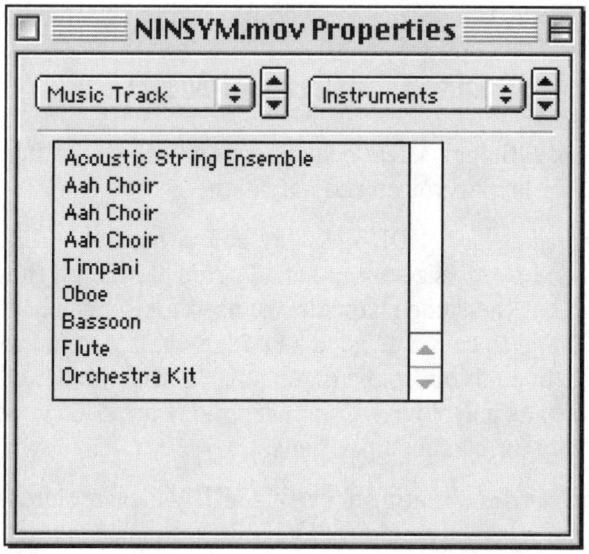

Figure 4.6. Information dialog box for MIDI file in QuickTime Pro.

Generating MIDI Files

There are many ways to find or generate MIDI files. If you are a musician, you can use sequencing software (such as Cakewalk or Cubase) that captures everything that you play on a synthesized instrument. The sequencing software can record and play back several parts or instruments in perfect synchronization—sort of like an old-fashioned player-piano roll. After the musical information is loaded into the computer, it can be edited or revised in relation to its rhythm, meter, tone, and many other parameters. With MIDI sequencing software, you can experiment with harmonies, record different parts, and play them back as a complete arrangement.

If you are not musically talented, you can still create MIDI files by scanning sheet music. Programs, such as SmartScore, work like OCR software—they scan the sheet music and translate the print notation into MIDI commands. Other music recognition software (such as AKoff Music Composer) will allow you to hum, sing, or play music to record a MIDI song.

Advantages of MIDI

- *Small file size.* MIDI files are a fraction of the size of digital audio files (up to 100 times smaller). This small file size results from the fact that MIDI music is *not* sampled and digitized like digital audio files. Instead, MIDI contains information *about* the sound, not the sounds themselves.

Many computer games store music in MIDI files rather than digital audio to conserve disk space.

- *Compatibility.* The MIDI standard provides for the interchange of files among all MIDI synthesizers, sound modules, and sound cards.

- *Editing.* MIDI software enables you to "edit an orchestra" by changing the parameters of the notes and the instruments. You can also edit individual channels or instruments.

- *Availability of files.* Internet sites, such as MIDI.com offer access to thousands of MIDI songs. Most of the files are small and easy to download.

Disadvantages of MIDI

- *Cannot create narration.* Although MIDI technology is great for creating sound effects and music, it is not appropriate for human voices and narration.

- *Playback may be unpredictable.* MIDI files may sound markedly different when played back through different sound synthesizers and sound cards. Although the General MIDI specifications help to ensure that the same channels are used for similar instruments, an inexpensive audio card is never going to sound as good as a high-quality sound module that was designed specifically for MIDI. In addition, sound cards differ in the number of voices they can produce simultaneously (known as polyphony). Common options provided by sound cards are 16, 32, or 64 voices—64 is plenty for most compositions.

- *Musical talent is recommended.* Creating or editing MIDI music requires some musical talent. For those of us who are not musically endowed, MIDI files can be obtained through bulletin boards, the Internet, or CD-ROM collections.

AUDIO ON THE INTERNET

The Internet is a great repository for the storage and transfer of audio files. Two basic methods can be used to access and play audio files on the web: 1) download and play the audio or 2) stream the audio. Each has its advantages and disadvantages.

Download and Play

Using search engines and other tools, you can easily locate audio files on the web (in WAV, AIFF, MIDI, MP3, or other formats), download them to your own computer, and then play the files. The benefit of this approach is that the files will stay on your hard drive so that you can play them again later (even without an Internet connection). Also, you do not need a plug-in or audio player because most web browsers can recognize many general audio file formats and play the files after they have been downloaded.

A disadvantage to the download and play approach is that you might have to wait until the entire file is downloaded before it will begin to play. For small files, this is not a major concern, but, for large files, the wait time can be enormous. For example, with a 28.8 modem, you could easily wait several minutes for a 3MB file to download.

When downloading audio files, you must respect copyright laws. Unless a site states that the music is public domain, check the copyright restrictions (most audio sites have a link to the copyright information). Some sites will allow you to download the files for personal use only.

Besides downloading audio files from web servers, it is possible to access audio files (such as MP3) on others' computers and transfer them directly to your own computer (this method is called peer-to-peer swapping). The most "famous" implementation of this technology was Napster, a web site that was sued by members of the music industry for providing the means for the illegal transfer of copyrighted music. After Napster was found guilty of copyright infringement, they were forced to use "audio fingerprinting" on the files (a technique that can check to see if they are copyrighted) before allowing the file transfer to take place.

Streaming Audio

If audio files are large, the process of downloading them before playing them can be frustrating. Streaming audio is a solution to the long transfer and wait time. When audio is streamed over the Internet, it can play as it transfers. In other words, when you access a streaming audio file, the audio begins to play almost immediately and will continue to play as it transfers. In this manner, you can listen to radio stations, or you can hear a "live" concert.

One of the disadvantages of streaming audio is the fact that most formats require a plug-in to be installed on your computer. In other words, many web browsers can't recognize and play the streaming formats (at this time). There are three popular streaming formats for audio; all three require a different plug-in or player application.

One of the reasons the formats have different plug-ins is they each use different *codec* (compression/decompression) protocols. In other words, in order to stream audio in real time, it must be highly compressed before it is sent on the Internet. On your computer at the receiving end, the file must be quickly decompressed as it is played. The plug-in matches the codec that was used to compress the audio, decompresses it, and plays it on your computer.

The three leading audio streaming formats include Real Media, QuickTime, and Windows Media. All are excellent, and all provide free downloads of their plug-ins; however, there are some differences.

Real

Real by RealNetworks, Inc. is the pioneer in the streaming field. "Way back" in 1995, they created a file format that allowed compressed audio files to stream across the web. Since then, they have expanded to streaming video, and offer a range of software tools for encoding, decoding, and sending the streaming files. Their low-end software programs (such as Real SlideShow) are free; upgrades have a price tag.

QuickTime

QuickTime by Apple Corporation was the original leader in digital video. It is a versatile program that can support many file formats and media. QuickTime is commonly used for streaming audio content in addition to audio/video content. QuickTime provides several options for a codec—if you want to stream music, use Qdesign; for voice, use Qualcomm. QuickTime Pro (used for production and editing purposes) costs about $30.

Windows Media

Windows Media Technologies is the term that Microsoft uses to define a wide range of products that provide the ability to create, deliver, and play streaming files in the ASF (Advanced Streaming Format). All of the encoding software is free, the streaming server is free (with Windows NT), and the files play in Windows Media Player (installed on most PCs). It is a good format if you are operating in a Windows environment.

Guidelines for Creating Streaming Audio Files

- Start with the highest possible quality recording, with quality microphones, speakers, and cables.

- Record at the highest-available sampling rate and size (44.1kHz with 16-bit stereo sound).

- Select the appropriate codec and transfer speed. Some formats (such as Real) allow you to create one file that will automatically adjust to different transfer rates (such as 56K modems, ISDN, T1, etc.). Other formats (such as QuickTime) require that you record a separate file for each target bandwidth.

SUMMARY

The goal of making the computer talk and play music has been achieved. Educators can easily use text-to-speech synthesis, MIDI, CD-Audio, and digital audio to include sound in their presentations, lessons, and computer programs. With computer-controlled sounds and music, no time is ever lost in rewinding a tape to find the correct starting point or in trying to place a phonograph needle on the right record groove. Random access to sounds, voice, and music is at the heart of multimedia instruction and presentations.

GLOSSARY

8-bit. An 8-bit audio card stores one of 256 values for each sample of sound.

16-bit. A 16-bit audio card stores one of 65,536 values for each sample of sound.

analog recording. A method in which the waveform of the recorded signal resembles the waveform of the original signal.

.AU. A common audio format for files that are linked to World Wide Web pages. These files will play on Macintosh, Windows, or UNIX computers.

audio chip. A computer chip that can produce sounds. Macintosh has built-in audio chips.

CD-Audio. High-quality audio stored on a compact disc in a linear format.

CD-ROM (Compact Disc-Read Only Memory). An optical storage device capable of storing approximately 650 megabytes of digital data (see Chapter 2).

channel. The paths over which MIDI information travels. MIDI can send data on as many as 16 channels with a single MIDI cable.

compression. Reducing data for more efficient storage and transmission. Compression saves disk space, but it also reduces the quality of the playback. Compression ratios of 2:1, 3:1, or 4:1 are often available for digitizing audio.

decibel. A relative unit to measure the ratio of two sound intensities.

digital recording. A method of recording in which samples of the original analog signal are encoded as bits and bytes.

dynamic range. The difference between the loudest sound and the softest sound. Dynamic range is measured in decibels.

frequency. The number of times per second that a sound source vibrates. Frequency is expressed in hertz (Hz) or kilohertz (kHz).

general MIDI. A MIDI standard that assigns each instrument a unique identification number.

HyperSound. A HyperCard stack that enables the user to record, store, and play sounds with a MacRecorder.

Hz (hertz). Unit of measurement of frequency; numerically equal to cycles per second.

kHz (kilohertz). Unit of measurement of frequency; equal to 1,000 hertz.

MIDI (Musical Instrument Digital Interface). A standard for communicating musical information among computers and musical devices.

polyphony. The number of simultaneous voices a sound card can produce.

RealAudio. A compression and transfer technique that allows audio files to play over the Internet as they are transferring.

resolution. The number of bits used to store sounds; 16-bit audio cards have higher resolution and produce a richer sound than 8-bit audio cards.

sampling rate. The number of intervals per second used to capture a sound when it is digitized. Sampling rate affects sound quality; the higher the sampling rate, the better the sound quality.

sequencer. A device that records MIDI events and data.

sound module. A peripheral for MIDI that uses an electronic synthesizer to generate the sounds of musical instruments.

synthesizer. A musical instrument or device that generates sound electronically.

text-to-speech synthesis. Sounds created by applying computer algorithms to text to produce "spoken" words.

voice recognition. The ability of computer hardware and software to interpret spoken words. The computer can react to commands or transfer the words to text.

.WAV. The extension, or last three letters, for sound files saved in Microsoft wave format. To be compatible with the MPC standards, all audio files must be stored with this format.

waveform. The shape of a sound depicted graphically as amplitude over time.

RESOURCES

AKoff Music Composer (MIDI scanning software)
http://www.akoff.com

Audio Media Online
http://www.audiomedia.com/

Audio Tutorial
http://www.cica.indiana.edu/cica/faq
/audio/audio.html

Audio Tutorial
http://www.summercore.com
/Audiotutorial.htm

Audio/Video Software News
http://www.idg.net/go.cgi?id=475626

Audio World Online
http://audioworld.com/

Cakewalk Music Software (MIDI sequencing software)
http://www.cakewalk.com

Cubase (MIDI sequencing software)
http://www.us.steinberg.net/

Digital Audio: Tutorials and Resources
http://k-12.pisd.edu/multimedia/audio/

Digital Audio on the Internet
http://www.manteno.k12.il.us/finearts
/tutorial/digaud.html

Digital Audio Tutorial
http://www.beatnik.com/software
/tutorials/daudio2.html

Encarta World English Dictionary
http://dictionary.msn.com/

English Express by Knowledge Adventures
http://www.knowledgeadventure.com
/educators/index.html

GoldWave—Digital Audio Editor by GoldWave, Inc.
http://goldwave.com

HyperStudio
http://www.hyperstudio.com

iCab—Internet Browser
http://www.icab.de/

Learn Spanish Your Way by Britannica
http://store.britannica.com/

Mac Digital Audio
http://www.macdigitalaudio.com/

Making More Music by Voyager
http://voyager.learntech.com/cdrom/

MIDI.com
http://www.midi.com

MIDI Farm
http://www.midifarm.com/

MP3.com
http://www.mp3.com

Music Ace by Harmonic Vision
http://www.harmonicvision.com/

NaturallySpeaking by L&H Dragon
http://www.lhsl.com/naturallyspeaking/

QuickTime by Apple Computer
http://www.apple.com/quicktime

RealOne Player by RealNetworks
http://www.real.com

Real SlideShow by Real Networks
http://www.realnetworks.com
/products/slideshow/index.html

SmartScore by Musitek
http://www.musitek.com/

SoundBlaster by Creative Labs
http://www.creative.com

SoundEdit 16 by Macromedia
http://www.macromedia.com
/software/sound/

SpeechViewer III by IBM
http://www-3.ibm.com/able/snsspv3.html

Tell Me More Kids
http://www.auralog.com/us/kids.html

Veritel (Voice Verification Biometric Technologies)
http://www.veritelcorp.com/

ViaVoice by IBM
http://www-4.ibm.com/software/speech/demo/

WeMedia—Talking Browser
http://www.wemedia.com

5

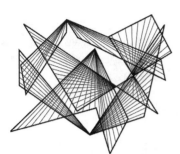

DIGITAL VIDEO

A Scenario

Marc ended up in the high school life-skills course for a common reason—he needed an elective and he had schedule conflicts with all the other courses. He really was a "techie," and had hoped for something a bit more glamorous than learning how to identify the bargains in a supermarket.

As it turns out, he is having a great time in the course. Yes, he learned how to price pickles by the ounce to determine where the cheap pickles were. He also showed his instructor how to load a simple program into a handheld computer to make data entry simple and to classify the results by supermarket chain.

However, it is sewing that really has his attention, especially the computer-controlled embroidery machine. He uses a computer drawing program to create fancy designs, or he selects and downloads images from hundreds that are already on web sites. A second program evaluates the designs and determines what colors of thread need to be loaded into the embroidery machine. Once this is done and an appropriate garment (t-shirts fit his budget well) is properly positioned, a simple click of a button starts the fast, almost magic, robotic machine. Within minutes, he has a custom-designed t-shirt. Dragons made with florescent thread on black t-shirts are becoming his trademark.

There is one catch. Threading that machine is a real pain. (It took over an hour the first time he tried, and he got it all wrong anyway.) After showing several other students the shortcuts and tricks he learned by trial and error, he has come up with a great idea. He will create a video that shows how to thread the machine. This will solve two problems. Not only will he save time by not having to show other students how to thread the machine, but he also has found a video production project for his digital media class.

Preproduction

Marc wishes to produce a digital video that clearly shows the process of threading this advanced sewing machine. He wants to end up with two versions of this video—one with high quality images and audio that can be distributed on a CD-ROM, and a second version that has lower quality—but still useful—images and no audio. This version must be a much smaller file because it will be placed on a web page for the Life Skills course. He has access to a DV camcorder and a simple production set with lighting and sound equipment.

After planning and developing a script, Marc decides to "shoot" the threading process from three different angles. First, he will need a medium "face-on" shot of the teacher introducing the process and starting the threading procedure. However, this shot will be too far away and from the wrong angle to clearly show the threading process. He will have to reposition the camera and take an "over the shoulder" shot that shows a clear view of the threading process from a "first person" perspective. Finally, he will have to reposition the camera a third time to show a close-up of one particular part of the process that can cause problems (getting the thread through the needle guide and the eye of the needle in the right direction).

Production: Shooting the Video

Marc mounts the camera on a tripod to minimize camera motion since unnecessary motion plays havoc with later digital compression stages. It takes three attempts to get the introduction (medium shot) down right, but that is minor because the camera is locked in position for the entire shot. He carefully notes the digital counter numbers (timecode) for the start and end of "Intro-Take3."

Next, Marc repositions the camera and tripod so that it looks over the left shoulder of the teacher. (He tried both shoulders and found the best view from this side.) He tilts, pans, and zooms in so that only the key parts of the sewing machine and the teacher's hands show. If he went in any closer, he would lose parts of the path the thread follows. It takes four tries before he gets a nice, smooth threading process from the spool through the eye of the needle and out. Marc carefully notes the counter numbers for "Thread-Take4."

Finally, Marc slides the camera and tripod up close to the sewing machine, lowers it down, and focuses right on the needle thread guide and needle eye (he remembered to pull the thread back out so that it wouldn't already be there when he started shooting). This shot is tricky. He finds that it is difficult to get the close-up without the teacher's hands getting in the way. It takes nine tries, but he carefully notes the timecode of the start and end of "Closeup-Take9."

Marc now has his video. After reviewing it, he finds that he is lucky because the best audio corresponds with his three best video shots. He will not have to "borrow" audio from the other attempts.

Postproduction

It is time to switch over to the computer side of making the video program. A variety of digital video editing programs are on the market, and they range from very professional and expensive to very basic and inexpensive. As it turns out, the iMac computer that Marc is using came with iMovie2 already installed. This is a popular program with school systems because it is easy to use, works very well, and comes already installed on many Mac computers.

Because Marc is using a DV camera, his video is in a format that is already compatible with his computer system. Although he does not have to go through an "analog to digital" capture process, he does have to transfer or "import" his video to the computer hard drive. First, Marc makes sure that he has plenty of file space on the hard drive of the school's video editing computer. Just to be safe, he also takes the time to use a utility program that defragments the drive to ensure that the capture process will run smoothly. Next, he connects the DV camcorder to the desktop digital video system through a FireWire connector.

While Marc could import the whole digital tape to the computer and then locate and edit just the shots he wants to use, this would consume a tremendous amount of hard drive space. To conserve space, Marc will import only the three shots that he needs.

One nice feature of the Mini DV camcorder and the iMovie editing software is that the computer has direct control of the camcorder. Marc uses the *fast forward*, *rewind*, and *play* buttons along with the digital counter to locate his shots. When he locates a shot that he wants to transfer, he clicks the "Import" button to save the shot as a file on the computer's hard drive. Importing his three shots takes less than 30 minutes.

Next, Marc previews all three of his imported shots to make sure he didn't cut anything off the start or end of each shot, including the audio. In fact, during production he had the teacher pause for about one second at the start of each take before he spoke, and he ran the action about one second beyond the end of the audio, so his audio is safely "inside" the video shots. Earlier, Marc created an animated title shot with an appropriate music background, so he locates that and makes certain it is ready to go.

iMovie uses icons to represent each video file, and a "timeline" to represent the editing process. First, Marc drags the title file to the timeline, followed by the other three files in their appropriate order. He can now see a "preview" of the complete project in a small video window. As he looks at the project, he decides that it would be good to have dissolves rather than straight cuts between all of the shots. Using the software, he selects the "dissolve" transition and drops one of the icons between each shot in the sequence. Because he was careful with his audio, he doesn't have to worry about two different audio tracks overlapping on the dissolves.

After saving his project, Marc decides to modify the show for the version that will go on the web. He doesn't want to use audio on the web version, so the "Intro" is a bit meaningless. Marc goes back to the timeline, and removes the "Intro" shot. The flow line closes up, so that the title is now set to dissolve right into the over-the-shoulder threading shot. Next, he "clicks off" the audio channel. Finally, he directs the software to save the resulting file under a new name with a smaller window size, fewer frames per second, and a different compression scheme. In a few minutes, he has a second finished file, which is quite a bit smaller than the first. All he has left to do is "burn" the CD-ROM and work with the school webmaster to get the second file onto a web page.

INTRODUCTION

Just a few years ago, the equipment required to shoot and edit a video project similar to Marc's would have required a room full of complex equipment that cost tens of thousands of dollars. Now a $500 camcorder and a desktop computer can produce video of a technical quality that equals or exceeds the expensive equipment of the past. Digital video production is now possible for schools, thanks to more powerful desktop computers; affordable digital camcorders; and sophisticated, yet inexpensive digital editing software. In this chapter we will cover the following topics:

- Analog video

- Digital video

- Preproduction: Planning your video project

- Production: Shooting video

- Postproduction: Nonlinear editing

- Distribution: Media options, file formats, and compression

ANALOG VIDEO

Though video exists nearly everywhere we look, it is surprisingly hard to define. In simple terms, video is an electronic image that is drawn (using fine lines of color) on a luminous screen. If the lines are redrawn fast enough with slight variations, the result is an image that appears to move. In the United States, video was defined as a standard by the National Television Standards Committee (NTSC) when television debuted in the 1940s. This standard designates the number of lines (525) required to create a complete image (along with synchronizing signals) and the number of distinct images (30) displayed each second.

Although the technology of video has advanced tremendously since it was first developed, nearly all standard television equipment used in the United States still follows the now ancient NTSC video standard. Only small changes have been implemented to accommodate color and other more modern innovations like closed captioning. Canada, Japan, South Korea, and Mexico also use the NTSC standard; other countries use other, incompatible formats (see Table 5.1).

Table 5.1. Analog Video Standards

Video Format	Countries	Number of Lines	Frames per Second
NTSC	USA, Canada, Japan, South Korea, Mexico	525	30 fps
PAL	Australia, China, Europe, South America	625	25 fps
SECAM	France, Middle East, Afric, Russia, North Korea	625	25 fps

Standard video is analog in nature, which means that it consists of continuous electromagnetic wave forms. When video is broadcast through the air or through standard cable systems as "television," the electromagnetic waves are similar to those of FM radio, but each station takes up more wave space (bandwidth) because the waves must contain visual information in addition to the audio.

Analog electromagnetic waves are everywhere. Standard AM radio, FM radio, television, short-wave radio, some cellular telephones, the energy in your microwave oven, and even some of the energy in lightning consists of analog electromagnetic waves. However, all these analog waves have a nasty habit of getting in the way of each other. When this happens, the results can be minor irritations, such as a bit of static in your television picture, or totally distracting, as when the cement truck driver breaks through on a wireless microphone circuit that is being used by a university president during commencement ceremonies.

The greatest problem with analog signals of any type is that they have a very strong tendency to go bad. The old LP record that you played and played until it finally wore out was an analog signal stored on plastic. The copy of a copy of a videotape that looks and sounds awful is another example of an analog signal gone bad. For a number of reasons, undesirable elements that we lump together and call noise invariably find their way into analog signals.

Analog signals, such as standard video, have another strike against them in the modern information age. To put it bluntly, computers are analog illiterate. Modern computers are completely incapable of working with analog signals; they can only work with numbers that represent distinct values. Thus, any analog signal must first be converted into numbers (digitized) before it can be stored or used by computers.

DIGITAL VIDEO

Video in digital form solves many of the issues related to analog video. For example, you can copy digital video files as many times as you like, and the copies will be just as clear and clean as the original. Also, computers operate in digital mode—meaning you can copy files or edit files, transmit them on networks, and save them on "permanent" media such as compact discs.

Digitizing video, however, is one of the most demanding operations that we ask of a desktop computer. Each frame of analog video is roughly equivalent to the resolution and color of a 640 x 480 computer screen, with 24-bit (16.7 million colors). If the video images were indeed digitized as a succession of 640 x 480, 24-bit color images, the digital files would be huge. Each image contains 307,200 pixels (640 x 480). Each pixel requires 3 bytes of data to provide its color information (24 bits are equal to 3 bytes). Therefore, a single digitized image of video requires 921,600 bytes of data. To simplify this discussion, let's round that up to 1,000,000 bytes, or 1 megabyte. We could assume that those "spare" data bytes are used to transport the sound that usually goes with video. With 30 images required for each second of motion video, a digitized stream of motion video requires the flow of 30 megabytes of information per second. A minute of video would then consist of 1,800 megabytes, or 1.8 gigabytes of data, and a 30-minute video would require 54 gigabytes!

Mass storage devices are improving rapidly, but there are still very few economical methods for storing 54 gigabytes of data for each half hour of video. This is part of the reason why digital video has not completely replaced the standard VHS videotape yet. An equally challenging issue would be to figure out how to move that much data through a computer at a steady 30 megabytes per second to produce the 30 frames per second required to present smooth motion. Even for the most powerful modern desktop computers, this is an astonishing amount of data to process.

However, digital video exists today, and, in fact, it is in common use. We use CD-ROMs that contain video clips; we teleconference over the web; and many of us now have DVD players as part of our home entertainment systems. What has happened? How have we managed the task of pouring way too many bytes of information through a funnel with far too small an opening? While the answer is not magic, in some ways it appears to be very close.

Digital Video Compromises

It simply is not practical to use current technologies to digitize all the "raw analog data" that a pure analog video signal provides. Instead, several compromises must be used to allow digital video images to be displayed on common computers and transmitted over the Internet.

Reduction of Image Size

A smaller image requires fewer bytes of data to create it. Instead of using the full screen for a digital video, it can be reduced to 1/4 or even 1/16 the size of the screen (see Figure 5.1). In teleconferencing and other video that is accessed through the web, it is common to see images as small as 120 x 160 pixels. Note that an image recorded at 640 x 480 will result in a file that is four times larger than the same file captured at 320 x 240.

Figure 5.1. Window sizes: 1/16, 1/4, and full screen.

Reduction of the Number of Frames Per Second

Analog video on television is always displayed at 25 or 30 frames per second (fps)—depending on where you live and which standard is in use. However, it is possible to produce relatively smooth motion with as few as 10 fps. The reduction in the frame rate will result in a corresponding reduction in the file size—if a video segment is captured at 30 fps, it will be twice as large as a segment captured at 15 fps.

Reduction of Color Depth

When you save a digitized video file, you can choose to save in black and white, grayscale, or with various numbers of colors. The more colors you use, the larger the file will be. The number of colors used to display an image is referred to as the color depth, because it denotes the number of bits of color for each pixel. The chart in Table 5.2 shows the number of colors in different color depths. Note that a video file stored in 24-bit color will be three times larger than an 8-bit video.

Table 5.2. A Comparison of File Sizes As They Relate to One Second of Motion Digital Video Without Sound

	16.7 Million Colors (24 bits)	256 Colors (8 bits)	16 Colors (4 bits)
Full screen; 30 fps	27.0MB	9.0MB	4.5MB
Full screen; 15 fps	13.5MB	4.5MB	2.25MB
1/4 screen; 30 fps	6.8MB	2.3MB	1.15MB
1/4 screen; 15 fps	3.4MB	1.1MB	0.55MB

Compression of Image Data

Compression is the most complex, but most effective, method to reduce the amount of data required to create motion images. Many techniques exist to compress data, but they fall into two broad categories—*lossless* and *lossy*. The technical details can be very complex, but the basic concepts are easy to understand. With lossless compression techniques, the data that is required to recreate an image is manipulated so that it can be stored as a smaller number of bytes. For example, an area of blue sky might have many adjacent pixels with the same color values. This information is combined in such a way that the area of blue sky is still precisely defined, but with fewer or a compressed number of bytes of information. When the image is re-created, the compressed data can be translated back into its exact, original form. This process is called lossless compression.

On the other hand, it is possible that an area of blue sky has many very similar pixels of blue, but they do, in fact, vary slightly in the precise shade of blue. It is possible to calculate an "average" blue for this area of sky, change the entire area to the average, and then treat it as described previously. However, when the image is re-created, only the average blue will be re-created. The subtle hues of blue will be lost. This is one type of lossy compression. (See Chapter 2 for more information on compression and pages 108–11 for information about specific video compression techniques).

Through combinations of the "digital video compromises," many levels of digital video are possible. They range from small, low-color, low-frame rate teleconferencing videos that work their way through the crowded Internet to the "better than VHS" digital images that are now delivered through digital television satellites, digital cable systems, DV camcorders, and DVD entertainment systems.

PREPRODUCTION: PLANNING YOUR PROJECT

Some schools have been fortunate enough to have had a television studio with video editing equipment for many years. This allowed a few students to learn video editing techniques, along with the planning, design, and delivery of video. Daily "news" shows were common, and video yearbooks were often developed. It was a great learning experience; however, it was usually limited to a select few students.

Desktop digital video opens the world of video to all students (potentially). No longer is a special place with expensive equipment needed. The equipment is relatively inexpensive, and can easily be moved from one room to another. However, as with other technologies, desktop video should be used only where it can meet an instructional goal. Careful planning (on the part of the teacher and students) will ensure that the technology is not a goal in itself, but another tool to enrich the educational experience.

The development of a digital video can be roughly divided into four, overlapping phases: preproduction, production, postproduction, and distribution (see Table 5.3).

Table 5.3. Phases for Digital Video Projects

Preproduction	Production	Postproduction	Distribution
• Select project idea/goal • Outline project • Write scripts and storyboards • Assign roles • Design sets (if necessary)	• Shoot video • Record audio • Create graphics • Digitize analog elements	• Import video, etc. into editing software • Edit video clips • Add transitions • Add title slides, etc. • Combine the clips into movie file	• Select media for distribution • Select file format • Select CODEC • Export video files

Selecting a Project Idea/Goal

Video projects can open a whole new realm for student creativity and collaboration. With desktop video, students are not passively learning, they can be actively constructing knowledge. Projects can be designed to foster critical thinking skills, encourage cooperative learning, and develop problem-solving skills. The project ideas listed below should be viewed as "story starters" —ideas that you and your students can build from to create (and carefully plan) video projects for your classroom.

- *Demonstrations/Tutorials*. As illustrated in the scenario, students can create demonstrations or tutorials for a particular topic. For example, students at Palmer Junior Middle School created a digital video movie about the Bernoulli Principle. The video involved five students demonstrating the principle through ping pong balls hanging on strings from the ceiling.

- *Field Trips*. Students love field trips, and what better way to share the experiences (with other classrooms or other schools) than to create a video? Battery-operated camcorders can go nearly anywhere, and students can collect video shots that will be edited later, when they return to school. Field trips can be created as class projects, or as individual projects when students travel with their families.

- *Creative Works*. Do your students write poetry, compose music, create drawings, or author stories? If so, they can create desktop movies to showcase and combine their works. For example, they may read their poem, while a music track plays and images related to the poem appear. Or they may embark on digital storytelling and "act out" their stories through audio, video, and graphics.

- *Video Yearbooks*. Video yearbooks offer students opportunities to showcase their accomplishments and activities. Although video yearbooks have been common in high schools (using an analog editing suite), they can now be created in a classroom, perhaps focusing on a specific group of students or classes.

- *Documentaries*. We view documentaries on television all the time. Now, your students can create their own documentaries. For example, they might conduct research into the water conditions in your area. Using video footage, interviews, discussions, and so forth, they can answer questions such as "What factors have lead to the current drought conditions?" or "What steps are being taken to minimize the pollution in the lakes?"

- *Community or School News*. Interviewing skills can be developed by creating a community news show. Patterned after television, students can research current events, talk to experts in the area, and synthesize the information into a short, concise video.

- *Oral History*. Every community, family, and region has older people and others with an enormous wealth of knowledge and experience. Capturing an oral history report can answer questions such as "What was it like when there were no cars?" or "How did you start this successful company during the Depression?" In addition to the chance to get to know community members, students can learn about real-world experiences.

- *Commercials*. Creating a commercial is an art. Students can create jingles, study the psychology of marketing, and delve into creative expression.

Planning the Project

Successful video projects require a lot of planning. Students should be encouraged to prepare detailed outlines, scripts, and storyboards before the first "shot" is taken. Although they will be editing the video later, proceeding without a plan generally leads to wasted time, energy, and file space. The complexity of the planning materials will vary, based on the project, the age of the students, and the anticipated outcomes.

Desktop video projects can be developed by individual students or groups. If it is a group project, you may want to assign (or have students select) roles for the project—appropriate roles might include interviewer, camera operator, director, lighting specialist, actor, actress, narrator, etc.

If a set or costumes are going to be used, they must be carefully planned. In some instances, you may need permission to use a particular location, release forms from actors (depending on where and how the video will be used), and copyright releases for music. Also, make sure you will have sufficient cameras, batteries, tapes, microphones, etc.

PRODUCTION

The production phase includes shooting the video, recording audio, and creating graphics. If you are using existing footage (such as a videotape), it should also be digitized during this phase.

Getting Ready for the Shoot

Many, many considerations go into shooting good video (far more than this chapter can provide). For example, technical and artistic issues relating to lighting and sound must be addressed. Proper lighting is extremely important with video, which explains why television and movie crews have lighting specialists. Some camcorders have a small built-in light on the front, which is effective when shooting subjects that are only a few feet away. If you are shooting indoors and have time to "set the stage," you might consider setting up additional lights. Professional lights can be expensive; however, you can find less expensive alternatives at hardware stores. The placement of the lights is also important—standard photography rules, such as "Don't shoot into the sun" and "Don't place a light directly above a person" apply. More information about proper lighting techniques can be found on the web at sites such as http://www.dv.com/magazine/1998/0998/lighting.pdf and http://www.elitevideo.com/10-2.htm.

Audio is another aspect that must be considered. Although all camcorders have a built-in microphone attached, this microphone is only useful if you are shooting a close-up, such as an interview. For shots with greater distance, you may want to consider purchasing some lavaliere microphones (like the ones worn on TV) with extension cables to the camera. Of course, if the audio is going to be added as a separate track (such as background music), you can record or capture that later—independent of the camera. For more information about audio, see http://pblmm.k12.ca.us/TechHelp/VideoHelp /aGoodStuffToKnow/Microphones.html.

Segments of video must be carefully planned so that the finished video will flow smoothly. For example, one shot might have an actor address another actor off-screen, and the next shot will have the second actor entering the scene. Video is not always shot in the exact sequence that it will eventually be shown. In this example, the second scene might be shot several days later. It would be very distracting if directions got messed up and the second actor entered from the opposite side that the first actor was looking. As you might guess, careful records must be kept so that the best "takes" can be quickly sorted from the dozens of not-so-good tries.

All of this does not come naturally, and if you have a third grade class creating a desktop video, issues such as lights and sets may not be as important. However, if you are serious about producing excellent video, but lack the experience, try to find a workshop or course related to video production, refer to the resources at the end of this chapter, or seek expert assistance until you learn the processes that are involved. In addition, books, such as *iMovie2: The Missing Manual*, *The Little Digital Video Book*, and *Digital Video for Dummies* provide excellent information about preparing for video shoots, lighting, sound, scripting, capturing video, and the like.

Digital Camcorders

Although video can be shot with an analog camcorder and later converted to a digital format, digital camcorders are now available at a very reasonable price. The real breakthrough took place recently when a number of video equipment producers established standards that opened the digital video recording world to consumers. The most important was an industry standard for consumer digital video, called DV—an abbreviation for, as one might suspect, digital video. While manufactures produce several variations of DV for different levels of users, they all produce an interchangeable format called *Mini DV*. This format uses a miniature cassette (2 5/8 x 1 5/8 x 1/2 inches) that is interchangeable between Mini DV camcorders and recording/playback decks of all manufacturers.

The size of the recording cassettes allow these camcorders to be very small, but they still provide some of the most impressive performance statistics of all consumer video equipment. They can record from 60 to 90 minutes per cassette, depending upon the cassette and the recording settings. By analog standards, they are capable of producing images of around 500 lines of horizontal resolution. "Lines" are the standard analog method of measuring video resolution, and it is still applied to digital recorders, because the images are often viewed on standard televisions. For comparison, VHS camcorders provide only 240 lines of resolution, and S-VHS and Hi-8 camcorders provide 400 lines. In addition, the Mini DV format is capable of recording stereo, CD-quality sound.

What makes Mini DV camcorders unique is that they use an industry standard called *IEEE-1394* to provide a simple data interconnection with computers. Also called *iLink* by Sony or *FireWire* by Apple, this connection permits the direct, very fast transfer of the digital video and audio data from one device to another.

The IEEE-1394 interface allows a computer program to control the copying of digital video from the camcorder, and after editing is finished, allows the computer to record the finished program back to the camcorder. In other words, the camcorder can function as an editing machine, although most manufacturers don't encourage this due to the resulting wear and tear on the camcorder. Fairly simple, inexpensive interface boards (such as DV Wonder by ATI or Studio DV by Pinnacle Systems) allow most computers to become IEEE-1394 compatible, and some computers (such as iBooks) are arriving with these interconnections as standard equipment.

With a Mini DV camcorder and an IEEE-1394 compatible computer, it is possible to record digital video and audio, transfer digital video to the computer for editing, and then record the edited program back to a Mini DV tape in the camcorder with no loss in quality of the original digital video. Most DV camcorders also have an analog video input—that means if you have videotapes or other analog sources that you want to digitize, then you can send it into the digital camera and out to the computer. All DV camcorders can also output in analog video, so the finished video can be viewed on a regular television or recorded to regular VHS tape (see Figure 5.2).

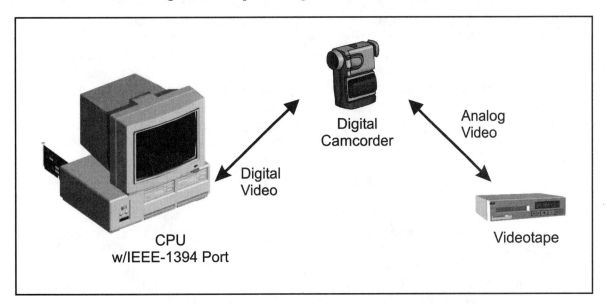

Figure 5.2. Digital camcorders.

If you have access to only analog camcorders, don't despair—although the video quality won't be quite as high, you can convert the analog video to digital through a device called a "video digitizer." This is usually an interface card that is added to a spare slot in a computer (or it can be an external converter box). Figure 5.3 illustrates the configuration of a video digitizing card. Examples of digitizing cards include All-in-Wonder by ATI and VideoBus by Belkin.

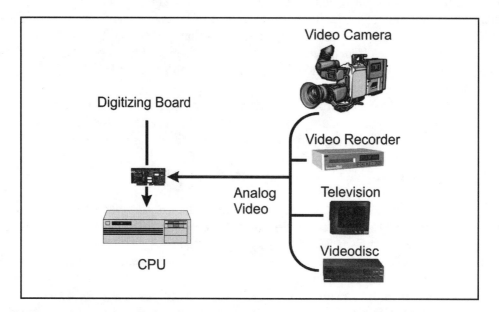

Figure 5.3. Configuration for capturing digital video from analog sources.

POSTPRODUCTION

After all the video has been shot and the other materials have been collected, another process called postproduction begins. Postproduction consists of editing the video—putting everything into the proper order, with the right transitions, to end up as a video program. With analog video, editing took place by copying "shots" from one videotape to another. If a video effect such as a dissolve was needed, then two source tapes were used at the same time. The tapes were positioned so that as one clip came to its end, the other clip started. Much of the time in the postproduction suite (the room where editing took place) was spent trying to get the tapes in just the right places for the next segment of video to be recorded. Since videotapes are a linear medium, they have to be fast-forwarded and rewound over and over again as the editing takes place. Editing analog videotape is called *linear* editing.

Nonlinear Editing

In some ways, editing digital video files on a computer is similar to editing videotapes. Individual clips are appended together to eventually end up with the video program. The difference is that the clips are digital files stored on hard drives attached to the computer, rather than on a strip of magnetic tape. There is no waiting for the tapes to be properly positioned. In fact, once the edit decisions have been made and assembled into a list, called an *edit decision list* or EDL, the computer can work away, nonstop and unattended, building the large digital file that becomes the finished video program. It is even possible to make changes in the middle of a program. The changes are made, and the computer simply rewrites the modified file back to the hard drive. The ability to edit anywhere in a digital video program gives rise to the term *nonlinear* editing.

Computer Hardware

Editing video requires a robust computer—in the Macintosh world that means either a G3 or G4; in Windows, it equates to a Pentium 4 or AMD Athlon. In both cases, you'll need at least 256MB RAM and as much hard drive space as you can afford (at least 20GB). You can roughly figure on being able to store four minutes of digital video on each gigabyte.

One of the weakest links in a digital video system lies with the high performance hard drives that provide the mass storage used for the digital video files. These hard drives must be capable of saving or reading files continuously for the entire length of a video segment. For example, if a 10-minute segment of video is being digitized, the hard drive must be capable of saving data continuously for the entire 10 minutes at the data rate generated by the video digitizing card or FireWire port. Only recently have drives, often called "AV" (for audiovisual) drives, been designed to handle such demands. Though earlier drives appeared to have the speed and capacity to process information fast enough, they were meant to write data in rapid, but short bursts, with frequent pauses to recalibrate the hard drive mechanics during the pauses. Such drives, although ideal for high-performance file servers, simply would not work properly to store video files.

Even AV hard drives can operate poorly if they are not set up and maintained properly. For example, limitations in many operating systems make one large, or "physical" hard drive appear to be several smaller "logical" hard drives. During some of the processes of editing digital video, the video data must be read from one drive, processed by the computer, and saved back to a hard drive. If two physically separate drives are used, each can perform at its maximum rate. However, if the two "logical" drives are really only one larger physical hard drive, then the average performance of each logical drive can be only one half of the maximum performance of the physical drive.

As a final illustration of the complexities of the capture and storage of large, continuous video files, one must consider the impact of an effect called *disk fragmentation*. As a hard drive does its job, files are created, changed, and deleted. As a new file is added to a disk, it is placed into the available space. When a hard drive is brand new, each new file goes into the next available space on the drive in a continuous manner until the drive eventually fills up. However, usually long before that happens, some earlier files are modified or deleted. This creates empty spaces, or "holes" in the material previously stored on the drive. To fully use the storage space, the hard drive system fills these holes with new files. If a new file is larger than a hole, the file is broken into pieces, or fragments, and then scattered around the hard drive until it is all finally stored. The drive system keeps track of the location of all the pieces in order to reassemble the file again when needed.

Unfortunately, it takes much longer to store or retrieve a fragmented file than it does with continuous files. In fact, after thousands and thousands of reads, writes, and deletes, a hard drive may have almost all of its files fragmented. At this point, the performance of the drive may drop to a small percentage of its real capabilities, so a badly fragmented hard drive will not work to capture digital video, no matter how good it is. Some operating systems have programs that examine a hard drive and rearrange, or defragment, the files so that almost all of them are put back together again. Other operating systems do not provide this service, so extra software must be purchased to do the job. The process of defragmenting a really messed up hard drive can take hours, during which time the computer can do little else. The best programs allow the process to be scheduled for a time when the computer is not in use, such as the early morning hours.

Software Editing Tools

Inexpensive, but easy-to-use software makes editing practical for schools. Although digital video editors (such as Adobe Premiere) have been used by professionals and amateurs for several years, a real impetus to desktop video's popularity in schools occurred in 2000 when Apple Computer released a Beta version of iMovie on the web. A subsequent program (iMovie2) is now included with the purchase of most Macintosh computers. A free video editor is also provided with Windows Millennium (called Movie Maker).

Although the features and interfaces vary, all of the editing software provides basic functions for editing video. The process consists of the following general steps:

1. Import the video and other media into the editing software

2. Edit the video clips to the desired length

3. Place the video clips on a timeline

4. Add transitions, such as dissolves and cuts between clips (if desired)

5. Add title slides and other media elements

6. Combine the clips into one movie file

7. Save the movie file in the desired format

8. Export the movie file to videotape, web server, DVD, or CD-ROM

For example, Figure 5.4 shows the editing window in iMovie. Note that the clips that have been imported are displayed on the right. A large preview window (on the left) is used to edit individual clips, and the timeline appears at the bottom of the screen.

Figure 5.4. Editing interface for iMovie.

As a comparison, Figure 5.5 shows the editing window in Movie Maker. Note that the features are basically the same, although they are rearranged. Both programs offer tutorials and abundant *Help* features to get started.

Figure 5.5. Editing interface for Windows Movie Maker.

Movie Maker and iMovie are great tools for video editing. If you find that you or your students need more features, there are several "high-end" editors on the market. Table 5.4 provides information on the most common editing tools used in education.

Table 5.4. Popular Digital Video Editing Software

Program	Cost	Platforms
Adobe Premiere	$500	Windows/Mac
FinalCut Pro	$1000	Mac
iMovie2	Free with Mac OS X $50 with OS9	Mac
Windows Movie Maker	Free w/Windows ME and XP	Windows

Another tool that should be mentioned is QuickTime Pro. Although this is not a video editor per se (you can't import raw video), it is a very powerful tool at a very low price ($30). With QuickTime Pro, you have access to simple editing tools (you can shorten a movie or combine two movies) and a wide variety of file formats (you can import numerous file formats and export to QuickTime, AVI, DV, or several other options).

DISTRIBUTION

The amount of choices you can make at the end of a project, related to how, when, and where the video will be shown, can be staggering. This section provides an overview of the different media (such as computer, videotape, or DVD) that can be used to disseminate your projects, along with the most common file formats and compression options.

Dissemination Media

After a video is edited, it can be disseminated via the web, CD-ROM, DVD, or videotape. Live webcasts can take place without editing. The production and postproduction processes must be planned around the intended end use of the finished video program because different distribution media may require unique production techniques. For example, web-based video that is delivered to a small "window" on a computer screen through an Internet connection is usually a much lower quality than the digital video that is stored on a DVD.

Web-Based Video

As we hear almost every day, applications on the web (including those with video) have grown at a phenomenal rate. Web-based video can be delivered to a remote computer in three ways—as a complete file, as a progressive download, or as a continuous stream of data. If a video is sent as a complete file, you can download the file and save it on your computer's hard drive for later viewing. Another advantage is that the quality will be better (because it will be playing from your hard drive, rather than over the Internet). However, video files are generally very large, and waiting for a download over a dial-up connection can try the patience of just about everyone. For example, a 10MB file (which is not an unusually large file even for compressed digital video) can take between 30 and 40 minutes to download with the fastest standard telephone modems that are currently in use.

Progressive downloads are an alternative to complete downloads in that the video files will begin to play after a portion is received by the remote computer. Many QuickTime files are configured this way (referred to as Fast Start). As illustrated in Figure 5.6, you can watch the gray status bar to see how much of the video has arrived, and you can play that portion. The downside of this approach is that, if there is a slow connection, the video will stop until the next portion is downloaded.

Streaming video provides a continuous stream of video that plays as it is received on your computer. In other words, you do not have to wait for the file, and the file is not saved on your hard drive. Streaming video is used with very large files and "live" events such as a press conferences or videoconferencing. Although the wait time for streaming video files is minimal, the quality can suffer—especially through a dial-up connection.

Figure 5.6. Status bar for progressive download.

CD-ROM-Based Video

The capacity and portability of CD-ROMs made them the first computer storage medium to simplify the production and distribution of quality digital video. As CD-ROM drives have become faster and the production costs of CD-ROMs have dropped dramatically, CD-ROMs with video are showing up everywhere. Games, application software, interactive courseware, and even "junk" CD-ROMs—those that arrive in the mail to promote a commercial product—are now commonplace.

The digital video on CD-ROMs can vary tremendously in quality, but it is usually much better than what is delivered over the World Wide Web. This is because modern CD-ROM drives can deliver video data to the computer more rapidly than most standard Internet connections. In many cases, the quality of the video and audio can approach that of a standard VHS videotape, although it usually displays in a small window on the screen.

DVD

While CD-ROMs opened the door for commercial digital video products, the technical limitations of CD-ROMs quickly became apparent. In particular, the storage capacity of a standard CD-ROM (approximately 650MB) was not sufficient for more than a few minutes of high quality digital video. In addition, a variety of different techniques were used to capture, edit, and store the video files on the CD-ROM. As a result, no assurance existed that a desktop computer would have the software needed to play back the video unless that software was also supplied on the CD-ROM. Even then, different CD-ROMs with different versions of the same software often conflicted with each other.

The time was right for a storage medium with both higher capacity and some defined industry standards for video. The DVD standard has now opened new lines of consumer video products because it can hold up to 17 gigabytes of information. Instead of renting movies on videotape, we can now rent them on DVD. Some high-end desktop computers also have the ability to create or "burn" DVDs. For example, Apple has created two programs—iDVD and DVD Studio Pro that can be used to create DVDs on G4 computers. Because the storage space is so large on a DVD, and the video will play directly from the DVD, very high-quality video can be stored on DVD. Using iDVD, you can create a DVD that offers 60 minutes of full-screen, full-motion video.

Analog Videotape

Digital video production and postproduction are often used to prepare videos that are recorded back onto standard analog videotapes. It might sound strange to go through all the trouble of digitizing video, and then export the finished video to an analog videotape. However, VHS videotapes are still a medium of choice for widespread distribution. The videotapes are inexpensive, easy to duplicate, and can play high-quality video (as compared to web-based video). Nearly all homes and schools have videotape players and recorders. Also, if you have a digital camera, it's very easy to hook up the VCR to the camera and export the finished video directly to videotape (thus freeing up the space on your hard drive).

Live Webcasts

Digital video can also be used to check the traffic at a busy intersection in town, or to participate in underwater adventures. A *webcast* is a "live" stream of video that is sent continuously through the Internet. For example, the Salem School District in Salem, New Hampshire, provides a live simulcast/webcast of its educational access cable television channel. Programming consists of live high school sporting events, board meetings, student productions, concerts, satellite feeds, and a message board. The Discovery Channel (http://www.discovery.com/cams/cams.html) provides webcasts to view animals, weather, cities, volcanoes, airports, and more.

If you want to create a webcast, you won't need digital editing software, but you will need a digital camera (webcam) and broadcasting software. A *webcam* is a video camera that is attached directly to a computer to transmit still or continuous (streaming) video images through the Internet for communication or research purposes.

With your own webcam, you can add photos to online documents or e-mail, send video letters, or use the conferencing software to turn your computer into a videophone. Various webcams include Logitech QuickCam (http://www.logitech.com) and Kodak Webcam (http://www.kodak.com). Software and hardware related to webcasts can be found at Nuspectra (http://www.nuspectra.com/products /index.htm). Additional links are at Webcam Central (http://www.camcentral.com/).

File Formats

If you are exporting or saving digital video for either web-based or CD-ROM delivery, you will need to select a file format (also referred to as architecture). Video file formats define the contents of a video file, such as how many streams of video and audio it contains, the resolution of the media, and the compression types. There are several formats available; different editing software offers different options, and many of the file formats are incompatible.

QuickTime (.MOV and .QT)

QuickTime, developed by Apple computer in the early 1990s, was the first popular program to "put it all together" for desktop digital video. QuickTime provided both authoring and playback interfaces for synchronized video and audio. Although first provided for Macintosh computers, QuickTime files can now be played and edited on PC-compatible computers as well.

QuickTime has maintained its identity through several major revisions, and it is still one of the most popular architectures for digital video on desktop computers. It has evolved to a point where it now works with virtually every kind of audio, still image, and video file format. The digital movies that are produced with QuickTime can be configured to play through CD-ROMs or the Internet with a wide range of image size, color depth, and frame rate options. They can be optimized for streaming, progressive download, or download and play.

If you are using iMovie, QuickTime is the only file format that you can use. In the higher-end programs (Premiere and FinalCut Pro), QuickTime is just one of many options.

Windows (.AVI, .ASF, .WMV)

Shortly after Apple released QuickTime, Microsoft introduced a similar, but incompatible product called Video for Windows, which uses an .AVI file extension. Since then, Microsoft has introduced other file formats, including .ASF (Advanced Streaming Format). The .AVI format is used primarily for download and play files; .ASF is for streaming. The newest format (.WMV) stands for Windows Media Video. It is highly optimized for streaming. The file can be streamed by Windows Media server and played by Windows Media Player.

If you are using Windows Movie Maker for your video editing, .WMV is the only file format that you can use to save your movie. In the higher-end programs, such as Premiere, Windows Media files are listed among many options.

Real (.RA and .RM)

Real Networks (and their predecessors) were the pioneers in streaming technologies when they introduced RealAudio in 1995. Since then, the Real formats (.RA for RealAudio and .RM for RealMedia) are widely used for streaming media on both Macs and PCs. Although neither iMovie nor Movie Maker offer these formats as options for saving their files, the high-end editors do include them. You can also use programs, such as Adobe Premiere, to convert files from one format to another —for example, from QuickTime to Real.

The advantage of Real is that their plug-ins are widely available and widely used. The compression is very good, and the quality is excellent. In addition, they offer tools, such as Real SlideShow and Real Presenter that can create streaming files very easily.

MPEG (.MPG and .MP3)

MPEG stands for Motion Pictures Expert Group. It is used as a file format as well as compression technique, and it is popular for high-end video applications. There are two MPEG file formats that are worth mentioning—MPEG-1 and MPEG-2. MPEG-1 is commonly used to store video files on video CD-ROMs. The quality is about the same as analog videotape, and the files are generally too big to transfer over the web efficiently. Support for MPEG-1 is now built into Windows and QuickTime.

MPEG-2 offers higher quality (and larger file sizes). It is used to create DVDs. It is also the format received by home satellite dishes, and the format to which all U.S. television broadcasts will convert for high-definition television (HDTV). MPEG-2 offers extremely high quality with a fast data rate; it is not used on the web.

MP3 is an audio-only offshoot of MPEG (consisting of the third layer of an MPEG audio stream). Using MP3, files for individual songs can be compressed down to sizes that are quite reasonable to send through standard Internet connections. The music can then be stored on hard drives and played back at any time. Portable electronic players with no moving parts (MP3 players) are now available. The songs are copied into the player, or they are inserted through portable compact memory chips.

This has opened up a whole new Internet industry—that of distributing high quality music files through the Internet. Through this technique, it is possible for artists to sell their music directly to consumers, thus bypassing the entire traditional music industry. It is also possible for pirates to steal copyrighted music and make it available to anyone who wants to download it.

Compression and Decompression—Codecs

As mentioned earlier, a finished video is not practical to deliver in its "pure" digitized form because the files would be exceptionally large. Therefore, when you export a video and select a file format, you may also have the opportunity to select a compression technique. In some programs, such as iMovie, you can select a "canned" export setting (instead of selecting a specific codec and other parameters). In other words, if you are saving as a QuickTime movie, you can select an option from the following list:

- Email Movie, Small
- Web Movie, Small
- Streaming Web Movie, Small
- CD-ROM Movie, Medium
- Full Quality, Large

iMovie will then select the best codec, frame rate, and window size for the application. For example, in Figure 5.7, "Web Movie, Small" was selected, and the parameters that will be used are:

- Codec: H.263
- Window Size: 240 X 180
- Frame Rate: 12 fps
- Audio Codec: Qdesign
- Audio Sampling Rate: 22kHz
- Audio Channels: Stereo

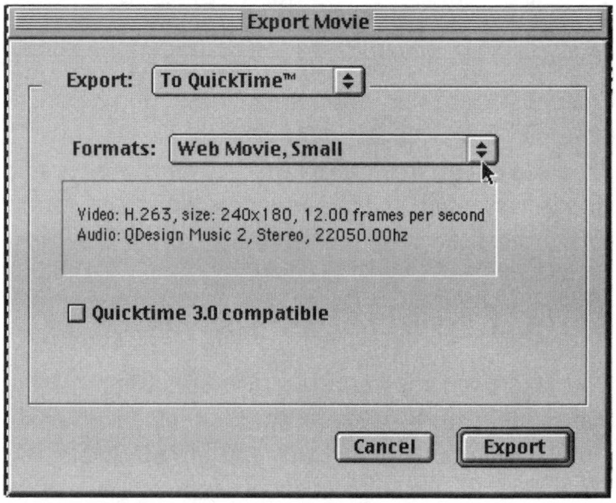

Figure 5.7. Export settings in iMovie.

There are times, however, when you may want to select a particular codec and other parameters for an application. This section provides an overview of some of the most popular codecs. Note that many of the codecs are limited to specific file formats—for example, the RealMedia format uses the G2 codec.

JPEG and MJPEG

A professional group called the *Joint Photographic Experts Group* (JPEG) developed this standard for the data compression of still pictures. It offers data compression of between two and 100 times, and three levels of processing are defined that range from lossless to very lossy encoding. In general, the greater the compression, the greater the amount of image information that is lost. JPEG is an open standard rather than a proprietary one, so it is very widely used for storing or transmitting still images (such as graphics on the web). See Chapter 2 for more information about JPEG.

MJPEG stands for *Motion JPEG*, and it extends the JPEG standard to motion images. The concept is simple in that every image making up the motion picture is encoded as a JPEG image. This is a popular compression standard for use in nonlinear editing systems because the data has a reasonable amount of compression, but the images are still very easy to work with.

MPEG

Another professional group called the *Moving Picture Experts Group* (MPEG) developed this compression technique specifically for digital motion images. This group's work builds upon that of JPEG, but it adds an important process called *interframe compression*. Interframe compression compares the sequential images of a motion picture and encodes only the information that changes from one image to the next. Thus, MPEG would encode only the moving lips of a nearly motionless "talking head" such as a really dry professor giving a lecture. While it isn't that simple because lots of things move slightly, even in a fairly static motion image, it does provide a basic understanding of why MPEG compression techniques can achieve incredible compression ratios during portions of a motion image when things are pretty much motionless.

However, MPEG encoding also carries with it some liabilities. For example, there is no simple way to start at a random point in MPEG encoded video. If you were to do this, the only thing visible at first would be whatever moved during the initial few frames. The entire image would gradually be created as additional things moved. However, since an edit point would usually create a major change from one frame to the next, the screen would almost instantly build if the playback started just before an edit, such as a change in scenes.

Because individual frame data is not always available, MPEG is certainly not a compression technique for storing motion segments that will undergo additional editing. However, there are ways to allow random access to a reasonable number of points within an MPEG encoded program. For example, every edit point could be compressed to start with a complete JPEG encoded image, and every so often—like once a second—a complete JPEG image could be embedded into the MPEG stream. This way, if a viewer wanted to go to any location in the program, he or she would never be more than a second away from a complete picture to start on.

MPEG-1 is a compression scheme that is designed to work at an average playback data rate of 1.2Mbps (megabits per second), the data rate of a standard CD-ROM. This is currently one of the most common motion image storage formats for computer games and instructional videos that are distributed through CD-ROMs. At best, its quality roughly matches that of a 640 x 480 VGA computer screen. One or two audio channels are available. MPEG-1 is not used for any broadcast applications.

MPEG-2 is not a single standard, but instead a family of inter- and intra-frame compression techniques designed to cover a wide range of requirements from VHS quality all the way to high definition television. MPEG-2 defines a range of compression levels that result in playback data rates that can range from 4 to 100Mbps. As you might guess, the lower playback rates produce the VHS quality images, while the higher rates are used with high definition television applications. MPEG-2 also provides many more options with the program audio than MPEG-1—up to seven audio channels are available, with higher frequency responses than those found in MPEG-1 video programs. In general, MPEG-2 provides higher image resolution, more accurate coloration, and better sound than MPEG-1. However, the tradeoff is that much more data is involved during playback of the program. As a result, a standard CD-ROM does not have enough storage capacity or data transmission speed to provide acceptable MPEG-2 programs. However, MPEG-2 is used for most DVD applications.

MPEG-4 extends the advanced MPEG compression techniques into other forms of multimedia. It is rapidly evolving, with a revised version soon to be available. Although it is a very difficult standard to explain, it treats a variety of multimedia components—natural sounds, synthetic sounds, still images, 3D images, and natural or synthetic motion images—as objects. MPEG-4 is designed to enable the delivery of the multimedia objects through networks, whether they are fast or slow. It includes techniques to synchronize multimedia objects, for example, so that a synthetic music component will start, play, and finish in harmony with an animated three-dimensional video clip. Two-way communications are possible so that users have much more ability to control or navigate through the MPEG-4 files coming over the network to them.

The JPEG and MPEG formats are called open compression standards because any developers can use the standards as long as they agree to follow them closely. This makes it possible for a wide variety of software from many different developers to share these open standard files.

Proprietary Codecs

Proprietary file compression formats exist that are much more closely controlled by a single company or small consortium. In most cases, other developers can't use proprietary formats unless they negotiate significant royalty payments with the copyright holders.

Sorensen is one of QuickTime's codecs that provides very high quality with excellent compression. Sorenson is used to compress files for both CD-ROM and web-based delivery. It is considered one of the best codecs available for digital video.

H.263 is a codec that was originally designed for videoconferencing (and is still used for that purpose). However, because of the tremendous compression it offers, it is also very useful for web-based video (especially if you are aiming for the dial-up users).

G2 is the codec that is used with RealMedia. The plug-in (RealOne) is very popular on the web and can decode files that are streamed with G2.

Cinepak was originally developed to play small digital "movies" at a time when computers were based on older Intel or Motorola CPU's. At that time, only standard or single-speed CD-ROM drives were available, so only a limited amount of data could flow through the computer. Cinepak's greatest strength is its extremely low CPU requirements. Cinepak's quality was considered very high when it was first released, but it does not compete well with newer codecs available today (like Sorenson). Newer codecs produce higher quality with the same data rates, or similar quality with lower data rates. However, newer codecs require high performance computers, so many will not work with older computers. If you still need to distribute digital video to a wide variety of computers, Cinepak is a codec to consider.

Indeo is a codec that was developed by Intel in the 1980s, and was originally known as RealTime Video because it compresses very quickly. Indeo is similar to, but not compatible with, the Cinepak codec. It is well-suited to CD-ROM and plays back on a wide variety of machines.

DV-NTSC and DV-PAL are two codecs that retain almost all of the quality of a digital file. They are used for back-up purposes and can also be used for DVDs.

SUMMARY

Digital video represents one of the fastest growing areas of desktop computing. Not only are computers increasing in power and storage capacity so that they can now easily work with the massive amount of data produced by digital video, but new video camcorders on the market are capable of recording in a digital video format. Now, the only limiting factors to continued growth of digital video on desktop computers are issues related to the portability of the images. The most practical method of moving a large video file from one location to another is by means of a DVD disc, but desktop DVD recorders are still relatively expensive.

The transportation problem becomes even more pronounced when we try to move digital video over LANs or the Internet. Full-screen, high-quality video is enough to bring most current LANs to a standstill, and trying to get even small, partial motion images through the Internet is still a major challenge. However, solutions are arriving. LAN technology is rapidly moving into the gigabit per second range, and with the arrival of cable modems and ADSL telephone lines, even Internet connections are much faster. As has been the case with most other media, video, too, will soon exist mainly in digital forms.

GLOSSARY

4-bit. A 4-bit video display card can display 16 different colors for each pixel.

8-bit. An 8-bit video display card can display 256 different colors for each pixel.

16-bit. A 16-bit video display card can display 65,536 different colors for each pixel.

24-bit. A 24-bit video display card can display 16.7 million different colors for each pixel, and it is often referred to as true color.

analog video. Video that is stored as an electrical signal with a continuous scale. Videotape and videodisc generally store analog video.

aspect ratio. The width-to-height ratio of an image. Changing the aspect ratio can make images appear out of proportion.

AVI (Audio Video Interleave). A Microsoft video file format that is used extensively on the Windows platform—especially for download and play files.

bandwidth. The transmission capacity of a telecommunications system. The greater the bandwidth, the greater the amount of digital information that can be transmitted per second.

capture. The process of collecting and saving text or image data. When an analog source such as a videodisc is used as a source to record a digital image on a computer, it is said to be "captured."

CD-ROM (compact disc–read only memory). A prerecorded, nonerasable disc that stores approximately 650 megabytes of digital data.

Cinepak. A technique for software-only compression. It requires considerable compression time but results in high quality.

clip. A short video segment.

codec (compressor/decompressor). Software (or hardware) that can compress and decompress audio and video content.

compression. Technique used to store files with fewer bits; therefore, less disk storage space is required. Lossless compression preserves all image qualities, while lossy compression sacrifices some image quality for greater compression ratios.

digital camera. A camera that records images in true digital form. The images are usually downloaded directly into a computer.

digitizing. The process of converting an analog signal into a digital signal.

disc. Usually refers to a videodisc or compact disc. Computer diskettes are generally referred to as disks (with a k), and optical storage media are referred to as discs (with a c).

DV (digital video). Video that is stored in bits and bytes on a computer. It can be manipulated and displayed on a computer screen. Often used to refer to the format used by a digital camcorder with DV tapes. Also used to refer to the compression type used by DV systems.

DVD (digital video disc). A second generation of the original CD-ROM format. It provides up to two layers of digital information on a compact disc. It stores up to 4.7 gigabytes for one layer; 8.5 gigabytes for two layers.

EDL (Edit Decision List). A list of all the start points (timecode) and stop points used in video production.

FireWire. The Apple Computer trace name for the IEEE-1394 standard that enables direct transfer of digital video between devices, such as a camcorder and computer.

fps (frames per second). Describes the frame rate—the number of frames displayed each second.

frame. One complete video picture.

frame rate. The number of video frames displayed each second.

full-motion video. Video frames displayed at 30 frames per second.

G2. The codec that is used with RealMedia.

H.263. A digital video codec that was originally designed for videoconferencing (and is still used for that purpose, as well as web-based video applications).

IEEE-1394. The Institute of Electrical and Electronics Engineers standard for high-speed ports and cables for a computer. Also known as FireWire and iLink.

iLink. The Sony trade name for IEEE-1394 standard.

image. A graphic, a picture, or one frame of a video.

Indeo. A software technique created by Intel to compress and decompress video.

interframe compression. A compression technique that stores only the differences between a frame and the subsequent frames.

JPEG (Joint Photographic Expert Group). An organization that has developed an international standard for compression and decompression of still images.

lossless compression. Compression programs that retain all the information in the original file.

lossy compression. Compression programs that discard some information during the reduction process.

MJPEG (Motion JPEG). Extends the JPEG standard to motion images. The concept is simple in that every image making up the motion picture is encoded as a JPEG image.

movie file. The file that is created by combining audio, video, and images.

MP3. An audio-only offshoot of MPEG (consisting of the third layer of an MPEG audio stream).

MPEG (Moving Picture Experts Group). Working parties for standardization of motion-video compression. MPEG-1 is used for linear video movies on compact discs, and MPEG-2 is designed for broadcast-quality digital video.

MPEG-2. A digital video standard designed for broadcast video.

nonlinear editing. Editing video through a random access medium (such as a computer) as opposed to a linear medium (such as a videotape).

NTSC (National Television Systems Committee). The U.S. standard for motion video of 525 horizontal lines per frame at 30 frames per second.

optical media. Media read with a laser beam. CD-ROM and DVD technologies use optical media.

PAL. The analog video standard used in Europe and South America. Uses 25 frames per second.

pixel. A single dot or point of an image on a computer screen. Pixel is a contraction of the words "picture element."

postproduction. The phase of a video project that includes editing the video.

preproduction. The planning phase of a video project—includes setting a goal, writing scripts, etc.

production. The phase of a video project that consists of shooting the video and compiling the media.

QuickTime. A file format that allows Macintosh computers to compress and play digitized video movies.

raster. The horizontal lines of light that make up an image on a standard computer screen. The number of pixels in each raster and the total number of raster lines dictate the screen's resolution, such as 640 x 480.

RealMedia. An architecture (file format) specifically designed for the web. A RealOne player plug-in is required.

resolution. The sharpness or clarity of a computer screen. Displays with more lines and pixels of information have better resolution.

SECAM. An analog video standard that is similar to PAL. It is used in France, the Middle East, and Africa.

Sorenson. A software technique created by Intel to compress and decompress video.

streaming. Files that can be played as they are sent over the web.

timecode. A track that assigns a specific number to each video frame.

timeline. A method for organizing the video clips in sequential order.

transition. The method of changing from one video clip to the next (can be dissolve, straight cut, etc.)

Windows Movie Maker. A software editing program that can be used to create digital movies. It is included with Windows Millennium Edition.

RESOURCES

10 Most Important Things to Know About Lights
http://www.elitevideo.com/10-2.htm

Adobe Premiere
http://www.adobe.com/products/premiere/main.html

All-in-Wonder (ATI)
http://www.ati.com

Desktop Video (About.com)
http://desktopvideo.about.com

Desktop Video Handbook
http://www.videoguys.com/dtvhome.html

Digital Movies in Education: Tips and Techniques
http://www.apple.com/education/dv/tips.html

Digital Video for Dummies (1999)
http://catalog.dummies.com/product.asp?isbn=0764508067

Digital Video Magazine
http://www.dv.com

Digital Video Primer
http://www.adobe.com/motion/events/pdfs/dvprimer.pdf

Digital Video with Windows Movie Maker
http://www.microsoft.com/WINDOWSME/news/articles/digitalstate.asp

Discovery Channel Webcams
http://www.discovery.com/cams/cams.html

DV Wonder (ATI)
http://www.ati.com/na/pages/products/pc/dv_wonder/

Education iMovie Gallery
http://www.apple.com/education/dv/gallery/

eMedia Magazine
http://www.emedia.com

Final Cut Pro (Apple)
http://www.apple.com/finalcutpro

iMovie (Apple)
http://www.apple.com/iMovie/

iMovie2: The Missing Manual
http://www.missingmanual.com

Kodak Webcam
http://www.kodak.com

Little Digital Video Book
http://www.peachpit.com

Logitech QuickCam
http://www.logitech.com

MacWorld iMovie Archive
http://www.macworld.com/subject/imovie/

Microphones for Video
http://pblmm.k12.ca.us/TechHelp/VideoHelp/aGoodStuffToKnow/Microphones.html

NuSpectra (Webcasting Products)
http://www.nuspectra.com/products/index.htm

Studio DV (Pinnacle Systems)
http://www.pinnaclesys.com

Video Format Conversion
http://www.manifest-tech.com/media_pc/vid_fmt_cvt.htm

Video Guide

http://pblmm.k12.ca.us/TechHelp
/VideoHelp/VideoGuide.html

VideoBus (Belkin)

http://belkin.com

Webcam Central

http://www.camcentral.com/

Windows Media Technologies

http://www.microsoft.com/windows
/windowsmedia/en/default.asp

Windows Movie Maker

http://www.microsoft.com/WINDOWSME
/guide/digitalmedia/moviemaker.asp

Windows Movie Maker Partners (Free Hosting Services)

http://www.microsoft.com/windowsme
/guide/moviemakerlarge.asp

6

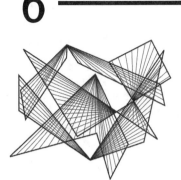

LOCAL AREA NETWORKS

A Scenario

It was 1985, and the administrators of Ridgewood High School took pride in the reputation they were building for their school. Ridgewood was fast becoming known throughout the state as a technologically progressive school. They had two rooms full of computers for their students. There were computers on the administrators' desks, most staff desks, and three computers were set up in the faculty lounge. Staff members had learned to use a spreadsheet program to manage the school budget, and letters to parents were typed on a word processor. A few of the teachers were typing and printing their own tests.

There was no question that the computers were popular among most of the students, staff, and administrators. The administrators were proud of their careful planning and the resulting positive results. Not only had they researched their computer hardware and software purchases very carefully, but they also had provided their faculty and staff with appropriate training.

More than 15 years have passed, and the administrators were now getting worried. The computers might, in fact, have become too popular. A technician had been employed part-time several years ago. The plan was for the technician to be temporary help to set up the computers and to train a staff member in techniques to keep things running. As it turned out, the technician is now a full-time employee who is clearly overloaded with responsibilities.

While there have been some hardware failures, the most common problems for the technician have centered upon software. Any time a program is updated the technician has to go to every computer that uses that program to install the updates. The student computers seem to need the greatest amount of attention because the students like to explore programs. Students often change settings and then are unable to get things reset again so that the program will work correctly.

Finally, the technician is spending more and more time trying to get a document or data created on one computer converted so that it can be used on another computer. This is a real problem because there are two incompatible brands of computers in use, and several versions of each brand depending upon when each computer was purchased. In some cases, there are hardware incompatibilities such as floppy disk drives that can't read the disks from other computers. In other cases, the incompatibilities are with software. For example, one version of a word processing program can't work with files from a later version of the same program.

The technician has suggested several times that he should attend a training session about local area networks (LANs) because he thinks a LAN could solve a number of the problems the school is having. He has even requested that a local vendor invite the school board members to visit a nearby factory that has recently started using a LAN throughout the factory building. The administrators have many questions. They don't really know what a LAN is, but they have heard that it requires connecting all the computers. They are certain this would be expensive, and they fear that it would just accelerate the school's rapidly spiraling technology costs. They are also concerned about security issues—what if the students were able to tap into the teachers' or principal's computers over a network?

Clearly, it is time for them to start gathering information!

INTRODUCTION

By the mid 1980s, one of the factors that added to the popularity of computers was their ability to operate independently of the cumbersome mainframe computers that ran businesses, governments, and schools. Although the mainframes had evolved to the point where display terminals were commonly used as input and output devices, these terminals were "dumb" in that they could only display what was going on inside the mainframe computer. The real power of the mainframe rested in its ability to run large and complex batch programs. A typical batch program might process a school district's payroll information in preparation for printing paychecks. Another might update the costs and quantities of inventoried items. While school employees might have had desktop terminals attached to their mainframe computers, the terminals were often nearly useless for mundane activities like word processing during the time the mainframe was running important batch jobs. As more staff members began to realize the independence that a computer could add to everyday processes such as typing or bookkeeping, they began to resent the limits imposed upon them by their restricted access to mainframes.

Then, microcomputers appeared on the market. They are controlled by the individual yet have enough power to handle word-processing and bookkeeping jobs. Almost over night, these small computers started to show up in offices in all kinds of business, government, and school settings. Employees were happy because they now had direct control over their own little computer, and mainframe computer services departments were happy to get rid of "nonproductive" computer nuisances such as word processing that were tying up their big machines.

Recently, however, the general climate of happiness started to wear thin. School administrators and business executives were finding their desks cluttered with equipment—often a dumb terminal was still needed to deal with the mainframe programs like payroll and inventory, but they also had a computer and monitor on their desks because it let them do simple day-to-day things. As more and more day-to-day things were conducted on personal computers, a greater problem became apparent. There was no easy way to get files and information from one place to another—each personal computer operated completely independently of the others, and each could only run the programs that were installed on it.

It quickly became apparent that the dynamics of computer usage and administration in corporate, government, and school environments were never again going to be what they had been. The personal computers changed everything—solving some old problems, but creating many new problems along the way. What was most needed was a structure that would add stability to the organization, storage, and distribution of the information created by computers, but at the same time allow each computer some level of independence from all others. Into this environment, local area networks (LANs) evolved. The topics of this chapter include:

- Overview of a LAN

- The OSI layer model of a LAN

- Physical layer: Cables, repeaters, and hubs

- Data link layer: Ethernet, network interface cards, and bridges

- Network layer: Ethernet, Token Ring, and ATM

- Transport and session layers: Network operating systems

- Wireless LANs

OVERVIEW OF A LAN

In simple terms, a local area network (LAN) is something that connects two or more nearby computers so that they can communicate with each other. The connections may be wire, fiber optic cables, radio waves, or infrared beams. No matter how the computers connect, the results are similar. The computers can share and exchange information.

A LAN allows the interconnected computers to share documents. A document that is created on one computer can be opened by another computer through the LAN. The second computer can then be used to review or modify the document. However, program compatibility is still an issue. For example, if a memo is typed in one word processing program and then opened by a computer that uses another word processing program, there is still no guarantee that the second computer will be able to display or modify the file.

To solve these program incompatibilities, a LAN also allows the interconnected computers to run or install programs from a single location. For example, an entire school might have more than one hundred computers that all use the same word processing program. The program is stored on a special computer called a *file server*, and all other computers go to the file server to load the word processor. Since all computers run the same program, the word processing files will be compatible with all the computers. In addition, when the word processing software is updated, it is updated on the file server where it is stored. There is no need to go to every computer with the new disks or CD-ROM.

A LAN allows the interconnected computers to share e-mail, audioconferences, videoconferences, and other multimedia forms of communication. Although the computers in a LAN are usually in the same building, buildings can be very large. It may be more productive for teachers to hold impromptu meetings through the LAN than to locate, schedule, and gather in a conference room. Current LAN technologies allow digital audio and video to travel from computer to computer.

Individual LANs can be interconnected to form larger networks that are called *wide area networks* or WANs. A WAN may involve computers in several buildings as in a school or university campus, or it might connect the computers of a state or large district. Perhaps the largest WAN of all is the rapidly expanding Internet, and because of this the "wide area network" phrase is being replaced with the term Internetwork.

There are standards, hardware, and software to create hundreds of possible LAN configurations. Although a few of the configurations are directly compatible with each other, many are not. Because this chapter is designed to help you understand the basic functions of a LAN rather than all the possible combinations, we will focus on a configuration that is currently one of the most popular. We will examine a network that runs Novell Netware over a 100BaseT Ethernet system. We will work with two school labs that will be called workgroups. Each workgroup has 20 computers, called workstations, that are connected together as part of the network.

The OSI Model

Discussions of LAN configurations quickly become technical and filled with jargon. It seems like there are almost endless variations—speed of the LAN, transmission media, LAN structure, LAN software, and so forth. Though technical terms are often necessary in discussions of these concepts, it is important to always use terms consistently through the definition of accepted standards. If there were no standards for LAN hardware and software manufacturers to follow, there would be no compatibility between LANs.

To help standardize all the concepts and buzzwords, in 1984 the International Organization for Standardization (ISO) created the Open Systems Interconnection (OSI) Reference Model that is outlined in Figure 6.1. Note that due to the International Organization for Standardization's activities in many nations, there is no single language interpretation of its name. For example, it is Organisation internationale de normalisation in French. "ISO" is not an acronym. Instead, it is a word that is derived from the Greek root "isos" that means "equal," and it is the short name that is used around the world for this organization.

As you can see, the OSI model outlines LAN structures by layers. These layers build upon each other as they progress from the most physical aspects of a LAN to the most application-dependent aspects. Each layer is designed so that the layers below it can be invisible to the layers above it. This allows changes to be made in single layers without impacting all the other layers. All the layers don't apply equally to every single LAN. Instead, the model is designed to extend to Internetworks that are composed of many individual LANs.

When reduced to very simple terms, the concepts of lower layers of the OSI model are fairly easy to grasp, while the upper layers involve more complex concepts. In the following pages, many of the basic concepts of LANs will be introduced, and they will be related to the appropriate layers of the OSI model. First, though, we will take a quick look at the model itself.

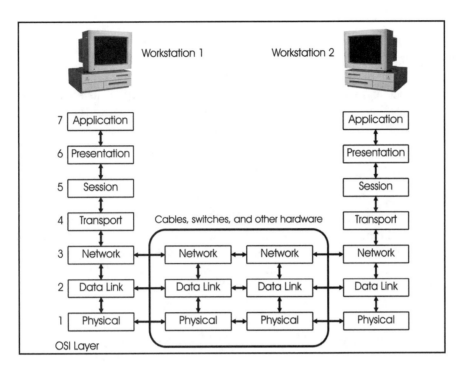

Figure 6.1. Open Systems Interconnection Reference Model.

OSI Layer 1—The Physical Layer

The physical layer of a LAN defines the most basic infrastructure of cable types, cable lengths, cable connectors, signal characteristics such as bandwidth, signaling (data transmission) rates, and the logistical shape or *topology* of the LAN. It is the most clearly defined layer, and it is also one of the most discussed. The "100BaseT" mentioned earlier defines one of a variety of possible structures for this layer.

OSI Layer 2—The Data Link Layer

A network works because it defines an orderly way for computers to share information. For example, any one computer has to know when it can transmit data, when it needs to wait to transmit, or when it is expected to receive data from another location. These rules are called the network *protocol*, or less commonly the network technology. Ethernet is an example of one of these network protocols. Layer 2 is where the specific protocol is implemented for each LAN. In addition, Layer 2 serves as the interpreter between various types of Layer 1 cabling that might be used in the LAN. For example, if two parts of a LAN use two different kinds of cables, these differences are dealt with at Layer 2, so that all higher layers are unaware of the differences. We will look much more closely at Ethernet and some of the hardware that is associated with it later in the chapter.

OSI Layer 3—The Network Layer

Many networks are not simple systems. Instead, they may link a variety of LANs, each with a different communication standard. One LAN may be Ethernet running at 10Mbps on twisted pair wire, another may be Ethernet running at 100Mbps on twisted pair wire, and a third may be Token Ring. OSI Layer 3 defines the device and software requirements that allow all higher levels to ignore these dissimilarities that are often found in a complex network. We will examine routers, which are Layer 3 devices, later in the chapter.

OSI Layers 4 and 5—Transport and Session Layers

These two layers vary in function from one LAN to another. In essence, they define the essential components of a network operating system (NOS), such as Novell Netware, that are not defined in lower levels. Among the functions that take place in these levels are the structuring of transmitted data in the appropriate "package," the control of users and file access to prevent data corruption, and a variety of other complex activities that are unique to a LAN. We will not go into any further detail about the specific components of these levels, but we will look at a popular NOS, Novell Netware, later in the chapter.

OSI Layers 6 and 7—Presentation and Application Layers

In addition to the NOS, every workstation that is connected to a LAN needs its own operating system, such as Windows 98, Mac OS X, or Windows NT. Each workstation must also have a small software module, called *client software*, that allows the NOS to "talk" with each workstation on the LAN.

Finally, applications that run through a LAN have different requirements than applications that run on free-standing computers. For example, if six users were each using a LAN-based word processor, and they each named a file they were working on as "resume," somehow the LAN must keep track of which resume goes to which network user. The NOS, the workstation operating system, and the word processing software must be capable of handling situations like this. We won't cover these layers any farther in this chapter, but this is where a variety of application-specific protocols define everything from file sharing to e-mail standards.

LAYER 1 DETAILS—CABLES AND REPEATERS AND HUBS

Layer 1 serves as the foundation of a LAN. It defines physical aspects of the LAN such as cables, repeaters, and hubs.

Signaling Rates

Much like individual computers, all LANs operate with their own internal electronic clock. As with computers, the primary purpose of the clock is to set a cadence that keeps all activities in step with each other. The faster the clock ticks, the faster data can be processed. Common telephone modems today can operate at speeds up to 56 thousand (Kilo) bits per second, or 56Kbps. Current popular LAN speeds are either 10 million (Mega) bits per second (Mbps) or 100Mbps. LANs with speeds of 1,000Mbps (or 1 billion Gigabit per second—Gbps) are just arriving and will become more common within the next few years. In our example, the "100" in 100BaseT represents Layer 1—the physical layer—running at 100Mbps.

Bandwidth

There are two ways to transmit information through a cable. One method uses the entire capacity of the cable to transmit a single stream of information. This method is called the *baseband* method and it is the most common in use today. It means that the cable that is used for the LAN can be used only to transmit the LAN data and nothing else. The "Base" in our 100BaseT example represents a physical layer that is running in a baseband mode.

A second technique splits the signal capacity of the cable into smaller components. One component might be used for the LAN, while another component might be used for a second LAN or for the transmission of television or telephone messages. In wire cables, this is usually done by designating specific frequency ranges of signals for specific applications. Cable television functions this way, with different frequencies representing different stations. With cable modem systems like Time Warner's RoadRunner, sophisticated equipment is used to create "channels" that carry computer data rather than standard television signals. This shared bandwidth process is called *broadband* technology and allows a single cable to serve multiple functions. It is not yet widely used outside of shared television and computer cable systems.

Cables

LANs can use a variety of cables—most are made of copper, but some are made of optical fibers. It is now even possible to use infrared beams or radio waves to create "virtual" cables. These wireless LAN technologies will be covered toward the end of the chapter.

Unshielded Twisted Pairs (UTP) of Wires

The cables used in telephone systems are made up of pairs of small wires that are twisted together. Usually a minimum of two pairs are enclosed in a thick vinyl outer sheath for the telephone wiring in a home, but the bundles of pairs can be much larger in cables that are used in commercial or office settings. Unlike some other types of cables, the vinyl covering offers no protection from outside electrical interference, so these cables are said to be *unshielded*. This combination—unshielded twisted pair of wires—is called *UTP cable*. See Figure 6.2.

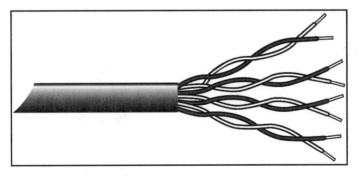

Figure 6.2. UTP cable.

UTP wiring is a very popular configuration for LANs because many schools already have communication cable bundles in place with spare wire pairs. Using these spare wires for the school LAN can be far less expensive than pulling new cables through the walls and ceilings of an existing building. The "T" in our 100BaseT example refers to a LAN that uses UTP wire as its cable system. However, there is more to the T than just some twisted wires.

Categories of UTP cable

As is the case with most aspects of technology, unshielded communication cable has evolved in capabilities over recent years. The original telephone wires of 30 or 40 years ago simply do not compare with modern communication cables. To help distinguish between types of UTP cable, the communication industry has developed the category listing that is depicted in Table 6.1.

Table 6.1. UTP Categories

Category	Maximum Data Rate	Typical Use
1	N/A	Telephone
2	1Mbps	LocalTalk
3	16Mbps	Ethernet
4	20Mbps	Ethernet
5	100Mbps	Fast Ethernet
5e	1,000Mbps	ATM

Categories 1 through 3 represent a period when voice communications were becoming more sophisticated, but data communications were still not a major issue. Category 1 does not really have any standards other than the thickness of the wire used. It is found in old buildings and is probably not even marked. It is not recommended for LAN use.

Category 2 also has few defined standards. It was used in the first integrated office telephone and alarm systems, and was installed for some early low-performance LAN systems, such as the original AppleTalk LAN. A category 2 cable has been tested for a maximum bandwidth of 1Mbps—perfectly acceptable for telephone applications, but way too low for a 100BaseT system.

Category 3 UTP was the first effort to apply modern communication standards to twisted wire cables. It is the best of the cables designed for telephone communications, and it is capable of handling modern telephone technologies such as ISDN and T1 lines. Although it is often referred to as modern "voice grade" cabling, it has been tested for a maximum bandwidth of 16Mbps—more than sufficient for a 10BaseT network. In addition, it has been certified to have a predictable impedance of 100 ohms. Older cables had highly variable impedances, making them much more susceptible to interference.

Category 4 UTP cables were the first designed specifically for network use. They are similar to category 3, but have been tested and certified to function at 20Mbps, providing a generous margin of error for a 10BaseT system.

Category 5 UTP is the current industry standard for network cable, and it is often referred to as "data grade" UTP cable. It has been constructed with higher standards that allow it to function up to

100Mbps. Now that 100BaseT systems are affordable and common, having the correct cable in place makes upgrading a 10BaseT system to a 100BaseT system far easier. Because the actual costs of category 4 and category 5 cable are almost identical, category 4 cable is now essentially obsolete.

Category 5e UTP is an extension of the category 5 cable standards that specifically addresses the higher speeds that 1000BaseT connections will bring in the near future. It is more expensive, but it should be considered in any new installation of cable. It is much less expensive to install now than it would be to tear out and replace lower performance cable in a few years.

If that is not enough, there is even a category 6 UTP cable standard in development. If development proceeds as expected, this standard will allow twisted wires to carry high speed communications for distances that are now possible only with coaxial and fiber optic cables.

Coaxial Cables

Twisted pairs of wires are not the only kinds of cables. Networks also can use coaxial cables that are like the cables found today in home cable or satellite television systems. A coaxial or "coax" cable has a center wire conductor that has a layer of insulation around it. A second conductor that acts as an electrical shield surrounds this layer. Figure 6.3 illustrates the structure of coaxial cable.

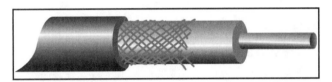

Figure 6.3. Coaxial cable.

Thicknets

Most early networks used a large coax cable that was about a half-inch thick, stiff, and difficult to work with. Connections were made by a tap that punctured the cable with a needle, making contact with the inner conductor. Moving either a tap or the cable would sometimes disrupt the entire LAN. Taps also required that the actual cable be directly accessible, so the result was that the cable often ran across the floor rather than through walls. Networks that used thick coaxial cable became known as *thicknets*, and the term was not totally complimentary.

Going back to our original example of a 100BaseT network, it would be called a 100Base5 network if the twisted wire were replaced entirely with thick coax cable. The "5" is derived from the fact that thick coax cable can be strung for 500 meters between connections—the greatest distance that any 100Mbps wire LAN can go without some form of amplification of the data signals. As a result, networks often use a 100Base5 component as a "backbone" line to go between buildings that are a distance apart. There is an added benefit in that coax cable is much less susceptible to electrical interference because of the electrical shielding characteristics built into it.

Thinnets

Thick coax cable was simply too expensive and too difficult to work with. It had great transmission characteristics, but it did not fit into an office setting well at all. As a result, a thinner (less than .25 inch) and far more flexible coax cable standard was developed. It was commonly called *thinnet* or even *cheapernet* because of its lower costs compared to thick coax cable. The proper name, however, when used in our example 100Mbps system is defined as the 100Base2 standard because it allows connections to be 200 meters apart. This standard also used connectors that were more user-friendly, making it easy to move networked computers from place to place. 100Base2 networks combine many of the flexible aspects of twisted wire networks with the security of shielded cables. Not only are they far less susceptible to electrical interference than twisted wire cables, they also radiate or "broadcast" less of what goes through them. Since it is possible to monitor LAN communications by using sophisticated antennas to capture a radiated signal, thinnet systems are preferable over twisted wire systems when security is an issue.

However, even thinnet coaxial cable is more expensive to install than category 5 UTP. Connections and repairs to damaged cables are also expensive. As a result, 100BaseT systems now far outnumber "pure" coaxial systems.

Fiber Optic Cables

Fiber optic cables have been in use for some time now. The most common applications are in long distance and underwater telephone cables, but even cable television companies are rapidly switching local communities to fiber optic systems. Fiber optics are also used in local area networks, but extremely high costs have limited their use. See Figure 6.4 for an illustration of fiber optic cable.

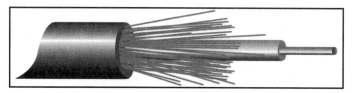

Figure 6.4. Fiber optic cable.

If the unshielded twisted pairs of wires in our example network were replaced with fiber optics, the system would be designated as a 100BaseF network. Such a network would have several advantages over any metallic wire system:

1. Fiber optic cables contain no metal, so they are not affected by lightning storms or even the electromagnetic pulse of a nuclear bomb blast.

2. Fiber optic cables have the potential to allow far more information to be transmitted per cable and for far greater distances than copper wire. Many of the emerging 1Gbps systems use fiber optic cables when long distances are needed. They can go up to 2000 meters between connections.

3. Because they don't transmit electricity, fiber optic cables don't radiate electronic signals. They are completely "bug-proof" unless they are tapped.

Currently, however, totally fiber optic systems are incredibly expensive. Not only must the expensive fiber optic cable be installed in the building, but also very expensive connectors and interfaces must be used. The result is that almost never is a pure fiber optic system installed. However, fiber optic lines are now commonly used in place of thick coax cable as the backbone of networks that span several buildings.

Fiber optic lines will almost certainly become far more cost-effective as greater capacity is needed on LANs. One Gbps is about the maximum for advanced metallic wire based systems, while fiber optics cables have the ability to exceed 600Gbps. Multigigabit fiber optic LANs are currently starting to emerge in data-intensive environments, such as military signal processing.

Ethernet Cable Summary

Table 6.2. Summary of Ethernet Cables

	Wire Type	Speed	Maximum Cable Length	Interference Susceptibility	Relative Cost
10BaseT	Twisted Pair	10Mbps	100 meters	Medium	Low
10Base2	Thin Coax	10Mbps	185 meters	Low	Medium
10Base5	Thick Coax	10Mbps	500 meters	Low	High
10BaseF	Fiber	10Mbps	2000 meters	None	Very High
100BaseT	Twisted Pair	100Mbps	100 meters	Medium	Low
100BaseTX	Twisted Pair	100Mbps	220 meters	Medium	Low
1000BaseFX	Fiber	1000Mbps	2000 meters	None	Very High
Wireless IEE 802.11	None	11 Mbps and higher	N/A	High	Medium

Topologies

Although it is becoming a less significant topic, the logical structure or *topology* of a LAN is still discussed now and then. This can be a very confusing topic because the real shape of a LAN rarely resembles its topology. In general, there are three basic topologies: bus, star, and ring.

Bus Topology

The structure of a thicknet LAN is a bus topology. It has workstations tapped onto a single, linear thick coaxial cable called the bus line (see Figure 6.5). The bus is snaked around the room or building, positioned so that each workstation would be close enough for a connection. If any break occurs in the bus, the entire LAN stops. Bus topologies are very clumsy and become more and more undependable as cables are tripped on, snagged by chairs, tapped and untapped, and so forth. As a result, the bus topology has now been relegated to the long, untapped cables that connect workgroups on different floors or in different buildings and these bus topologies are often called *backbones*.

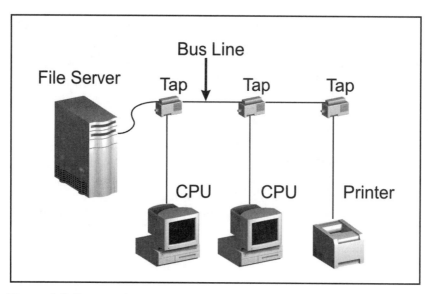

Figure 6.5. Bus topology.

Star Topology

The *star topology* is used by 10BaseT and 100Base T systems, so it has become very popular. All workstation connections converge upon a central point, where a hardware device called a hub or switch is located (see Figure 6.6). Individual workstations can usually be connected to or disconnected from the hub without interrupting the rest of the LAN.

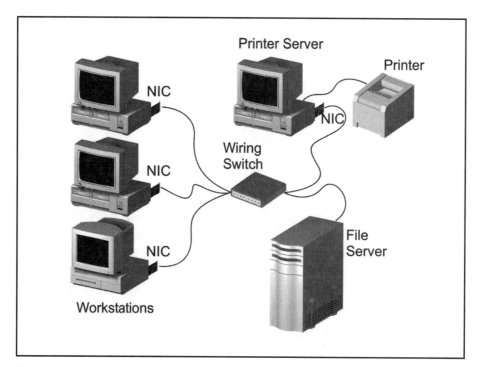

Figure 6.6. Star topology.

Ring Topology

The *ring topology* looks similar to a star topology in that it often uses a central hub for connections. However, all workstations become part of an electronic ring once they are connected. As with star topologies, workstations can usually be connected or disconnected without interrupting the functions of the LAN.

Repeaters

Most of Layer 1 focuses on the cables and connections that make up the foundation of a LAN. There is one piece of electronic hardware that functions within Layer 1, however. As mentioned during the discussion of cables, a signal can't move through wire or fiber optic cable forever without getting weak and mixing in with interference. If the length of a cable segment is too long to permit a strong signal to pass through it, a *repeater* is used in the middle to strengthen the signal so that it can get to the other end. Repeaters don't analyze or alter the original data, but just amplify the signal and filter interference. They make it possible to extend the distance that a LAN can cover.

Network Hubs

As mentioned a bit earlier, star topologies such as 10BaseT use a special type of repeater called a network *hub*. The visible effect of a hub is to remove the main network wiring from the immediate vicinity of the workstations. Instead of a vital cable going from workstation to workstation as in 10Base5, the hub allows critical cables to stay in closets and walls, with only thin connecting cables going to the workstations.

A hub acts like a repeater, but instead of having only two connections (in and out), it can have eight, sixteen, or even more connections that are commonly called *ports*, with each port accommodating a computer, another hub (called *stacking*), or a connection to a network bus. Any incoming signal is amplified, cleaned up, and supplied to all the ports on the hub.

LAYER 2 DETAILS—ETHERNET, NICS, AND BRIDGES

A network can be a very crowded place. Hundreds of computers, printers, and other devices can be connected to it. Each will send or receive information at various times. Unless rules are carefully followed, it will be like a crowded cafeteria at lunchtime. There will be so many "attempts to talk" going on at any one instant that no single conversation is intelligible. The second layer of the OSI model defines the rules for communication in such a crowded environment.

Layer 2 is really made up of two "sublayers," only one of which will be discussed in this text. This most visible sublayer is called the *Medium Access Control* or MAC component of Layer 2. The MAC controls the flow of data across the network by synchronizing the data and recognizing errors when they occur. The MAC contains precise specifications, or *protocols*, for the procedures that the network follows to handle potential conflicts that might occur in a busy network. Because of the importance of these protocols to a network, they are often simply called the *LAN protocols*.

Any new idea for a LAN protocol usually does not catch on unless it gets the backing of an important organization. The Institute of Electrical and Electronic Engineers (IEEE) is the dominant organization of this type, and the two most popular LAN protocols that they support today are Ethernet and Token Ring. Because Ethernet has become the more popular of these two, we will focus on it.

Basic Ethernet—A History

In this environment of short-lifespan technologies, it is unique that Ethernet is one of the oldest, yet the most popular, LAN protocols in existence today. There are a number of factors that have influenced this, but probably the most important has been the adaptability of the underlying concepts of Ethernet itself. It was designed so that it could grow, and it has indeed grown in step with the technologies that use it.

Ethernet has its origins as a *wireless* or radio data transmission system that was developed at the University of Hawaii in the 1960s and called ALOHA. By the early 1970s, it was being used to connect mainframe computers at the university with card readers and terminals at remote locations—even on ships at sea. The key to the system was a shared communication channel. This single channel allowed all the hardware to be designed to operate on the same frequency, greatly simplifying the design.

Soon the ALOHA system was being adapted to a fully cabled system to interconnect rapidly evolving computers with printers and other peripherals. By the mid-1970s, Bob Metcalfe and David Boggs, two Xerox researchers, had refined ALOHA and coined the name "Ethernet" for the refined system. Soon after, they demonstrated Ethernet on a network of over 100 connections.

By the early 1980s, the IEEE was finalizing the clearly defined Ethernet standard that is now called IEEE 802.3, and in 1989, Ethernet became an international standard when the International Organization for Standards (ISO) adopted Ethernet as a communication standard.

Basic Ethernet—The Fundamentals

The fundamental concepts of Ethernet are not complex. In fact, they are easy to understand. Ethernet is designed to allow a whole bunch of computers, printers, and other odds and ends to communicate with each other through one set of cables. To do this, some basic rules are required. Every device that is connected to the network follows these rules:

1. *Listen before transmitting.* Before a device tries to transmit, it first checks to see if any other device is transmitting.

2. *Transmit when quiet.* If the network is quiet for a specific period of time, the device that wants to send information then transmits it.

3. *Wait for quiet.* However, if the network is currently handling data, the device that wants to send waits and listens. It continuously listens until a quiet interval occurs. Then it follows Rule 2 above.

4. *Listen for a collision.* Once a device finds the quiet period so that it can send its data, there is no guarantee that one or more other devices have not done exactly the same thing. The result is that two or more devices can start to transmit at the same instant, and a "collision" occurs. All conversations are garbled in a collision. To detect this problem, all devices are designed to listen as they transmit. If a device detects a collision, it immediately stops transmitting.

5. *Tell everyone a collision took place.* Although all devices should have detected the collision, it might not happen in certain circumstances. To make sure that the word gets out, any device that detects a collision sends out a jam signal. This is sort of like the air horns on a big truck. Every device is warned that scrambled data just went out on the network and to discard it.

6. *Back off and wait a bit.* This is the key to Ethernet's success. Every device that tried to send at the instant that the collision took place backs off and waits a bit. However, each device has a random "wait" algorithm that causes it to wait a slightly different period of time before returning to Rule 1 at the top. Thus, if a collision does happen, one of the colliding devices will try to retransmit its data before the others, thus preventing a second collision because the other devices will then hear the first device when they listen.

Network Interface Cards

While the basic concepts of Ethernet are pretty simple to understand, actually implementing them has been a challenge that has constantly taxed the limits of the evolving digital technologies. The hardware that was required to carry out the Ethernet LAN protocols was originally bulky and expensive. Early 10Base5 systems used a couple of "black boxes" for each workstation. One box tapped directly into the thick cable at the point where it came close to a workstation site, while another black box was positioned next to or inside the workstation itself. A short but complex cable connected the two.

By the time Ethernet evolved to UTP wire in the 10BaseT or 100BaseT modes, the miniaturization of electronics had moved forward. This allowed the much more flexible hub structure to replace the original taps into the network cable. A device, called the *Network Interface Card* (NIC), was developed to connect the cable from the hub to the electronics of the computer. The NIC fits directly inside the workstation. As a result, the only visible connection between the LAN and a workstation is a simple "telephone-like" cable.

NICs are really combinations of several "layer" components of a LAN, but they are basically Layer 2 devices because they are designed for specific communications protocols, such as Ethernet or Token Ring. As a result, an Ethernet NIC will only work on an Ethernet LAN, and then it must have appropriate connectors for the specific type of Ethernet LAN that is in use at the computer's location. For example, a NIC for a 10BaseT LAN will not have the proper connectors for a fiber optic cable LAN.

Two Ethernet Layer 1 topologies—10BaseT and 100BaseT—use exactly the same connectors, however. In this case, it is possible to design a single NIC that will detect and work properly with either LAN speed. Dual speed NICs are now very inexpensive, so it is common for LAN administrators to buy and install dual speed NICs in their workstations even if their LAN currently runs only at 10Mbps. If the LAN is upgraded in the future to a 100BaseT system, the NICs will recognize the change to the higher speed and instantly adapt to it with no further action required at the individual workstations.

Ethernet Bridges

As mentioned earlier, groups of computers in an Ethernet network are often connected together through the use of hubs. A hub is best thought of as a multiple port repeater. It simply takes every bit of data that comes into it from any port, amplifies it, and sends it back out all the other ports. The result of this is a division of the total capacity (bandwidth) of the network among all the workstations that are actively attempting to communicate at any point in time. For example, if 20 workstations were all connected into a LAN through a hub or two (they can be stacked together) and all computers were attempting to communicate at the same instant, a 100BaseT network could at best only provide an ideal of

5Mbps of data flow to each workstation (the maximum LAN speed divided by the number of computers attempting to communicate). In reality, because of collisions and other network limitations, the average flow to each workstation would be less than the ideal.

Bridges are a bit different. They were originally developed to connect workgroups of workstations together through dissimilar Layer 1 topologies. For example, one workgroup might use Ethernet on a 10BaseT system, but the cable (backbone) that connects the workgroup to the rest of the network might be 10Base5 bus topology. A bridge was originally a device that connected the two cable systems.

In addition to connecting dissimilar wiring structures, a bridge has some intelligence built into it. It examines the data that is flowing into it, and it sends only the data that is intended for other locations out to the backbone. As a result, each bridge has an effect of "breaking off" a workgroup so that it is its own smaller local area network. For example, if there were two groups of 20 computers (like two labs) that were connected to a backbone through hubs, the maximum simultaneous transmission rate would drop to 2.5Mbps. per computer. However, if the two labs were connected to the backbone through a bridge, only the data that crossed from one lab to the other would flow between them. Each workstation in a workgroup (lab) of 20 would have an average bandwidth of 5Mbps when communicating within the workgroup, and the backbone would be used only when communications were needed between workgroups.

Ethernet Switches

The ability of a bridge to expand the data flow capacity of a network caught on very quickly. Large networks with hundreds of workstations were quickly broken down into multiple workgroups, each with their own hub and bridge to the backbone of the network. To save space and simplify wiring, hubs were soon built with the bridge within them.

Soon, however, network engineers figured out yet another improvement. If bridges could insulate the whole network from communications that were intended just for one workgroup, why not build a "multiport" bridge to completely replace the hub? Soon this piece of equipment became called the *Ethernet switch*. It does for a workgroup what the bridge does for a network. Every piece of incoming data is examined, and it is then switched only to the port where it needs to go. Thus, every workstation in the workgroup has the full bandwidth available to it as long as it is communicating with another computer in the same workgroup.

In a 100BaseT system with Ethernet switches, data coming from one workstation in a workgroup can move to another workstation in the same group at a full 100Mbps. At the same time, other pairs of computers in the same group can be doing the same thing. In effect, an Ethernet switch multiplies the potential total bandwidth of a workgroup by the number of pairs (or one half the total) of computers in the workgroup.

Switches represent the current "state of the art" in Ethernet systems. They allow tremendous increases in network capacity with a minimum of additional expenses. In most cases, the original wiring is all kept in place, and hubs are simply replaced with switches.

LAYER 3 DETAILS—THE NETWORK LAYER

As mentioned earlier, Ethernet defines a process, or *protocol* of communication. It is the most common LAN protocol in use, so we have applied it in most of our examples. There are less common protocols such as Token Ring, which was promoted heavily by IBM in the early 1990s.

Token Ring differs from Ethernet in that all workstations in the workgroup are electrically wired into a ring topology. A token (think of it as a little green flag) is passed endlessly around the ring. When a workstation wants to communicate, it simply waits until it gets the green flag. It then holds it until after it sends out its data. At that point, it releases the green flag (token) for the next workstation in the ring. If the next workstation doesn't want to communicate, it passes the token on again. This is a very simple, yet elegant process to control communication on a network. However, for various reasons, Token Ring never became as popular as Ethernet. It is now rapidly fading from view, with few new installations taking place.

Ethernet is established, adaptable, and popular. However, there are new LAN protocols challenging it fairly often. For example, a promising prospect is the *Asynchronous Transfer Mode* (ATM) protocol. While Ethernet's roots are about 30 years old, ATM is being designed right now. It leverages off the strengths of Ethernet, but proposes solutions to some of Ethernet's weaknesses. For example, from the beginning, ATM is designed for speed. Demonstration networks have utilized fiber optic cable to run at 662Gbps! ATM is designed for networks that span the world—something only imagined when Ethernet first came into use. Finally, ATM is designed to adapt to the needs of the data that is being transmitted. For example, digital video or audio can be assigned top priority to minimize interruptions, while archival data can be given a low priority so that it flows through the network during less busy periods. At the present, however, ATM is new, evolving, and very expensive. Its current primary application is as a high bandwidth backbone for very large networks.

Routers—Speaking Multiple Languages

We have now reached the point of discussing the reason for existence of Layer 3. While ATM can function as an excellent high bandwidth backbone right now, very few workgroups are running ATM. Somehow, those Ethernet (and maybe a few Token Ring) workgroups need to be translated to and from ATM to use that high-speed backbone. This is the function of a router. Not only does it identify which data needs to exit the workgroup to get to another location, but it translates that data into the appropriate LAN protocol, as needed. Routers are among the most complex network devices in use today because of the translation demands that are placed upon them. They are also critical to the operation of the Internet, the largest network of all. Routers are nearly always the link between local area networks and the Internet.

Network Servers

Many LANs use at least one computer that is dedicated to the process of running the LAN. This computer is often called a *server* because, among other things, it "serves" files to the rest of the LAN. In smaller LANs, a single server may perform multiple functions, while in larger LANs, servers may be set up for specialized purposes. A server runs an operating system, called the *network operating system* or NOS that is different than the operating systems that run on workstations. The functions of a NOS will be discussed in greater detail in just a bit. However, we will first discuss LANs that function without a server at all.

Life Without Servers—Peer-to-Peer LANs

Many small networks that exist mainly to interconnect the workstations within a workgroup do not use servers at all. These networks are called *peer-to-peer networks* because all parts of the network are workstations that are equal to each other. An example of a peer-to-peer LAN is illustrated in Figure 6.7 on page 134.

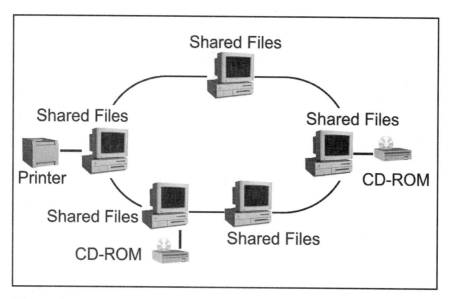

Figure 6.7. Peer-to-peer LAN.

A peer-to-peer LAN is very effective at transferring files from one workstation to another. Printers or modems on one workstation can be used by other computers on the LAN. With proper software, workers can exchange calendars and e-mail as well. However, there are real limits to the functionality of the serverless, peer-to-peer network concept.

To better understand the functions of a server, it is best to use an example of life without one. Let's say that three different people in a peer-to-peer workgroup are working on a complex report. Without a server, there are three ways to deal with the report.

1. *Separate copies.* First, the complete report could be stored on each workstation so each worker would have full access to the complete report. While this is very convenient, it also guarantees that within a very short time there will be three very different versions of the report! Trying to figure out how to get the three versions back into a single report might take as long as it took to write the initial versions!

2. *Separate assignments.* A second strategy would be to assign separate sections of the report to each of the three workers. This would avoid the problem of three separate versions evolving, but it would likely result in three separate "minireports" within the whole report. Depending upon writing styles and coordination, it is possible that formats would vary, facts and figures would vary, and even three different printers might produce different fonts on three different types of paper. These things have happened all too often. Usually one person gets stuck spending a great deal of time trying to make the three minireports look more like one coordinated report.

3. *Single source.* A third strategy would be to store the document on a single workstation, and then use the network to access the document from the other workstations. This would ensure that the final product would be a single, coordinated version of the report. However, there are still some potential problems. What happens if the software does not know that

three people are working on the same document at the same time? Let's say that it is lunchtime, and each person saves what they have done before they go to lunch. Because they are accessing a file on a single workstation, they save back to that workstation. Does the second person to save the file wipe out the version that was saved by the first person? Does the third person wipe out what the second person saved? Clearly, special software is needed to coordinate the concurrent use of a single file.

Another problem can evolve with such basic logistics. If the report is stored on a single workstation, clearly that workstation must be running in order for anyone to access the report. What happens if it is Monday morning and the individual assigned to that workstation calls in sick? Does someone else have the authority to go into that office to start the computer and printer? Are there passwords that must be used? Once again, this is not a simple solution!

Life with a Network Server

Network servers solve the above problems. They are dedicated computers that generally are not used as workstations. They are never turned off, and they have the appropriate software to control access to files. The workstations are now called *clients* that are "served" by the servers. The servers can be thought of as a level above the workstations. They are often more isolated than the workstations—sometimes residing in locked, climate-controlled closets. They are often cared for by a single network administrator.

In this environment, if multiple access to individual files is requested, the server uses appropriate software to deal with potential conflicts. In smaller networks, printers are often attached directly to network servers. If they are, then any workstation can access that printer. In the above example, the result would be a report that multiple workers can access, modify, and print on a single printer.

Specialized Servers

Two functions of a server have been mentioned—controlling access to files and providing shared printers. Many other activities can also be handled by a server. In fact, as a network grows, a single server is sometimes expected to do more than one computer can handle efficiently. As a result, servers often become specialized. A single, but large school LAN might have the following servers:

- *Network server*. This is the original server. It runs the network operating system, which will be discussed in the next section of this chapter.

- *Printer server*. When printers are used in school labs, they can demand a tremendous amount of processing power. Quite often, separate computers are set up in a network as printer servers just to handle the printing activities. This way, a computer can quickly pass a print job through the network to a print server and then go on to other things, while the print server deals with the details of getting the job printed. Many of the newer, more powerful printers have the equivalent of a print server built directly into them.

- *Database server*. Many schools use complex sets of data to manage inventories, payrolls, and the like. To provide network access to this information, the data must be stored on a server. If a single network server is used and many workers attempt to access database information, other duties of the network server can suffer. As a result, databases are often stored and manipulated by a separate database server.

- *Web server*. The Internet has placed new demands upon LANs. All those pages that you visit as you surf the Internet come from computers that are configured as web servers. Many schools actively develop their own web pages for external (Internet) and internal (intranet) purposes. For this reason, many LANs have separate web servers integrated into them. These web servers are sometimes also configured with network router hardware and software to help control access to the web server.

- *Others*. The list of specialized servers continues to grow. E-mail has become so heavily used that it can overload a network server. Separate e-mail servers are now quite common. Multimedia distribution is the most demanding activity in a typical LAN. That is why still image, video, and audio servers are being developed.

LAYERS 4 AND 5—NETWORK OPERATING SYSTEMS

As we go higher through the layers of the OSI model, it becomes much more difficult to point out specific hardware or software items that clearly fit into one layer. This is the case with Layers 4 and 5 of the model. Not only is it difficult to provide appropriate examples, few experts will agree on just where the examples fit, In these two layers, it is possible to argue that software as diverse as network operating systems and web browser media plug-ins fit . . . somewhere.

Several times during this chapter, we have mentioned the *network operating system* (NOS). This is a generic term that refers to the package of software programs that runs a LAN. A typical NOS has a number of things to do:

- Provide controlled access to data files.

    Don't let files be accidentally overwritten.
    Lock or unlock files to control access to them.
    Store files within a logical structure that allows easy access.

- Distribute shared programs to the workstations that request them.

    Allow users to access programs on the server, just as if they were on workstation hard drives.
    Keep track of the number of workstations that are using a program at any one time and limit it to the number of approved licenses.

- Execute workgroup programs such as e-mail and database management systems.

    Run directly on the server those programs such as e-mail that serve the entire network.
    Supply access to these programs in versions appropriate for a variety of workstations.

- Manage network printers and print jobs.

    Direct print jobs to appropriate printers.
    Store print jobs, if necessary, until the printer is ready.

- Provide security for the network.

  Control who can access the network.
  Control what portions of the network individual users can access.

- Provide management programs for the network.

  Provide "performance meter" software that will indicate system loads.
  Provide simple methods for managing users passwords and access rights.
  Allow the network administrator to manage the network from a single location.

Figure 6.8 depicts a typical management screen that might be part of a network operating system.

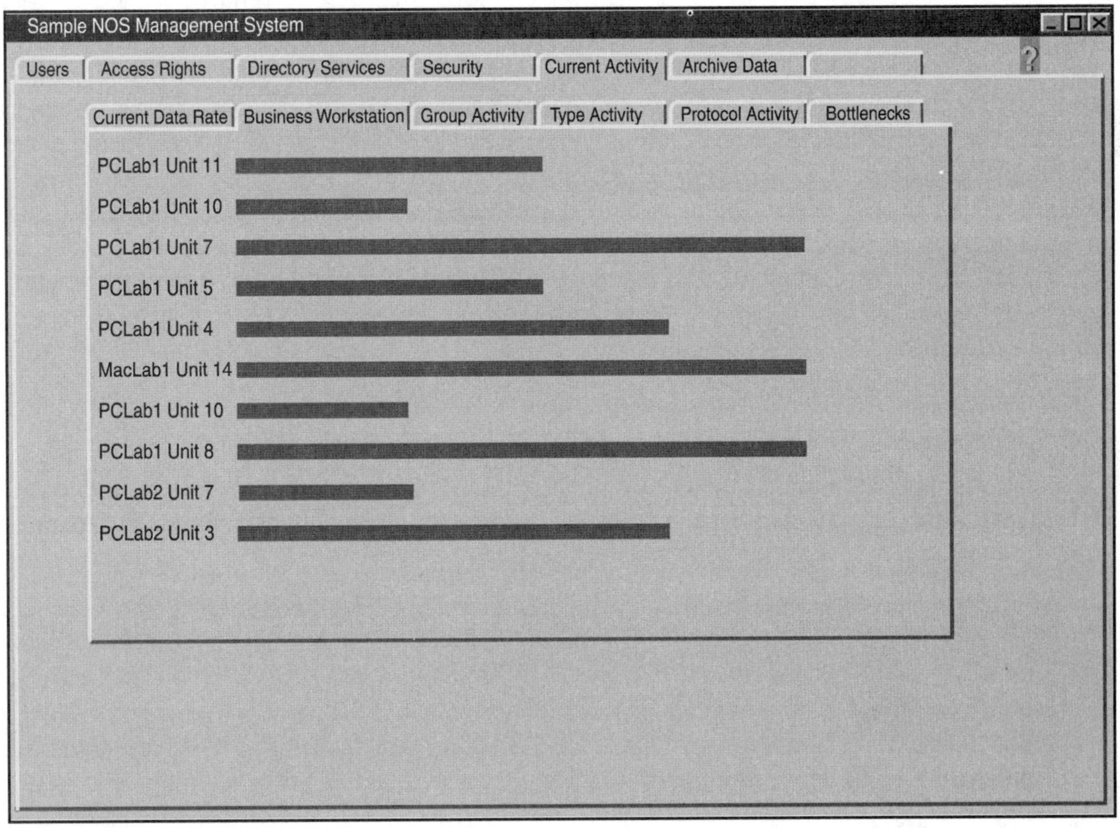

Figure 6.8. NOS management screen.

Novell Netware

Several commercial network operating systems exist. The most popular is Novell Netware, but Microsoft Windows NT Server is also widely used, and some systems use AppleShare. Unix is often found in advanced networks, and, an upstart, almost-free version of Unix, called Linux, is rapidly gaining attention as a very capable, yet very inexpensive challenger. However, to keep this discussion short, we will focus on some of the attributes of Novell's product. Many of its characteristics are also found in other NOSs.

The current Novell NOS is called Netware 6. It provides all the services that were outlined previously. In fact, it provides so many services that, like other current network operation systems, it tends to blur distinctions between local area networks and the Internet.

There are several enhancements found in Novell Netware 6. One of the most interesting is called Novell iFolder, and it is a big step beyond the hard drive file directories that most people work with. Novell iFolder allows an individual to log into the Internet from any location to access a personal folder. This permits the individual to work directly on document files that are stored on the server. The practice of e-mailing a file as an attachment so that it can be loaded and edited at another location is no longer necessary. The process of e-mailing files always creates the danger of confusion as multiple versions of the file evolve. Novell iFolder allows a person anywhere in the world to work with the files in his or her private folder.

A second enhancement is Novell eDirectory. This management software provides a unified, cross platform (compatible with different brands of computers) guide to the entire network of the school system or company. It uses a graphical user interface (GUI) to represent all interconnected network resources. The resources are organized into a hierarchical directory tree and managed by pointing, clicking, and dragging icons as needed throughout the directory tree. This is a summary of some of the capabilities of Novell eDirectory:

- *Access all network resources with a single login.* No matter how complex the network, users and network supervisors only have to log in once with one password to be authenticated to the entire network, instead of logging in to each file server or other network resources separately.

- *Allow any network user to access any appropriate network resource, such as other users, servers, printers, and even disk drives.* Once authenticated, users have access to all the network resources to which they have rights, regardless of the size of the network and where the users or resources are physically located. The individual network user has a profile of network resources that follows him or her anywhere on the network. If the user logs in from a computer in office, the same resources are still available. eDirectory combines with iFolder to work for users who share PCs, as well as for users who roam from PC to PC, anywhere on the Internet.

- *Allow authorized people to manage all the resources.* The system administrator is able to manage thousands of users from a single, centralized computer. Users can be grouped into a variety of workgroups, depending upon physical location, job assignment, individual project assignments, or any other grouping that might be imagined. Every group can have specific resources assigned to it, and each individual user automatically has access to the sum of all resources from all groups he or she belongs to.

In a large school network, the process of printing something out can get to be a real challenge. Many computers in labs, for example, will not have their own dedicated printers. If the school has a wireless network for laptops and portable labs, many of those computers will not be set up with printers.

With Netware 6, Novell has introduced new print serving software called iPrint. This software allows any authorized user to use schematic drawings of buildings to select a printer from any room, floor, or building that is part of the school network. The user can print to that location, and if appropriate drivers are not currently installed on the user's computer, iPrint assists with the process of downloading and installing the needed printer drivers.

Novell ZENworks

As powerful as a network operating system can be, it is next to useless if it is very difficult to use. Novell has integrated Netware 6 with a more general graphical desktop manager for networked computers. ZENworks, short for Zero Effort Networks for users, automates desktop management by using the network to provide access to application management, software distribution, desktop management, and computer maintenance.

In other words, a network administrator can perform a number of functions from one location. For example, if a particular spreadsheet program is installed on a number of computers that are connected to the LAN, an administrator can identify those computers and even install a spreadsheet update to every computer without going to the individual locations.

In a similar manner, software that is not properly licensed by the school can be searched out, identified, and removed. While this seems sort of "big brotherish," schools are now painfully aware that they are responsible for what their employees do. If an employee "borrows" software from a friend and installs it on his or her office computer, the school is responsible for the unlicensed use of that software. A network directory, with an easy-to-use desktop interface, makes it much easier to ensure that only properly licensed software is used within the school.

WIRELESS LANS

Situations do exist where standard LAN technologies simply don't work. In most cases, the limitations are with Layer 1, the physical structure of a LAN. Old buildings don't have the appropriate cables in place, and, in fact, may not have any simple way to put the appropriate cables into place. In commercial buildings, cables often require metallic conduit or other techniques to prevent flammable cable coverings from turning into the equivalent of candlewicks during a fire. More than once, unprotected cables have caught on fire and transmitted the fire along the length of the cable. If empty metallic conduits are not available, the cost of installing new ones is extremely high.

At other times, it simply isn't practical to provide LAN cables to every possible location where they might be needed. An old college classroom building, for example, might have 30 or 40 classrooms in it. While it would be nice to wire every room in the building for a LAN, it wouldn't make much sense to do it if four mobile computers are the only classroom computers used in the entire building. At the most, only four classrooms would be using a computer at any one time.

These "wiring challenged" applications are those that are ideal candidates for wireless LAN solutions. While it is extremely rare for an entire LAN to be wireless, it is now common for at least one workgroup in a LAN to be wireless. This workgroup is comprised of the mobile computers in the building housing the LAN.

Wireless LANs have the advantage of allowing a mobile computer to access the LAN in the same way as a "wired" computer, but without the connecting cable. A cart-based wireless LAN computer can be moved from classroom to classroom without any concern over available LAN connections.

Types of Wireless LANs

Wireless LANs can utilize either microwave frequency radio waves or infrared beams, but the microwave systems clearly have the majority of the market share. Microwaves can penetrate walls, so it is much easier to use a microwave wireless LAN to provide coverage throughout a building than it is to use an infrared wireless LAN. Infrared systems work only in "line of sight" applications, and anything opaque blocks the various components of the infrared wireless network. Microwave wireless LANs are growing rapidly in popularity because they are simple to install and relatively inexpensive. Until they become so common that they "crowd themselves out of the market" by creating too much interference with each other, they will continue to dominate infrared systems.

A major factor that has accelerated the growth of wireless networks is the establishment of industry standards. The Institute of Electrical and Electronic Engineers (IEEE) organization has defined a standard called IEEE 802.11 that clearly specifies all the characteristics of a wireless system that currently operates at a maximum speed of 11Mbps. Since the standard is published and open to the industry at large, all equipment that adheres to the standard is interchangeable. As a result, an Apple computer with an IEEE 802.11 wireless card can surf the Internet on an IEEE 802.11 wireless network right along with PC's using IEEE 802.11 wireless cards made by other manufacturers. Figure 6.9 illustrates a typical wireless LAN.

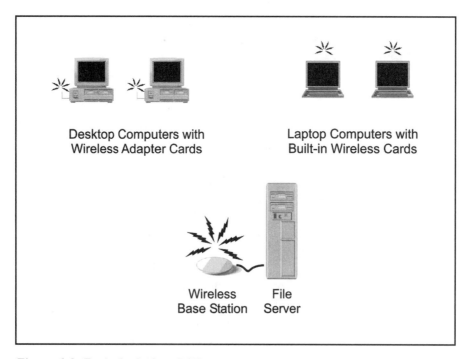

Figure 6.9. Typical wireless LAN.

Components of a Wireless LAN

A wireless LAN has two essential components—a connection to the LAN backbone and a connection to the computer. These components are provided by a variety of manufacturers with a range of capabilities and costs. One common, relatively inexpensive system that is often found in schools is the Apple AirPort system that is marketed by Apple Computers.

Apple AirPort Base Station

The Apple AirPort Base Station connects the wireless network to the wired network, a cable modem, or a high-speed telephone connection through an Ethernet 10BaseT or 100BaseT port. There is also a 56Kbps modem built in that allows Internet connections through a standard telephone line when a wired LAN is not available.

The AirPort Base is typical of most IEEE 802.11 base station equipment in its ability to create an effective radio wave "sphere" with a radius of about 150 feet, depending upon the number and type of walls or floors in a building. Any appropriately equipped computer can communicate with the base station if it is within this sphere.

Wireless base stations are like wired LAN hubs in that computers must share the available bandwidth. If a single computer is accessing the base station, it can use the entire 11Mbps bandwidth. On the other hand, if ten computers are accessing the same base station, each computer will get an average of 1.1Mbps of bandwidth. While there is no clearly defined limit to the number of computers that can use a single base station, Apple states that a realistic limit for its AirPort Base is 10 computers that are using the Internet on an AirPort Base directly connected to a network. If only activities with low data demands (reading e-mail, chat, online research, etc.) are taking place, then more computers can use the AirPort base with satisfactory results.

For areas with more intensive computer use, wireless base stations can be "stacked" so that their radio spheres overlap. For example, the AirPort system allows up to three base stations to operate within the same 150 foot sphere on separate channels. Each of the stations provides 11Mbps of bandwidth access, so the three together will provide the area with 33Mbps of network access. This would allow a rolling "laptop lab" of 30 wireless laptop computers to be used in almost any room of a typical school building.

Apple AirPort Card

All computers that use a wireless system must have an appropriate wireless interface. If the system is IEEE 802.11 compatible, then any 802.11 interface card will allow a basic connection to the wireless LAN. However, even the 802.11 standard creates the potential for some incompatibilities. There are options for data encryption, setting up "private" wireless LANs, and options for wireless "roaming" from one base station to another without losing the Internet connection. Not all systems use all these options. Therefore, it is necessary to make sure the wireless cards for the computers are fully compatible with the base stations. One way to do this is to use cards that are provided by the same company as the base stations.

The Apple AirPort Card is available only for current models of Apple computers. Wireless cards need small antennas to send and receive radio signals, but the AirPort card is unique in that it does not have any. Instead, all current Apple notebook and desktop computers have the antennas built directly into them. When the AirPort card is installed, it connects directly to the internal computer antennas.

The result is a design that does not have troublesome little antennas sticking out of the side of the computer, just waiting to get caught on something.

Software

All wireless LAN systems require management software. To a great extent, the ease of use and effectiveness of the wireless system will depend upon this software. Apple provides AirPort Base software (which runs only on an Apple computer) to set up and manage the AirPort Base stations. Though other brands of computers can use IEEE 802.11 cards to access an Apple AirPort base station, only an Apple computer that runs the management software can manage the station.

In addition, Apple provides software to set up the AirPort cards in each computer that will use the wireless system. This software also allows two AirPort-equipped Apple computers to communicate directly with each other without the use of an AirPort base system. This allows the direct transmission of files between the two computers, or the operators of the two computers could be playing shared interactive games.

Security

Microwave wireless systems transmit their signals very much in the same manner as cell telephones. That means that anyone with a IEEE 802.11 standard laptop can enter the zone of a wireless base station and log on to that system if it is an "open" system. Steps can be taken to create "closed" systems by requiring standard login IDs and passwords. Base stations can also be programmed to "connect" only to specific machines.

However, wireless signals go everywhere, and a person with appropriate equipment can detect and capture the signals of the wireless network as long as they are within range of the signals. Without logging into a closed wireless system, it would still be possible to "eavesdrop" on all the communications within that system. Even with fairly simple equipment it would be possible to capture account numbers, IDs, passwords, and all sorts of private information.

To prevent this, the IEEE 802.11 standard provides for an advanced 40-bit encryption process that can be configured to function at all times. It is also possible to use software with added encryption. Most current web browsers, for example, have the capability of using 128-bit encryption. If a web browser were using 128-bit encryption over a wireless system that has its 40-bit encryption turned on, it would take a supercomputer to decode any data that might be captured! However—it is still possible.

SUMMARY

Basic discussions about LANs and even fundamental LAN management activities are well within the capabilities of a technologically competent teacher, but there are many aspects of LANs that are very complex and require formal training to master. To help organize our short discussion of LAN basics, we have used a design model, the Open Systems Interconnection (OSI) Reference Model. As the layers of the model progress from basic wiring through more complex issues, we have deliberately reduced the amount of detail that was covered. The functions of the top-most OSI model layers (6 and 7) are so diverse that we have only indirectly discussed them.

Local area networks have become key players in most schools and businesses. They allow each computer to maintain a degree of independence from the others and they provide many benefits that were found before only in mainframe systems. In particular, they provide a direct route to allow students and teachers to access the Internet, read e-mail, or conduct audio or videoconferences. They make it easy to exchange files or to work collaboratively on projects. For administrators, local area networks offer benefits as well. All computers can be managed from a single location through LANs. New software can be installed, and licenses can be controlled without requiring personnel to travel to each workstation.

There are some negative aspects to LANs as well. First, they quickly become crucial to any school or business. If a LAN fails for any reason, courses can be brought to a halt. For this reason, the critical components of most LANs, such as the hard disk drives and the power supplies, are designed to be redundant. Most of the time, if a hard drive fails, duplicate drives continue to operate while the defective drive is replaced. The same applies to power supplies. In the case of a total power failure, a LAN usually has enough backup power to allow itself to shut down without losing data.

Sophisticated LANs can be very expensive. In addition to the hardware and software costs, they often require full-time personnel just to manage them. However, many studies have shown that in a large business or school, it is much more cost-effective to manage the many computers through a LAN than without a LAN. If a LAN is not used to manage computers, it is common to find that there is no central control of software licenses, software or hardware purchasing, or maintenance of computers.

GLOSSARY

10Base2. A standard that defines a thin coaxial cable system, sometimes called thinnet. It can transmit signals up to 10Mbps with a distance limit of 200 meters per segment.

10Base5. A standard that defines a thick coaxial cable system, sometimes called thicknet. It can transmit signals up to 10Mbps with a distance limit of 500 meters per segment.

10BaseF. A standard that defines a fiber optic system, which can transmit signals at 10Mbps up to 2000 meters per segment.

10BaseT. A standard that defines a twisted-pair cable system. This is an inexpensive cable system that is often used in LANs and office telephone systems. It can transmit signals up to 10Mbps with a distance limit of 100 meters per segment.

100BaseFX. A standard for fiber optic cabling that can transmit data at 1Gbps with a distance limit of 2000 meters per segment.

100BaseT. An extension of the 10BaseT standards that defines much faster LAN data transmission over twisted pair cabling. Can transmit data at 100Mbps, with a distance limit of 100 meters per segment.

100BaseTX. Similar to 100BaseT (twisted pair cabling) that can transmit data at 100Mbps, with a distance limit of 220 meters per segment.

AppleTalk. A proprietary LAN by Apple that has a data speed of 230.4kilobits per second. AppleTalk interfaces are built into Macintosh computers.

ASCII (American Standard Code for Information Interchange). An established code that defines all characters, punctuation marks, and digits in binary form.

ATM (Asynchronous Transfer Mode). A network protocol that transmits data at a speed of 155Mbps and higher. It is most often used to interconnect two or more local area networks.

backbone. A cable to which multiple nodes or workstations are attached.

bandwidth. The range between the upper and lower limiting frequencies that a cable can transmit.

baseband. Digitally encoded information transmitted in such a way that the entire capacity, or bandwidth, of the cable is utilized.

bit (binary digit). A basic unit of computer information expressed numerically as a 0 or a 1.

bit-transfer rate. The number of bits transmitted per unit of time. Frequently stated in millions of bits, or megabits, per second for LANs.

bridge. A LAN computer that links two similar networks.

bus topology. A network in which all workstations are connected to a linear transmission cable.

byte. A grouping of eight bits. A byte provides sufficient information to define one ASCII character.

cable. One or more conductors contained within a protective shell.

client/server network. A networking system in which one or more file servers (server) provide services; such as network management, application and centralized data storage for workstations (clients).

coaxial cable. A cable made up of one central conductor surrounded by a shielding conductor.

collision. A simultaneous transmission of data by two or more LAN workstations.

Ethernet. A baseband LAN communications standard developed by Xerox. Data transmission speed is typically 10–100megabits per second.

FDDI (Fiber Distributed Data Interface). A network protocol that is used primarily to interconnect two or more local area networks, often over large distances.

fiber-optic cable. A cable that contains a fine strand of glasslike material. Light, not electricity, is conducted through the cable.

file server. The computer in a LAN that stores and distributes the files for the workstations.

gateway. A computer in a LAN that links two dissimilar LANs. It is capable of translating data between the two LANs.

Gigabit Ethernet. An Ethernet protocol that raises the transmission rates to 1Gbps (gigabits per second). It is primarily used for a high speed backbone of a network.

gigabyte. One billion bytes. Equal to 1,000 megabytes.

GUI (graphical user interface). The technique of using a mouse and icons to select computer functions.

hub. See wiring hub.

infrared. Electromagnetic waves whose frequency range is above that of microwaves, but below that of the visible spectrum.

Internet. A worldwide network of networks that exchanges information using the TCP/IP protocol.

intranet. Network internal to an organization that uses Internet protocols and browsers.

ISDN (integrated services digital network). A new technology for telephone systems that is totally digital. Computer data can be intermixed with voice communications.

LAN (local area network). An interlinked microcomputer system, the dimensions of which are usually less than two miles. Transmission rates are usually above one megabit per second.

LocalTalk. A network standard used by Apple Macintosh computers. Uses shielded or unshielded twisted-pair wire at a relatively slow data-transfer rate of 230.4kilobits per second.

megabit. One million bits. Network speed is usually measured in megabits per second (Mbps).

NIC (network interface card). The interface card that is added to a computer to make it a LAN workstation. It determines the LAN standard for the network cable. Common standards are Ethernet and Token Ring.

node. End point of a network connection. Nodes can include devices such as file servers, printers, or workstations.

NOS (network operating system). Operating system designed to pass information and communicate between more than one computer. Examples include AppleShare, Novell NetWare, and Windows NT Server.

packet. A grouping of binary digits, often a portion of a larger file. Treated within a LAN as an entity.

packet switching. A transmission technique commonly used in LANs. Packets are transmitted in an intermixed manner, with each one going to its predetermined destination. This allows all workstations on a LAN equal access to files.

peer-to-peer network. A network in which resources and files are shared without a centralized management source.

printer server. A computer on a LAN that runs software to control one or more shared printers.

protocol. Refers to the complete structure of the information that is going from one computer to the other.

RAID (redundant array of inexpensive disks). Two or more disk drives are used as mirror images of each other. This provides an effective method of automatically backing up data.

ring network. A LAN topology in which data are transmitted among workstations in one circular direction.

star network. A LAN topology in which all workstations are connected directly to a central location, often a file server or hub.

thicknet. Thick coaxial cable used to connect parts of a LAN that are separated by long distances.

thinnet. Thin coaxial cable used to connect parts of a LAN separated by medium distances, such as between floors of buildings.

token. A special message or flag used in some LANs. The token is passed from workstation to workstation, and the workstation that has the token can transmit. This prevents data collisions.

Token Ring. A network standard that uses token-passing techniques to prevent data collisions. Transmission rates are 4 or 16 megabits per second, depending upon interface cards and type of cable.

topology. There are two types of topology related to networks: physical and logical. The physical topology refers to the configuration of cables, computers, and other peripherals. Logical topology is the method used to pass the information between workstations.

twisted pair cable. Two wires twisted together. This type of cable is often used for telephone communications.

UTP (unshielded twisted-pair) cable. Two wires twisted together. This type of cable is used for telephone communications and many LANs. Categories 2 through 5 are in use, with the higher numbers allowing faster LAN data transmission rates.

WAN (wide area network). A network of computers that is spread out over large distances. Usually high-speed telephone lines are used to interconnect the computers.

wireless LAN. A LAN that uses infrared light beams or radio waves to interconnect the computers. This allows portability and ease of placement of workstations.

wiring hub. The central connecting point for a number of computers on a LAN. Wiring hubs simplify LAN connections and allow computers to be added or removed without interrupting the LAN itself.

workgroup. A collection of workstations and servers on a LAN that are designated to communicate and exchange data with one another.

workstation. Individual microcomputer on a LAN that is used by students and teachers to run programs.

RESOURCES

Apple Airport
http://www.apple.com/airport/

Charles Spurgeon's Ethernet Web Site
http://wwwhost.ots.utexas.edu
/ethernet/ethernet-home.html

Education (un)Wired
http://www.apple.com/education/k12
/networking/

free-ed.net
http://free-ed.net/

InternetWeek
http://www.internetwk.com/

Network Computing
http://www.nwc.com/

Network Magazine
http://networkmagazine.com/

Networking Primer, IBM
http://www.networking.ibm.com
/primer/primerintro.html

Network World
http://www.networkworld.com/

Network World Fusion
http://www.nwfusion.com/

Novell Support
http://support.novell.com/

Standards Overview, Siemon
http://www.siemon.com/standards
/default.asp

Technology Information
http://www.cisco.com/univercd/cc/td/doc
/cisintwk/index.htm

Understanding OSI
http://www.isi.salford.ac.uk//books/osi
/all.html

Web66 Network Construction Set
http://web66.umn.edu/Construction/

Windows Magazine
http://www.winntmag.com/

7

Telecommunications

A Scenario

It wasn't long ago that Nora became a homebound student. Her mother recalled how depressed and isolated Nora felt, believing she would no longer be able to interact with her classmates and share in class projects.

To her parent's surprise, her school was well prepared to address the needs of homebound students. They provided Nora with the technology to remain in contact with her classmates and school assignments. With a laptop computer and a connection to the Internet, Nora could keep in contact with her classmates, work on collaborative projects using the class web site, and stay on top of all the assignments (and gossip!).

Her teacher, Mr. Nickelson, made sure that class assignments were posted on the web and that he was available to answer his students' questions via e-mail—no matter where the students were located. His class web site included online discussion boards for class projects, a calendar of upcoming events and assignment due dates, and links to Internet sites for specific assignments.

Using videoconferencing technology, Nora was able to see, hear, and participate with others during class discussions. Nora appreciated having the virtual classroom online, as well as Mr. Nickelson's belief that learning should be able to take place anywhere. She felt confident that when she was able to return to school, she would be right in step with her classmates.

INTRODUCTION

The Internet provides many resources and opportunities for communication and research. Although the Internet has been around for more than 40 years, it wasn't until the introduction of the World Wide Web that most educators and businesses began to take advantage of the world of telecommunications. With its point and click graphic interface, the web has attracted millions of users, including government agencies, K–12 schools, universities, and commercial enterprises. Topics focused on in this chapter include:

- Overview of the World Wide Web

- Internet research in the classroom

- Communication activities

- Benefits and concerns related to classroom use of the Internet

- Internet access options

- Resources for further information

OVERVIEW OF THE WEB

The growth of the Internet is perhaps the single greatest contributing factor to the communications explosion. The Internet is a worldwide telecommunications network that connects millions of other, smaller networks. It began in 1969 as a U.S. Department of Defense project that was called the Advanced Research Projects Agency Network (ARPANET). In 1986, the National Science Foundation formed NSFNET, which replaced ARPANET, and built the foundation of the U.S. portion of the Internet with high-speed, long-distance data lines. The Internet is now commercial, and almost any individual, school, or company can subscribe to a service that connects to the Internet, as well as register a unique domain name (i.e., www.mysite.com), receive automatic information updates, and transmit and receive video and audio.

Because the original purpose of the Internet was for efficient military communications, it was designed to get the message through even in the worst of conditions. Messages (e-mail, data files, images, and so on) are broken into small packets that contain the address for the destination and a sequence number that allows reassembly of a complete file when it gets to the destination. Once a file goes into the "net," each packet is on its own. The Internet seeks out the most efficient path at any instant, and packets can scatter all over as they look for a clear path to their destination. Once at the destination, they reassemble into the correct sequence of the original file. The protocol, or language, that is used on the Internet to send and receive packets of information is called *TCP/IP* (transmission control protocol/Internet protocol).

The first wave of public access to the Internet was through programs such as telnet and gopher that were alphanumeric (text and number), line-oriented programs that often required cryptic text commands. The concept of the World Wide Web—often shortened to web—was created in Switzerland in 1991 to allow hyperlinks within documents. In other words, while you are reading one document, there may be words or buttons that you can choose or click on to take you to another document or file. When multimedia web sites are accessed, sounds, pictures, or motion images can result from a mouse click. See Figure 7.1 for an example of a web screen.

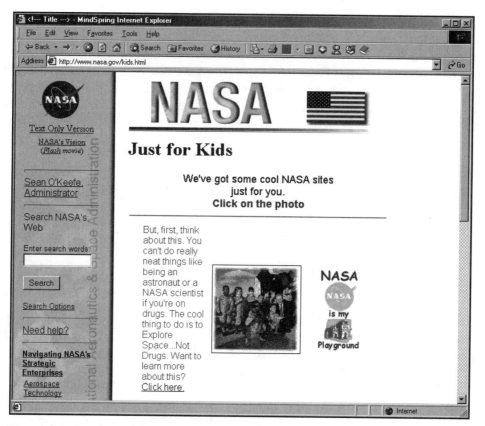

Figure 7.1. Sample web page.

Web Pages

A web page is a file written in *hypertext markup language* (HTML). Web pages can contain text, sound, video, and more. If a web page serves as a focal point or main menu for an individual, group, or organization, it is called a home page. For example, a person might say that the home page for the multimedia program HyperStudio is at http://www.hyperstudio.com/. The web address (http://www .hyperstudio.com/) is called a *uniform resource locator* (URL). Every Internet location that stores and provides access to web pages must have a unique URL.

URLs for web sites begin with *http* (hypertext transfer protocol) followed by a colon, two slashes, and the address for the web page or site. At the end of the address, another slash may appear, followed by a path and file name. For example, http://www.yahooligans.com/content/tg/index.html is a URL that will take you to the first page of the Yahooligans' Teacher's Guide—the name of the page is index.html and it is stored in the "tg" directory. (Note that in some cases the addresses may be listed as a series of numbers rather than letters.)

Web Browsers

To display web pages, you will need a *web browser*, such as Netscape or Internet Explorer on your computer. Web browsers are software programs that can "read" the HTML text file and convert it into a page with clickable links like the one in Figure 7.1. Although many web browsers are available,

Netscape Communicator and Microsoft Internet Explorer are by far the most common. Luckily, both of these programs are free and can be downloaded from the web.

Web browsers contain many built-in functions, such as the ability to go "Back" to the previous page, go "Forward" to the next page, or set bookmarks to return quickly to sites of interest. Web browsers continue to be updated and released, offering new features with each release. If you or your students are creating web pages, it is important to test the pages using both of the popular browsers, including all versions that have been released in the past two years.

Plug-ins

Web browsers were designed to interpret HTML and to display specific graphic formats (GIF and JPEG). As the browsers have matured, a few additional capabilities have been added, such as the ability to play sounds that are stored in common formats (WAV and AIFF). There are, however, many file formats that web browsers do not recognize and are not able to interpret. For example, if you access a page with a QuickTime movie, you may see a message similar to: "QuickTime plug-in is required to view this page."

Plug-ins are small programs that can be installed on your computer and used as part of your web browser, expanding its capabilities. Plug-ins are often needed to play music, display video, interact with objects, and play games that may have been created in commercial programs such as Macromedia Director, QuickTime, HyperStudio, and others. After a plug-in is installed, the browser will recognize it automatically, and its function will be integrated into the file being displayed. Common plug-ins required for multimedia files include:

- Apple QuickTime (http://www.apple.com/quicktime/download/)
  This plug-in provides you with access to QuickTime animation, music, MIDI, audio, video, and virtual reality scenes in a web page.

- Macromedia Flash Player (http://www.macromedia.com/software/flashplayer/)
  This plug-in enables you to view content created with Macromedia Flash.

- Macromedia's Shockwave for Director (http://www.macromedia.com/software/shockwaveplayer/)
  Shockwave Player displays web content that has been created by Macromedia Director Shockwave Studio. This includes interactive games, online learning applications, multimedia, graphics, and streaming audio.

- RealOne Player by RealNetworks (http://www.real.com)
  RealPlayer lets you play streaming audio, video, animations, and other formats on the web.

- HyperStudio Plug-in (http://www.hyperstudio.com/quickstart/index.html)
  This plug-in allows you to view HyperStudio stacks on the Web.

- Net2Phone (http://home.netscape.com/net2phone/index.html)
  This plug-in lets you turn your PC into a phone so you can call anywhere in the world.

Another popular file format that requires a plug-in is the Adobe Portable Document Format (PDF). This file format is used when the exact style of a document must be retained. For example, if you wanted to download a tax form, such as the1040A, with checkboxes and specific page numbers, it would have to be in exact IRS style and format. Therefore, the IRS posts this document in PDF format (and you will need a plug-in to view it and print it). Other common uses of the PDF format include online journals and magazines. The Adobe Acrobat Reader plug-in is available at http://www.adobe.com/products /acrobat/readstep2.html. Visit Netscape at http://home.netscape.com/plugins/index.html for more information and links to other plug-ins.

Searching the Web

If you do not know the URL of the site you need, search tools are available on the Internet to help find a web site. These search tools, including Yahoo, Lycos, AltaVista, and others, will supply a list of sites that match the search criteria that you enter. (See the resource section at the end of this chapter for a list of some of the educational sites on the web.)

There are two main categories of search tools: *subject directories* and *search engines*. Subject directories generally organize the topics by categories for people who want to browse through a list. Yahoo is the most popular subject directory. With Yahoo, you can type in a search word or find the information you want by clicking on various topics and subtopics. All of the sites listed on Yahoo have been reviewed. Yahoo also provides a directory, Yahooligans, for school-age children, as well as its own search engine.

Search engines are powerful tools that index thousands of web sites through a computer program. The indexes are updated almost continuously. When you enter a keyword into a search engine, you will receive a list with the number of "hits" (links to related sites). The number of hits you receive may vary a great deal among different search engines because some of the engines are created based on the titles of web sites and others are based on the full text of the web sites. Also, some of the engines index several hundred million documents and some index fewer than one million. Major search engines on the web include:

- AltaVista (http://www.altavista.com)
- Excite (http://www.excite.com)
- Google (http://www.google.com)
- Hotbot (http:// hotbot.lycos.com)
- Go.com (http://www.go.com)
- Lycos (http://www.lycos.com)
- WebCrawler (http://www.webcrawler.com)

Some search engines provide the results from simultaneous searches of several search indexes. These comprehensive tools are known as metasearch engines. Examples of metasearch engines include MetaCrawler, Dogpile, and PlusSearch.com.

Besides using the search tips or hints provided by various sites, you can minimize your search by using specialized content search engines. These are selective about what part of the web is searched and indexed. For example, TeachTarget (http://www.techtarget.com/) indexes only sites related to technology. Lists of specialized content search engines can be found at Easy Searcher (http://www .easysearcher.com).

Search engines designed especially for children are available. These sites screen for inappropriate material and link to sites appropriate for children. Using these sites helps to narrow the scope of hits and ensures that students will not accidently end up viewing pornographic material. Search engines designed for children include Ask Jeeves for Kids (www.ajkids.com), OneKey, and Yahooligans.

"Localized" search engines are also found on individual web sites—especially those with large databases of information. For example, online journals, catalogs, and corporations (such as Microsoft) usually include a search engine to index and retrieve the content of their own site. Just about anything you are looking for can be found on the web. Fortunately, there are many tools available to help you find the information.

Effective and efficient web searches depend on careful selection of keywords and proper use of search commands. However, the commands and techniques used to limit the number of hits varies among the different search tools. For best results, read the search tips or hints that are provided at each search site. Also, note that there are some commands that are fairly common across sites. For example:

- *Phrase searches*. On most search engines, quotation marks are used to designate a phrase search. For example, if you want information about compact disc technology, you should enter "compact disc." Otherwise, you may also retrieve web sites about disc brakes in compact cars.

- *Inclusive searches*. Adding a "+" sign before a word usually means that it must be found on each web site that is retrieved. In other words, to retrieve sites that have information about panthers in Florida, you should enter +Florida +panther.

- *Exclusive searches*. The "–" sign is used to exclude words from searches. For example, to locate web sites with information about Martin Luther (and NOT Martin Luther King), you could enter "Martin Luther"–King.

- *Truncation*. Some search engines allow you to use the "*" sign for multiple endings to a word. If you wanted to retrieve sites with information about Texas or Texans, you could enter Texa*.

For more information about searching techniques, review the instructions at each site or visit http://infopeople.org/search.

INTERNET RESEARCH IN THE CLASSROOM

The Internet provides a wealth of information for research, including access to international libraries; government databases; and collections of text, graphics, sounds, and digital video. Information on virtually every topic is available on the Internet and is usually more up-to-date and extensive than the information in the libraries or textbooks. Educational research activities using the Internet can be divided into three broad categories or levels: basic, advanced, and original. Although these categories are not exclusive, they can be used to help classify Internet projects based on the number of sites visited, the sources of the research, and the complexity of the research questions (Barron and Ivers 1999).

Basic Research

Basic research involves finding and comparing facts from a single or several preselected sources and reporting the information. In most cases, students' initial explorations of the Internet involve basic research. For example, they may be instructed to access the Library of Congress or the CIA World

Factbook to write a research report. A good starting point for basic research is My Virtual Reference Desk at http://www.refdesk.com/.

When conducting research on the Internet, students should be encouraged not only to practice their research skills to find the information they need, but also to analyze the results of their searches, compare the facts, and report them appropriately. They should also begin to question the data and reject poor, incomplete, inaccurate, and unimportant facts.

A popular form of basic research is a WebQuest. WebQuests are appealing because they provide structure and guidance both for students and teachers. WebQuests guide learners as they research a specific issue and blend the results of the research into a product or project. The following six components are essential for WebQuests (see Figure 7.2). For more information on WebQuests, along with hundreds of examples, visit http://edweb.sdsu.edu/WebQuest/.

1. Introduction—Background on the activity to be completed.

2. Task—Description of main research question and anticipated end product.

3. Process—Steps for completing the task.

4. Resources—Web sites that provide information relative to the task.

5. Evaluation—Guidelines for evaluation (often includes a rubric).

6. Conclusion—Opportunities for reflection and extension.

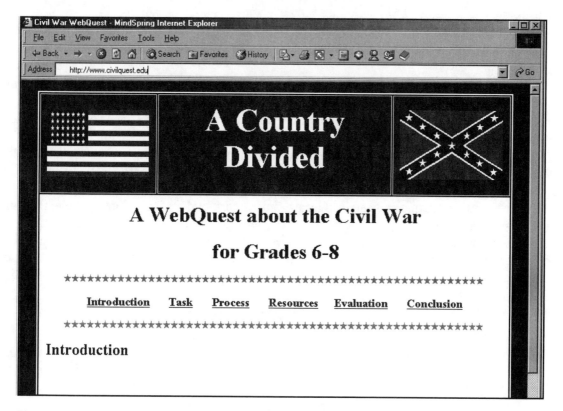

Figure 7.2. WebQuest related to the Revolutionary War.

Advanced Research

Advanced research includes a wider variety of sources, including several sites on the Internet as well as print or CD-ROM sources. Another difference is that the sources in advanced research are not preselected. In other words, the students determine which source or sources to investigate. Advanced research consists of a six-step cycle.

1.   Questioning—Before going online, students structure their research questions.

2.   Planning—Students develop a search strategy and a list of sites to investigate.

3.   Gathering—Students go online to collect information.

4.   Sorting—After signing off the Internet, students analyze and categorize their data.

5.   Synthesizing—Students integrate the information and draw conclusions.

6.   Evaluating—Students assess the results; if necessary, the cycle begins again with a refined research question.

Another critical element at this level is to ensure students can distinguish between reputable and nonreputable sites, between fact and fiction, and whether or not the information is the result of a single opinion or documented evidence. Students should also learn to triangulate gathered information by comparing the data obtained from multiple sources.

Original Research

The Internet is an excellent place to conduct original research through surveys and collaborative experiments. For example, students may conduct surveys through e-mail messages as they collect and compare food prices or other items from around the world. After the information is compiled, it can be graphed, analyzed, and reported. Cooperative experiments can also be performed. For example, students from different geographical locations may collaborate to plant the same kind of seeds on the same day. They follow the same directions for care of the plants as they grow, measure the plants, and send data to other participants. The data are then used for graphing, analyses, and drawing conclusions.

Many web sites exist that can serve as focal points for original research. For example, the Online Science Experiment site at http://www.cbt.virginia.edu/Olh/exp.html supplies information and data that students can manipulate as they learn the scientific method. Penny Toss at http://www.fi.edu/fellows/fellow7/mar99/probability/penny_toss.shtml is another example of a web site that is devoted to original research. In addition to having fun and conducting research, students learn the basics of probability.

COMMUNICATION ACTIVITIES

A major advantage of the Internet is the potential for worldwide communication. Never before have students had the opportunity to interact with others throughout the world on a daily basis. This section presents information on the most popular methods used for global communication in K–12 schools: E-mail exchanges, videoconferencing, and web publishing.

Communication via E-mail

One of the most common forms of Internet-based communication is *e-mail* (electronic mail). E-mail messages are created by a person on a computer workstation or digital device, transmitted to other computers, and read by others on their computer workstations or digital devices. E-mail is possible when a group of people have their desktop computers networked through a local area network, the Internet, or an intranet. E-mail messages can be addressed to an individual, a group, or the members of an entire organization.

To send e-mail messages through the Internet, you must meet some basic requirements. First, you must be able to access a host computer at an *Internet service provider* (ISP). Second, you need an account that provides an Internet user address. Such an address might be something like barron@ usf.edu. This address would be spoken as "barron at usf dot edu." The address is made up of two parts. To the left of the @ sign is the identification or name of the user on the system where he or she has an account. To the right of the @ sign is the Internet designation of the user's system, called the host name or the domain name.

The host name follows a predefined structure. The last right-hand component (edu in this case) represents a type, or domain, of organization or country. Some common domains are provided in Table 7.1. The remainder of the host name identifies a specific computer or service provider. For example, usf identifies the University of South Florida. If you use the Internet through a commercial vendor, you might have an address like smith@aol.com, where smith is the identification of the user on the commercial America Online system. Note that each e-mail address must be unique. Therefore if another "Smith" wants an account on AOL, he or she would need to be something like: smith1@aol.com or jsmith@aol.com.

Table 7.1. Types of Organizations and Their Internet Identifiers

ID	Major Domains
EDU	Education
COM	Commercial Organization
MIL	Military
GOV	Government Sites
NET	Special Network Resources
ORG	Other Organizations
UK	United Kingdom
CA	Canada

Variations of e-mail allow group communications on the Internet. A *listserv* is simply a group address list that automatically distributes information. Any message that is sent to the listserv is sent to all names on the list. Some listservs are private; most have automated procedures that allow anyone to subscribe or unsubscribe. Take care in joining listservs because they may generate dozens of messages a day.

Electronic bulletin boards and newsgroups are also available on the Internet. On these services, users can post messages and read messages that others have posted. USENET is a popular bulletin board system that has more than 10,000 special-interest groups. Many school districts do not allow access to newsgroups because of the potential for adult-oriented material and information.

E-mail Activities

E-mail activities can provide numerous opportunities for students to practice their reading, writing, research, and computer skills; learn about others; and write for an audience. The following are a few ideas for incorporating e-mail into your classroom.

> *Pen-Pal Activities.* Perhaps the most common form of e-mail projects is electronic pen pals, or e-pals. Students can learn from others in a risk-free environment both within and beyond their communities, practice written communication skills, become aware of other cultures, practice foreign language skills, and make new friends. If you are looking for classrooms and students to communicate with, try the Intercultural E-mail Classroom Connections site at http://www.iecc.org/ or epals.com Classroom Exchange at http://www.epals.com/.

> *Peer-to-Peer Tutoring.* Another form of electronic communications is peer-to-peer tutoring or mentoring. These exchanges provide a formal use of e-mail that specifically pairs students with other students or with adults who can provide one-on-one assistance and guidance routinely.

> *Ask An Expert.* E-mail can also bring students into direct contact with distinguished authors, national figures, or other notable people. An Ask An Expert site is available at http://www.askanexpert.com, where students can send questions to experts in a multitude of different fields.

> *Round-Robin Stories.* In a round-robin approach, a participating class starts a story with one paragraph. The story starter is sent to a predetermined class (class one sends its story to class two, and so on). Students work in small groups to add a new paragraph to the story. The story variations then rotate to the next class, and that class adds to the story before forwarding it. This cycle continues until the story returns to the first class in the round.

Synchronous Communication via Videoconferencing

E-mail communications can be referred to as asynchronous because there is usually a time difference between when a message is sent and when it is read. With better connection speeds and compression rates, *synchronous communications* (those that take place at the same time) are increasingly possible for schools.

One type of synchronous communication is Internet chat. Internet chatting enables two or more people to type on a "collective" computer screen. They can see what they are typing as well as the input from others—all at the same time on the same screen. Chatting can be very helpful to education; however, it should be carefully monitored and restricted to chat rooms designed for students only.

Imagine having your students practice their French by speaking directly to students in France! Another form of synchronous communication, called *videoconferencing*, makes this possible. This allows you to see, hear, and interact with others in real-time. Depending on the speed of your Internet connection, the quality of the audio and video can vary from excellent to dismal. If the connection is not fast enough to support both video and audio, many schools have found the audio only conferences to be productive. Videoconferencing and audioconferencing are covered in more detail in Chapter 8.

Communication via Web Publishing

Communication using the Internet can also take place when a student or a class posts a story or other document on a bulletin board or web page. There are two ways to publish on the web—students can submit their products to someone else's web site, or the students can create web pages and place them on their school's site.

If you decide to send the students' works to another web site (rather than hosting at your school), you will find there are many sites designed to highlight students' stories, songs, artwork, and other creations. Table 7.2 is a list of web sites that encourage students to submit their products. Visit these sites to learn about their submission procedures and criteria.

Table 7.2. Web Sites for Student Publications

CyberKids	http://www.cyberkids.com/
The Diary Project	http://www.diaryproject.com/
Global Show-N-Tell	http://www.telenaut.com/gst/
Kids' Space	http://www.kids-space.org/
TeenLit.com	http://www.teenlit.com/
Yahooligans! Publishing on the Web	http://www.yahooligans.com/School_Bell/Language _Arts/Writing/Publishing_on_the_Web/

Many districts, schools, classes, teachers, and students have also published their stories, songs, and the like on their own web sites. A school web site can serve as an information center for the community. The school calendar, building layouts, special events, course materials, and even the school song can be part of the site.

There are two fundamental stages to creating a web site or web pages. First, the page files and all associated images, sounds, and so forth must be created in the proper format and tested. Second, the files must all be transferred to a host computer called a web server.

Web page files must adhere to a specific format or language, called *hypertext markup language* (HTML). HTML uses tags to define how information is formatted on a screen:

<H2>Home of the Dolphins</H2>

In this example, <H2> and </H2> are tags that represent the beginning and ending of a line of text. The <H2> tag is a command to start a second level headline—a single line of text. Headlines have six levels available, with one being the largest and six being the smallest. The </H2> is the instruction to cancel the headline style and return to the normal font. If the </H2> were not used, all following text would continue to be displayed in the headline font. See Figure 7.4 to view the HTML file that creates the web page in Figure 7.3.

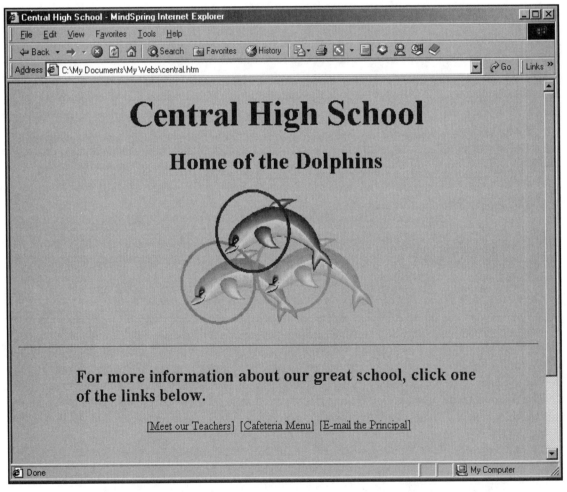

Figure 7.3. Sample web page.

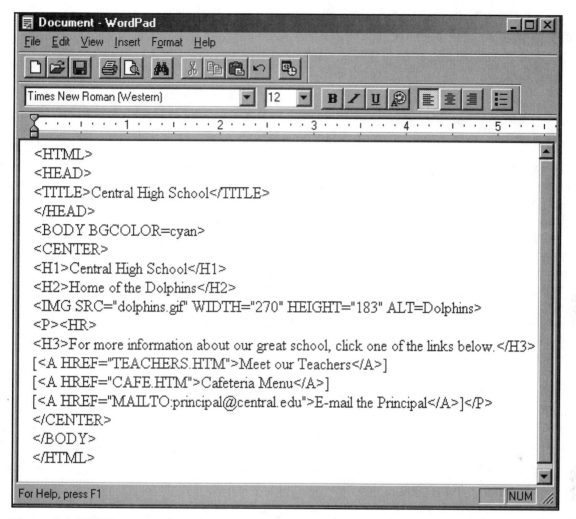

Figure 7.4. HTML tags used to create the sample web page in Figure 7.3.

About 50 common HTML tags are in use, but companies such as Netscape continue to develop their own enhanced or extended tags. Although all web browsers can correctly interpret the basic tags, enhanced tags are sometimes unique to specific browsers.

Creating a web page by using the HTML language may appear to be intimidating, but even elementary school students can do it. In many cases, students learn a dozen or so basic HTML tags and then gradually expand their "vocabulary" as they become more experienced. In other cases, students rely on HTML editors that insulate the author from most of the HTML tags. The editors allow the author to concentrate more on the content and form of the page and less on the mechanics of HTML. FrontPage, DreamWeaver, and Netscape Composer are popular programs that can easily create web pages—without knowledge of HTML. Many HTML tutorials are online to help get students started (such as http://www.coedu.usf.edu/inst_tech/publications/html), and many applications (e.g., Microsoft Word and PowerPoint) have built-in functions that allow users to save their work as web page (html) documents.

Once a web page and its associated materials have been created and tested, they must be transferred to a location, or host, on the World Wide Web so that all can access it. The host machine is usually maintained by the network administrator (at a school or university) or an Internet service provider (ISP).

BENEFITS AND CONCERNS OF USING THE INTERNET IN THE CLASSROOM

Many benefits come with using the Internet in the classroom. Barron and Ivers (1999) note that telecommunications can benefit education in many ways. For students, the Internet opens doors to multicultural education, establishes real-world learning experiences, helps to improve writing skills, encourages higher-level thinking skills, and increases motivation, achievement, and positive behavior. Benefits for teachers include useful tools for teaching research skills and instant access to educational research, curriculum sources, lesson plans, programs, online experts, discussion centers, and teacher forums. Other benefits include timely information, flexibility in the creation and delivery of documents, online classes and tutorials, and communication with the community through school web sites and e-mail.

There are, however, many things to consider before choosing to use the Internet in your classroom. These include Acceptable Use Policies, filtering software, privacy issues, and implementation techniques.

Acceptable Use Policies

Acceptable Use Policies (AUPs) define and address the responsibilities associated with using the school's network. A well-written AUP focuses on responsible use of computers, computer networks (including the Internet), and the transfer of information in school settings. Most AUPs include the following:

- A description of the instructional philosophies and strategies to be supported by Internet access in schools.

- A list of the responsibilities of educators, parents, and students for using the Internet, including a code of conduct for behavior on the Internet.

- An explanation of what constitutes acceptable and unacceptable use of the Internet.

- A discussion of the consequences of violating the AUP.

- A disclaimer removing the school division, under specific circumstances, from responsibility.

- A statement reminding users that Internet access and the use of the school's computer network is a privilege.

- A signature form for teachers, parents, and students indicating their intent to abide by the AUP.

It is important that everyone using the school network reads, understands, and agrees to the established AUP. Example AUPs can be found at:

- http://www.hasd.k12.pa.us/aup.shtml (Hazelton Area School District)

- http://www.richmond.k12.va.us/users/policies/aup.html (Richmond Public Schools)

- http://www.nps.k12.va.us/Norfolk/aupform.html (Norfolk Public Schools)
- http://mustang.coled.umn.edu/Started/use/Dist833pol.html (South Washington County Schools)
- http://wombat.cusd.chico.k12.ca.us/aup/ (Chico Unified School District)
- http://netizen.uoregon.edu/templates/model_policy.html (Responsible Netizen)

Filtering Software

Besides AUPs, administrators and teachers need to consider *filtering software*. Filtering software stops users from accessing material that is offensive or objectionable. The Guide to Parental Controls/Internet Safety Products (http://microweb.com/pepsite/Software/filters.html) provides descriptions and links to over 50 filtering programs. In addition to blocking undesirable sites, filtering software can track students' Internet activities; filter e-mail messages, news, and chat; set Internet access time limits; prevent personal disclosures; and allow custom-editing.

Another way to control web access is through programs such as Blue Squirrel's WebWhacker (http://www.bluesquirrel.com/products/whacker/whacker.html). WebWhacker allows educators to save layered web content to a computer's hard drive, creating a "virtual web" that does not require direct Internet access by the students. Not only do such programs give complete control of the content to educators, but they also allow them to transfer the information to other computers that may not have Internet access.

Privacy Issues

AUPs and filtering software cannot guarantee a child's safety. It is important that the student (and teacher) understand the need for anonymity on the web. In the case of the child, it is critical that he or she does not post or send his or her personal information (full name, home address, telephone number, e-mail address, age, etc.) without parental consent. The child must understand that "anonymity" also refers to others on the web—there is no guarantee that a person is whom they say there are. Unfortunately, pedophiles exist on the Internet, using gathered information to arrange an encounter that could risk a child's safety. Disclosure of personal information may also result in harassment, negative legal or financial consequences, and unwanted solicitations.

It is important that educators consider the students' anonymity as well. Instead of posting a student's picture on the web with his or her name, the teacher may consider using the student's initials. Teachers should obtain parent, administration, and student permission before posting students' work or picture on the web.

Implementation Techniques

Other than being familiar with district and school policies regarding the use of the Internet, educators must consider how they will organize instruction when using the Internet in the classroom. They need to think about where the computers with Internet connections are, when and how often they are free, which projection devices are available, students' experiences with using the computer and the Internet, and how to manage the classroom.

Many schools restrict Internet access to the school's Library Media Center. Media specialists are often available to assist students with their research and basic Internet research skills. Library Media Centers may be open before or after school, allowing students more time to do their research. Background information and initial instruction for an Internet project may begin in the classroom, but continue in the Library Media Center with the assistance of the media specialist. If computers with Internet access are limited, students could be sent in groups to begin their Internet research.

Teachers with classroom Internet access can demonstrate basic Internet skills to small groups or the whole class if a projection device is available. A rotation schedule can be created to allow students to work on the computer, but this may take a lot of time if only a few computers are available in the classroom. Teachers may opt to place students in cooperative groups instead of requiring individual projects. If Internet access is also available in the school's Library Media Center, the teacher can make arrangements with the media specialist for additional computer time.

In their book, *The Internet and Instruction: Activities and Ideas*, Barron and Ivers (1999) provide several implementation techniques for using the Internet. These include:

- Focus on the curriculum. Use the Internet as a tool to enhance the curriculum, not as an end in itself.

- Preview Internet resources on all computers that will be used to view them. This ensures that the computers have the hardware and software to support the site.

- Make alternative plans. Be prepared if sites are unavailable, the server is busy, or the system crashes.

- Conduct some activities offline. E-mail messages, stories, and so on can be created in a word processor before going online. Web information can be saved to a disk or pasted into a word processor for offline reading.

- Provide instruction in basic computer and Internet skills. Make sure students have the skills and knowledge to use the tools that are required of them.

- Respect the rights of others. Ensure students understand copyright issues, and how to conduct themselves on the Internet with others (netiquette).

Educators must also consider issues of equity. It is unfair to assign an Internet assignment for homework if students do not have adequate access. First, determine which resources are available at home for your students, as well as in your school and community.

ACCESS OPTIONS

A few years ago nearly everyone connected to the Internet through standard telephone lines, a "slow" modem, and a desktop computer. Now, there are many affordable options. This section presents information on various access options, including standard modems, fax modems, DSL, cable modems, and satellite.

Internet Service Providers

Regardless of the type of connection you obtain to the Internet, you will need an *ISP* (Internet service provider). An ISP is a company or organization that maintains high-speed connections into the Internet. Usually, they also provide e-mail addresses and storage. For example, if America Online is your ISP, you will connect to the Internet through their servers, your e-mail messages will be stored on their servers, and they will allow you a few megabytes of storage space to host a web page.

In some cases, an ISP may be a university or educational system that provides free access to students and faculty. Another option is to subscribe to an ISP that operates through the telephone or cable company. Most of the providers will supply all the software you need to connect and a local or toll-free telephone number for your modem.

Connection Speeds

Before exploring the various options for Internet connections, it is best to have an understanding of the available connection speeds (also referred to as *bandwidth*). Over the years, manufacturers have been able to increase greatly the transfer rate or speed of modems. Although this has been partly because of improvements in telephone lines, the largest improvements have come through discoveries about how to send and receive more information over telephone lines and how to correct common telephone-line interference.

Baud—named after Emil Baudot, who invented a telegraph teleprinter code in 1874—is a term often used to define the speed of modems. A modern measurement, *bits per second* (bps), has replaced baud as a measurement of speed for telecommunications. A bit is a binary digit having a value of 0 or 1. The more bits a modem can process per second, the faster it can send or receive data.

Bits define each character and the spaces between characters; it takes about 10 bits to transmit or receive a single character of information. A 56Kbps modem can transmit or receive about 56,000 characters per second. This sentence, which is 107 characters long (counting spaces), would require about 0.02 seconds to transmit.

Until recently, a modem that operated at 56Kbps was considered fast. Now, however, with DSL and other digital and wireless options, even faster speeds are possible. In fact, instead of measuring speed in Kbps (kilobits), we now measure it in Mbps (megabits). The chart in Table 7.3 shows some of the connection speeds discussed in this section.

Table 7.3. Transmission Speeds

Technology	Speed	
56K Modem	56-Kbps	
ISDN	128-Kbps	
Satellite	400-Kbps	
T1	1.5-Mbps	
ADSL	9-Mbps	
Cable Modem	10-Mbps	

Standard Modems

A standard, analog modem might seem like a complicated device, but it performs two simple processes. Most standard telephone lines transmit only analog audio tones, such as those in human voices. A computer manipulates digital information in a binary code of 0s and 1s. The modem translates, or modulates, the 0s and 1s of an outgoing message into a fluctuating tone that goes through the telephone line. At the same time, the modem listens for a different tone that comes from the distant computer's modem. As this tone comes through the telephone line, the local modem translates, or demodulates, it back into the 0s and 1s of the digital language of the local computer. Thus, the modem—modulator-demodulator—allows the two computers to behave as though they are connected directly even though they might be thousands of miles apart.

If everything goes well, the digital stream of 0s and 1s going out of one computer is translated into an analog tone. This tone is transmitted through the telephone line, and at the other end the distant modem translates the tone back into the identical, digital pattern of 0s and 1s that earlier departed the original computer. (See Figure 7.5.)

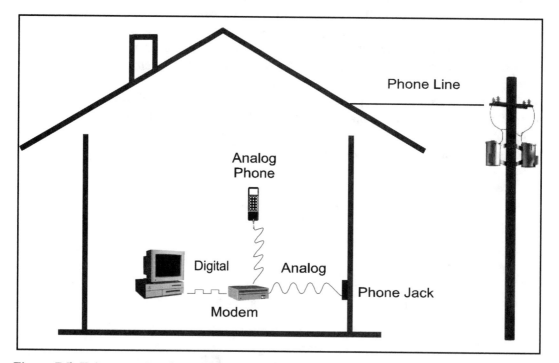

Figure 7.5. Using a modem for telecommunications.

Modems have settings that must be matched so that two modems can communicate. Some of these settings are automatically determined by the modems when the telephone call connects; other settings must be established manually. (The ISP usually provides the settings.)

The standard speed for modems now is between 28.8Kbps and 56Kbps. Those speeds can provide effective communications via e-mail and web sites that do not have extensive graphics. Advantages of standard modems include low cost and compatibility with standard telephone lines.

Although the bandwidth and speed of modems continues to improve, they are far too slow for most video applications. Other factors, such as the amount of congestion on the Internet, also affects the transmission rate.

Fax Modems

Facsimile machines, or fax machines as they are frequently called, have become almost as common as modems. Fax machines are used to send copies of paper documents from one location to another. The machines function in much the same way as modems in that they generate tones sent over standard telephone lines.

A *fax modem* allows one computer to connect to another to share data, but this type of modem can also connect to a distant fax machine. When it operates as a fax machine, it can receive a picture or image of whatever the fax machine at the other end is sending. With proper software, this image can be printed, stored, or immediately displayed on the computer screen. The image might contain text, numbers, line drawings, or photographs. If the image is entirely text, the text cannot be fed directly into a word processor for further editing unless optical recognition software (OCR) is installed. OCR software converts the image into a text file. A more efficient method of sending text documents that require modification is through the e-mail system. E-mail messages are already text so they can be edited immediately in any text editor or word processing program.

Fax modems can also be used to send information from a computer to a distant fax machine. The information must be either an image or a text file that is stored in the computer. After the appropriate software converts the file to a format that is compatible with fax machines, the distant fax machine is dialed and the file is transmitted. At the other end, the image of the page comes out of the receiving fax in the usual manner.

Integrated Services Digital Network (ISDN)

An *Integrated Services Digital Network* (ISDN) provides digital transmission over ordinary telephone lines. It is a dial-up connection much like standard modem access, but all similarities end there.

ISDN provides a raw data rate of 144Kbps on a single telephone line. This 144Kbps channel is partitioned into subchannels: two 64Kbps B (for bearer) channels and one 16Kbps D (for data) channel. The B channels carry customer voice or data signals. The D channel carries signals between your ISDN equipment and the phone company's central office. The combined B channels can transmit data up to 128Kbps. Splitting the available bandwidth into two parts (64Kbps each) allows one channel to be used for data transmissions, while the other channel is used for a standard voice telephone call.

ISDN is generally available from your local telephone company. Two services are available: the *Basic Rate Interface* and the *Primary Rate Interface*. The Basic Rate is designed for homes and small businesses and consists of two B channels and one D channel. The Primary Rate is designed for larger users and consists of 23 B channels and one D channel.

Your computer connects to an ISDN line via a terminal adapter (similar to a modem). Your access provider must have a network adapter to receive the ISDN signals. Hence, ISDN requires an adapter at both ends of the transmission, so both you and your access provider need to install an ISDN adapter.

Another form of ISDN is broadband ISDN (BISDN). It transfers information through fiber optic and radio media at two megabits per second and higher. Even so, this does not compare with the transfer speed of DSL. DSL is expected to replace ISDN in many areas, as well as compete with cable modems in bringing multimedia and other Internet features to homes and small businesses.

Satellite Technology

The same digital satellite technology that makes small dish antennas possible can also be used to send computer data to specific receivers. Using satellite Internet access, home users can currently receive (or download) information at speeds up to 428Kbps. This is strictly a one-way communication; standard telephone connections and modems are used to send data from the home back to the Internet service provider. Satellite offers high-speed access where cable access and DSL are not yet available. Users can run their Internet access and satellite TV through the same dish.

T-Carrier System

Bell System introduced the T-carrier system in the U.S. in the 1960s. It was the first successful system that supported digitized voice transmission. The T-1 line has a data transmission rate of 1.5Mbps, while the T-3 line provides transfer rates of 44.7Mbps. Both are used by Internet service providers. The T-carrier system is completely digital. The system uses four wires—two for sending and two for receiving data at the same time. Originally a pair of twisted pair copper wires, the four wires may now include coaxial cable, optical fiber, digital microwave, and other media. A T-1 line requires a digital connection device—a customer switching unit/digital switching unit (CSU/DSU)—to connect the four wires to carry the information. T-1 lines are usually used to connect to the Internet backbone; the Internet backbone consists of T-3 lines. T-1 lines are expensive; hence, businesses rather than individuals typically lease them.

Digital Subscriber Line (DSL)

Digital Subscriber Line (DSL) is a high-speed data service. With DSL, digital data is transmitted to your computer directly as digital data, allowing the phone company to use a much wider bandwidth for transmission. DSL shares your existing telephone line with the analog signal by using a different frequency range; so analog signals and DSL (digital) signals can be transmitted at the same time (see Figure 7.6). DSL technology can transmit data at rates up to nine megabits per second. This rate varies according to the length of the copper (phone) wire, the wire's gauge, and so on. Common home use speeds are 256Kbps to 2Mbps.

DSL for home use is technically called an *Asymmetric Digital Subscriber Line* (ADSL), but usually the "A" is dropped. The asymmetrical part of ADSL refers to the various bandwidths for sending and receiving data. There are three asymmetrical pipes (streams) of data on a DSL line:

- A POTS (Plain Old Telephone Service) for analog signals like voice and fax
- A medium-sized, digital upstream pipe
- A large, digital downstream pipe

The "upstream" pipe is used for the information that you send to the Internet and the "download" pipe is used for the information you receive from the Internet. The amount of information you send upstream is usually much less than the information sent to you downstream, so ADSL allocates more bandwidth for downstream data and less bandwidth for upstream data. These three distinct pipes send analog information directly to the Public Switched Telephone Network (PSTN) and digital data to the packet-switched network, allowing both networks to work faster and more efficiently.

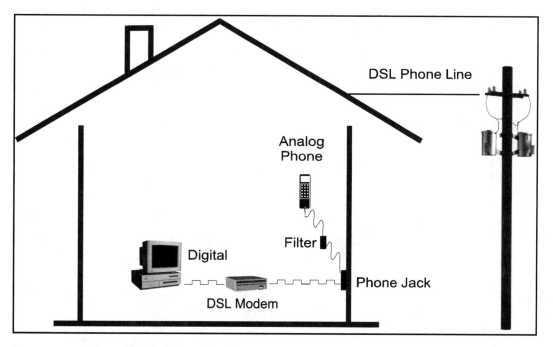

Figure 7.6. Using DSL for telecommunications.

In order to get a DSL line, special equipment must be installed in the telephone company's central office near your home, allowing you to connect to the voice and data networks. The closer you are to the central office, the greater the available speed of the DSL line. Next, the telephone wire outside your home must support DSL. If not, new wiring may need to be installed.

Once DSL is installed to your telephone service, the telephone line is connected to a DSL modem, which, in turn, is connected to your computer through an Ethernet cable. With DSL, your computer will be able to access the Internet in what will appear to be nanoseconds. In addition, unlike traditional access, you'll be able to use the telephone at the same time you are accessing the Internet. For more information about DSL availability in your area, contact your local telephone company.

Cable Modem

A cable modem is a device that enables you to connect your computer to a local cable TV line and receive data at about 1.5 megabits per second. The upper limit of cable, 52Mbps, is available to ISPs. Personal PCs' internal limitations and local providers' Internet connections limit the speed of the data to households.

A cable modem can be added to or integrated with a set-top box that supplies your TV set with channels for Internet access. Usually, cable modems are furnished as part of the cable access service. Like DSL, cable modems allow continuous access to the Internet, so dial-up and connection wait times are eliminated.

A cable modem has two connections: one to the cable wall outlet and the other to a computer (using a standard 10BASET Ethernet card) or to a set-top box for a TV set (see Figure 7.7, page 168). A cable modem modulates between analog and digital signals, but it is a much more complex device than a telephone modem.

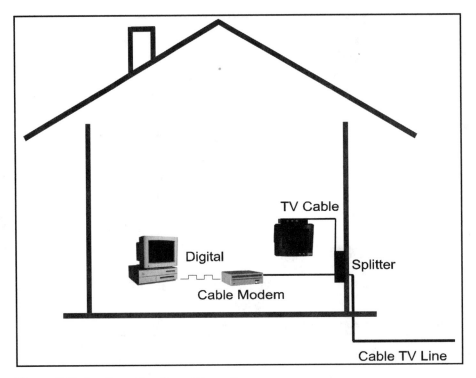

Figure 7.7. Configuration for cable modem.

Users with cable modems share the same cable line that is connected to their local cable company. This may slow the rate of data transmission if several users are online at the same time. Cable modem operators include Cox Communications, Time Warner Cable, Comcast, and AT&T Broadband. For a directory of cable modem providers, visit Cable Datacom News at http://www.cabledatacomnews.com/.

WebTV

WebTV is perhaps one of the least expensive ways to connect to the Internet. WebTV is a device similar to a set-top box for cable TV, except it uses a modem and standard telephone line to receive and transmit signals. It uses your TV as an output device. Transfer rates are similar to 56Kbps modems. Users need to sign-up with the WebTV access service and browse web pages using WebTV's browser. Besides speed, WebTV's limitations include incompatibility with certain audio and graphic files, plus it does not currently support Java, PDF files, and various fonts.

Wireless Technology

The term *wireless* refers to telecommunication in which electromagnetic waves carry the signal over part or all the communication path. Common examples of wireless devices include cellular phones and pagers, global positioning systems, cordless computer peripherals (e.g., mice, keyboards), wireless local area networks (LANs), and so on. These devices use transponders, or wireless receiver/transmitters, that are moving (satellites) or fixed (on Earth).

Wireless Internet access is becoming more common in today's society. Most cellular and personal communication services offer Internet access as part of their communication services. Unlike viewing colored and graphic web pages on your computer desktop, however, sites are viewed via your cellular telephone as text.

Personal digital assistants (PDAs) and laptop computers can have wireless Internet capabilities as well. In addition to a wireless modem, users need a subscription to a wireless ISP. Speeds are still slow, and it is possible that your ISP will charge roaming charges for service outside of your coverage area, if it is available.

Gigabit Ethernet

Gigabit Ethernet can transfer voice, video, and Internet data at speeds of 1 billion bits per second—one gigabit. Using fiber optic wires and cable lines, consumers are able to access television, telephone, and Internet services from one pipe going into their home. Internet access is about 1,000 times faster than a cable modem. Although this technology can transmit speeds of one billion bits per second, today's computers are not capable of accepting one gigabit Internet transmissions. Competisys Corporation, the first to offer this technology, offers Internet speeds of one to six megabytes, which can increase as the technology allows.

Internet2

Recently, Internet2 was launched. Led by more than 180 U.S. universities working with industry and government, Internet2 is an advanced network that supports complex applications and technologies for research and higher education. The universities are connected to one another through regional networks over Abilene—a superfast nationwide backbone—developed with Qwest Communications, Cisco Systems, Nortel Networks, and Indiana University. Abilene operates at over two and a half gigabits per second. Ten sets of encyclopedias can move over the fiber-optic lines in one second flat. Universities connect to the network at gigabit portals (called gigaPoPs) that have transfer rates of at least one gigabit. Internet2 is capable of supporting applications that would be impossible over the regular Internet. These include high-definition television and complex multicasts. Internet2 also supports the next generation of Internet Protocol —IPv6. IPv6 adds more digits to Internet addresses, expanding exponentially the number of devices that can be connected —that is, cell phones, appliances, even your wristwatch!

Internet2 recreates the partnership of academia, industry, and government that helped foster today's Internet in its infancy. Unlike today's Internet, however, Internet2 is not open to the general public. Researchers are using its advanced technical capabilities, security, speed, and capacity to test real-time, bidirectional full-screen video and audio streams for surgical collaboration, live music performances, holographic images, studying astronomy, linking high-power electron microscopes to the Web, and more. One of the goals of Internet2 is to guarantee 30-frames-per-second synchronized video across multiple networks without delays, jerkiness, or dropped frames. Many of the new technologies now in the experimental stage on Internet2 will eventually be offered over the global Internet.

SUMMARY

The variety of applications for telecommunications seems unlimited. New technologies are allowing us to access information at increased speeds, almost anywhere, at any time. The Internet allows us to access libraries after they are closed, bank on national holidays, and send messages to people no matter where they are. It allows us to create web pages for school communications, academic exchanges, and other publications. It is a nonsleeping world of endless resources, current events, and meeting places where groups of people separated by local, state, or even national boundaries can work together to solve common problems. As telecommunications technologies advance, so will the type and complexity of applications that can be run over the Internet.

GLOSSARY

Acceptable Use Policy (AUP). Defines and addresses the responsibilities associated with using the school's network.

Acrobat Reader. A plug-in that enables browsers to view PDF files.

ADSL (Asymmetric Digital Subscriber Line). A high-speed data service that allows analog signals and digital signals to be transmitted at the same time over a standard telephone line.

advanced research. A method that includes a wider variety of sources than Basic Research that are not pre-selected and includes a six step cycle: Questioning, Planning, Gathering, Sorting, Synthesizing, Evaluating.

AIFF (Audio Interchange File Format). A file format developed by Apple Computer for storing high quality sampled audio and musical instrument information.

ARPANET (Advanced Research Projects Agency Network). The government research network that served as the basis for the Internet.

ASCII (American Standard Code for Information Interchange). A standard that establishes the structure of binary 0s and 1s that define the letters of the alphabet, digits, and common punctuation marks.

asynchronous communication. Communication that does not take place at the same time (i.e., e-mail—messages can be sent and read at different times).

audioconferencing. A conference conducted via standard telephone lines and speaker phones.

B channel. The "bearer" channel of an ISDN line that carries the main data.

bandwidth. Bandwidth refers to: (1) how fast data flows on a given transmission path and (2) the width of the range of frequencies that an electronic signal occupies on a given transmission medium.

basic research. Research that involves finding and comparing facts from a single or several pre-selected sources and reporting the information.

baud rate. A term sometimes used to define the speed of serial data transmissions, such as those found with modems. The term is derived from Emil Baudot, a nineteenth-century inventor. The term is being replaced by bits per second (bps).

BBS (bulletin-board system). An electronic bulletin-board system (EBBS, sometimes shortened to just BBS). A computer-based equivalent of the traditional bulletin board. Most BBSs also offer an option for private E-mail.

bit (binary digit). The smallest unit of information in a digital computer. It is usually represented with values of 0 or 1.

bps (bits per second). A common method of measuring the speed of a modem. Modems range in speed from 1,200 bits per second (bps) to about 56,000bps. Modem bps rates must match before they can communicate with each other.

broadband ISDN (BISDN). A form of ISDN that transfers information through fiber optic and radio media at two megabits per second and higher.

bulletin board. A location or system that can be reached by computer forsharing or exchanging messages or other files.

cable modem. A device that enables you to connect your computer to a local cable TV line and receive data at about one and a half megabits per second.

chat. An option on some telecommunications systems that makes it possible for a user to communicate directly with the system operator or other users. The chatting is not vocal, however; the information typed into each system keyboard is displayed on the other computer monitor(s).

communications software. See telecommunications software.

conferences. Bulletin boards on a telecommunication system that are labeled for specific topics. A number of conferences (sometimes called discussion groups) might be available on a typical BBS, and users may select those in which they are interested.

D channel. The "delta" channel of an ISDN line that carries control and signaling information.

dedicated telephone line. A normal telephone line that is used for nothing but telecommunications. This reduces the likelihood that someone will pick up an extension or otherwise interrupt while the modem is online.

discussion groups. See conferences.

domain. A set of network addresses organized by levels.

download. To receive a file through a telecommunications system. Normally the system does not allow any other activity while the file is being transferred.

DSL (Digital Subscriber Line). A technology for bringing high-bandwidth information to homes and small businesses over ordinary copper telephone lines. A DSL line can carry both data and voice signals and the data part of the line is continuously connected.

E-mail (electronic mail). Mail or communications sent and received through electronic, nonpaper methods. Usually a mainframe, a LAN, or a BBS is the vehicle.

exclusive search. A type of Internet search whereby a "-" is used next to a word (i.e., "math lesson"-geometry) to exclude words from searches.

fax modem. A modem that can connect to a distant fax machine as well as connect one computer to another to share data.

filtering software. Software to stop users from accessing material that is deemed offensive or objectionable.

firewall. A set of related programs, located at a network gateway server, that protects the resources of a private network from users from other networks.

GIF (graphic interchange format). A common file format supported by the web, used for images with few colors (i.e., simple cartoons).

Gigabit Ethernet. A technology capable of transferring voice, video, and Internet data at speeds of one billion bits per second—one gigabit.

GUI (graphical user interface). Software that allows an individual to make selections by simply pointing and clicking with a mouse. A GUI often incorporates images as active parts of menus.

host computer. The computer one calls when initiating telecommunications. It might be a mainframe, a LAN, a BBS, or just another personal computer.

HTML (hypertext markup language). Coding language used to create hypertext documents to be posted on the Web. HTML code consists of embedded tags that specify how a block of text should appear or how the word is linked to another file on the Internet.

HTML editor. A software tool that allows the HTML authors to concentrate more on the content and form of the page and less on the mechanics of HTML.

http (hypertext transfer protocol). The protocol for moving hypertext files across the World Wide Web.

inclusive search. A type of Internet search whereby a "+" is used next to words (i.e., +math +lesson) indicating the words must be contained in the result of the search.

Internet. A group of networks connecting governmental institutions, military branches, educational institutions, and commercial companies.

Internet address. A series of letters or numbers that identifies a unique node on the Internet.

Internet2. An advanced network that supports complex applications and technologies for research and higher education.

ISDN (Integrated Services Digital Network). An enhancement to telephone switching systems that allows telephone lines to transmit voice and data in digital form.

ISP (Internet service provider). Organizations that provide connections to the Internet. They may be universities or private companies.

JPEG (Joint Photographic Experts Group). A graphic file format supported on the web, used for images with lots of colors (photos).

Listserv. A group address list that automatically distributes information.

metasearch engine. A search engine that provides the results from simultaneous searches of several search indexes.

modem (modulator-demodulator). Modems are used to link computers through telephone lines. Modulation is the process of changing computer data into tones that can be sent through a telephone line, and demodulation is the process of changing the tones back into computer data.

NSFNET (National Science Foundation Network). The high-speed "network of networks" that serves as the Internet backbone in the United States.

online. Having a computer connected via modem and telephone lines to another computer.

original research. Research through surveys, collaborative experiments, and other data collection procedures to arrive at an original solution or result.

PDF (portable document format). A file format that captures the elements of a printed document as an electronic image, allowing you to view, navigate, or print the document.

phrase search. A type of search where quotation marks are placed around two or more words (i.e., "Charlie Brown") , limiting the search to the exact phrase contained with the quotation marks.

plug-in. Small programs that can be installed on your computer and used as part of your web browser, expanding its capabilities.

protocol. A special set of rules that computers in a telecommunications connection use when they communicate. Each must recognize and observe the same protocol.

satellite technology. A digital technology that uses small dish antennas to send data to specific receivers.

search engine. A tool that index thousands of web sites through a computer program.

set-top box. A device that enables a television set to become a user interface to the Internet and also enables a television set to receive and decode digital television broadcasts.

SIG (special-interest group). In bulletin-board systems, about the same as a conference. Some BBSs are set up so that selecting one SIG automatically selects all appropriate conferences on that BBS.

stop bits. Every character of information that goes through a modem ends with one or more stop bits. Most common telecommunications systems use one stop bit. Communications software has a menu selection to set the number of stop bits.

synchronous communication. Communication that takes place at the same time.

system operator. The person in charge of maintaining a BBS. The "sysop" monitors the system, answers questions, and checks files that are uploaded.

T-carriers. A digital system that uses four wires—two for sending and two for receiving data—at the same time.

TCP/IP (transmission control protocol/Internet protocol). The rules, or protocols, for data transfers on the Internet.

telecommunications software. Program used to allow the computer to communicate through a modem. Most software of this type dials the requested number and sets the modem for the system that is being called.

truncation. A searching strategy whereby you shorten or cut off the end of a word with an asterisk (e.g., tele*) to allow more possibilities for a related result (e.g., telephone, telegraph, telecommunications).

upload. The process of sending a complete file to the host computer.

URL (uniform resource locator) . The address structure for the World Wide Web. A unique URL identifies each web site, allowing others to locate it.

USENET. A popular bulletin board system that has more than 10,000 special-interest groups.

videoconferencing. A form of communication that allows you to see, hear, and interact with others in real-time via technology.

WAV. An audio file format, created by Microsoft, that has become a standard PC audio file. A Wave file (.WAV) format stores information about the file's number of tracks (mono or stereo), sample rate, and bit depth.

web browser. A computer program designed to make it easy for an individual to use the World Wide Web portion of the Internet. A web browser almost always uses a graphical user interface (GUI).

webcasting. The ability to use the web to deliver live or delayed versions of sound or video broadcasts.

WebQuest. A structure and guided research activity designed to guide learners as they research a specific issue and incorporate the results of the research into a product or project.

WebTV. Similar to a set-top box for cable TV, WebTV is a device that uses a modem and standard telephone line to receive and transmit signals, and uses your TV as an output device.

WebWhacker. A software program that allows users to save layered web content to a computer's hard drive, creating a "virtual web" that does not require direct Internet access.

wireless technology. Telecommunication in which electromagnetic waves carry the signal over part or all the communication path.

World Wide Web. Hypermedia-based Internet information system. Graphical user interfaces allow users to click a mouse on desired menu items, resulting in text, sound, pictures, or even motion video from all over the world.

RESOURCES

Resources for Teachers

Education Index
http://www.educationindex.com
/education_resources.html

Exworthy Educational Links
http://home.socal.rr.com/exworthy/

Kathy Schrock's Guide for Educators
http://school.discovery.com/schrockguide/

National Teacher.Com
http://www.nationalteacher.com
/index.shtml

Pro Teacher
http://www.proteacher.com/

School.Net
http://www.k12.school.net/home.html

Sites for Teachers
http://www.sitesforteachers.com/

Skewl Sites
http://www.skewlsites.com/

Teachers.net
http://www.teachers.net/

Teachers@work
http://www.treadwell.co.nz/

Teachers Xpress
http://www.teacherxpress.com/

teachnet.com
http://www.teachnet.com/

Tools for Creating Web Pages

Dreamweaver by Macromedia
http://www.macromedia.com/software
/dreamweaver/

Frontpage by Microsoft Corporation
http://www.microsoft.com/frontpage/

Golive by Adobe
http://www.adobe.com/products/golive
/main.html

HomeSite by Macromedia/Allaire
http://www.allaire.com/Products
/HomeSite/

Netscape Communicator (Composer)
http://home.netscape.com/browsers/

SiteCentral by Knowledge Adventure
http://www.sitecentral.com/

Miscellaneous Web Sites

Ask an Expert
http://www.askanexpert.com

Cable Datacom News
http://www.cabledatacomnews.com

Cable Modem Primer
http://www.cable-modem.net/tt
/primer.html

ePALS.com
http://www.epals.com/

HTML Tutorials
http://www.coedu.usf.edu/inst_tech
/publications/html

HyperStudio
http://www.hyperstudio.com/

Intercultural E-mail Classroom Connections
http://www.iecc.org

My Virtual Reference Desk
http://www.refdesk.com

Online Science Experiment
http://www.cbt.virginia.edu/Olh/exp.html

Penny Toss
http://www.fi.edu/fellows/fellow7/mar99
/probability/penny_toss.shtml

WebQuests
http://edweb.sdsu.edu/WebQuest/

WebWhacker
http://www.bluesquirrel.com/products
/whacker/whacker.html

WorldVillage/Parental Controls
http://www.worldvillage.com/family
/parental.html

Yahooligans!
http://www.yahooligans.com/

Plug-ins

Adobe Acrobat Reader Plug-in
http://www.adobe.com/products/acrobat/readstep2.html

Apple QuickTime
http://www.apple.com/quicktime/download/

HyperStudio Plug-in
http://www.hyperstudio.com/quickstart/index.html

Macromedia Flash Player
http://www.macromedia.com/software/flashplayer/

Macromedia's Shockwave for Director
http://www.macromedia.com/software/shockwaveplayer/

Net2Phone
http://home.netscape.com/net2phone/index.html

Plug-in Information from Netscape
http://home.netscape.com/plugins/index.html

RealOne Player by RealNetworks
http://home.netscape.com/plugins/get_real.html

Search Engines

About.com
http://www.about.com/

AltaVista
http://www.altavista.com

Excite
http://www.excite.com

Go.com
http://www.go.com/

Google
http://www.google.com

Hotbot
http://hotbot.lycos.com

LookSmart
http://www.looksmart.com

Lycos
http://www.lycos.com

WebCrawler
http://www.webcrawler.com

Metasearch Engines

Dogpile
http://www.dogpile.com/

MetaCrawler
http://www.metacrawler.com/index.html

PlusSearch.com
http://www.metacrawler.com/

Specialized Search Engines

Easy Searcher
http://www.easysearcher.com

Searchwin2000.com
http://searchwin2000.techtarget.com

Search Engines for Kids

Ask Jeeves for Kids
http://www.ajkids.com

OneKey
http://onekey.com/

Yahooligans!
http://www.yahooligans.com/

Search Strategies

Infopeople
http://infopeople.org/search/

Student Publication Sites

CyberKids
http://www.cyberkids.com

The Diary Project
http://www.diaryproject.com

Global Show-N-Tell
http://www.telenaut.com/gst/

Kids' Space
http://www.kids-space.org

TeenLit.com
http://www.teenlit.com/about.htm

Yahooligans! Publishing on the Web
http://www.yahooligans.com/School_Bell
/Language_Arts/Writing
/Publishing_on_the_Web/

Sample AUPs

Chico Unified School District
http://wombat.cusd.chico.k12.ca.us/aup/

Hazelton Area School District
http://www.hasd.k12.pa.us/aup.shtml

Norfolk Public Schools
http://www.nps.k12.va.us/Norfolk
/aupform.html

Responsible Netizen
http://netizen.uoregon.edu/templates
/model_policy.html

Richmond Public Schools
http://www.richmond.k12.va.us/users
/policies/aup.html

South Washington County Schools
http://mustang.coled.umn.edu/Started
/use/Dist833pol.html

8

DISTANCE LEARNING

A Scenario

Carla turned on her computer to teach her virtual Trig class. She was beginning to really enjoy teaching her high school students this way. She loved the flexibility it offered her (she could work at home and save on child care expenses), as well as the options it opened up for the students. Individually, she knew that none of the small rural schools could justify a Trig class on their own. Together, they were able to support her salary and give students a chance to prepare for college. Most of her students participated in the course while attending a physical high school; however, she also had three students who were homebound for medical reasons, five who were being home-schooled, and one who had been suspended from school.

As she logged into the classroom site, her first step was to read and respond to the private e-mail messages from her students. Larry wrote that he didn't understand the last assignment, and Rodney thanked her for her recommendations on a new graphing calculator. She made a note to call Tammy's parent later because Tammy had not responded to her "Where are you?" messages for the past ten days.

Next, she checked the bulletin board, where students could post messages for everyone in the class to read. Then she downloaded and assessed all of the assignments that had been sent to her drop-box. After she was finished evaluating the assignments and sending e-mail messages to the students regarding their work, she posted the grades in the virtual gradebook. She knew, all too well, that the students would be checking the gradebook almost continuously (or so it seemed) to check their progress.

Today's lesson was in two parts—one synchronous and one asynchronous. The synchronous portion consisted of a virtual classroom session through HorizonLive. Carla had prepared a PowerPoint presentation for the class, along with questions that she could ask during the session. At precisely 2:00, she launched the program and waited for the students to sign on before beginning the lesson. She really liked using synchronous communications for some of the more complex and abstract portions of the curriculum. She was able to speak to the class (via streaming audio) just as if they were in the same room. She could also ask them questions (via polling techniques) and receive immediate responses. They could raise their virtual hands to ask her questions at any time.

The other part of the lesson was asynchronous. For this portion, she used WebCT, where she had placed the instructional materials and assignment, created a new topic on the bulletin board, and posted links to other relevant web sites.

Even though Carla had not met some of her students in person, she felt that she knew them—perhaps even better than she would if they were in a "regular" high school. She interacted with them individually every day and knew their strengths and weaknesses in relation to trigonometry and other topics. Distance education did not seem nearly so "distant" anymore.

INTRODUCTION

Teaching and learning are no longer confined to the walls of a classroom or to specific hours in a day. There are many technologies that make it possible to provide interaction, assessment, and collaboration, no matter when, where, or how the instruction is distributed. This chapter provides an overview of distance learning possibilities that range from sending a videotape to a homebound student to developing a virtual high school. Topics of this chapter include:

- Definition of distance learning

- Educational applications

- Audio technologies for distance learning

- Video technologies for distance learning

- Computer technologies for distance learning

DEFINITION OF DISTANCE LEARNING

The term *distance learning* has many synonyms (such as e-learning and distributed education). This chapter will define distance learning as instruction that takes place when the teacher and students are separated by distance or time. The focus will be on interactive exchanges that involve the use of technology.

Approaches to distance learning can be roughly classified as synchronous or asynchronous. *Synchronous* means "occurring at the same time." In other words, the instructor and the student are communicating in "live" discussions, even if they are miles apart. Synchronous communication provides immediate feedback; however, it also requires that the students and teacher schedule a meeting time, which can be difficult to do in multiple time zones.

Asynchronous communications occur at different times. For example, when you send an e-mail message, it is not usually read until much later. Asynchronous instruction is easier for students and teachers to fit into their schedules, but may involve delayed feedback. Table 8.1 presents common synchronous and asynchronous technologies that will be discussed in this chapter.

Table 8.1. Common Synchronous and Asynchronous Technologies

Technology	Synchronous	Asynchronous
Audio	Audioconferences (telephone) Audioconferences (Internet)	Audiotapes Streaming audio
Video	Satellite videoconferences Desktop videoconferences Microwave television	Videotapes Cable and broadcast TV Streaming video
Computer	Internet chat Shared whiteboards Application sharing	E-mail Instructional web sites Informational web sites

EDUCATIONAL APPLICATIONS

Distance learning initiatives have been common at universities and colleges for many years; now, we are witnessing an increased implementation in K–12 schools. The major benefits of distance learning include the convenience and flexibility it offers for students to interact with instructors and educational content. Several studies have found that distance learning is equal to or more effective than traditional instruction when the following criteria are met (Moore and Thompson 1990; Verduin and Clark 1991):

1. The method and technologies used are appropriate to the instructional tasks.

2. There is student-to-student interaction.

3. There is timely teacher-to-student feedback.

Several applications exist for distance education in K–12 schools. Although some applications, such as delivering instruction via the web, require minimal expenditures, other applications, such as the contract delivery of courses, require major curricular decisions and significant financial commitments.

Homebound and Home-Schooled Students

One of the original educational applications of distance education was to provide a classroom connection for students who were homebound because of illness or injury. As the number of home-schooled children increases, their parents are looking for instruction via a distance. There are several options. For example, assignments and activities can be shared through web sites, videotapes of classroom presentations or lectures can be sent, or Internet videoconferencing can be used.

Virtual High Schools

Several states and school districts now offer classes through a virtual high school. In most cases, these are web-based programs where the students participate via e-mail, bulletin boards, chat, and file transfers with a teacher/facilitator. These programs are designed to meet the needs of homebound students, home-schooled students, students who are suspended, as well as those who simply want to take courses that are not offered at a physical high school. Virtual high schools are increasing in popularity; it is possible to earn an entire high school diploma online.

The Classroom Guest Speaker

Video and audioconferencing allow the instructor to bring into the classroom a guest who would normally be unable to visit. Long distances, difficult travel conditions, or busy schedules make it impractical for many individuals to visit school classrooms as guest speakers. A telephone line into the classroom and a good speakerphone can solve these problems. Prominent persons are usually more willing to take 15 minutes to talk with a class by telephone than to spend a couple of hours traveling to and from the school. Numerous web sites also offer access to experts via e-mail and chat.

Distance Tutoring and Mentoring

Some school systems have begun distance-learning initiatives to give students access to tutors during the early evening or weekend hours. The tutors can usually work at their homes or at a central location and communicate with the students via e-mail, chat, or videoconferencing. Active community programs often encourage students and parents to become involved in the tutoring program.

Distributed Classes

A number of school districts in less-populated areas are using distance learning to share teachers among several schools. In this way, the few students who need a course in each school can add up to a single class large enough to justify the cost of a teacher. The teacher stays at one school, but classrooms in several other schools can be linked through the Internet, telephone, or video to the teacher's classroom. Proctors or teacher's aides supervise the students in the remote classrooms, distribute learning materials, and administer tests.

Contract Courses

Some companies now provide selected courses to schools that cannot offer those courses in the traditional manner. Foreign-language and advanced math topics are among the most common. These courses are normally delivered through satellite television channels with audio teleconferencing for student interaction. Examples include the Satellite Educational Resources Consortium (SERC) and StarNet.

Staff Development and In-Service Programs

Distance learning offers many opportunities for staff development and training. Some districts are using local cable television stations to reach teachers in off-hours; others are designing web-based training courses. All these options are appealing to teachers, who dedicate long hours each day at school, and may not have the time to travel to the district office or local university for more training.

AUDIO TECHNOLOGIES FOR DISTANCE LEARNING

Standard telephone technologies have been in use since the 1940s to provide educational opportunities to people who are separated by distance. The audio component of a distance-learning course can be as simple as a telephone call, or it can be as complex as an audioconference with microphones, telephone bridges, and speakers.

Audiotapes

Audiotapes (cassettes) are inexpensive, easily copied, and versatile. If a student misses class for a week or so, the best option might be to tape some of the classroom presentations. Audio is especially useful in courses that require the nuances of inflection, such as foreign languages.

When using audiotapes for instruction, be sure to record them using the best equipment possible. A low hiss during the recording process may result in a major distraction when the copy is played. Also, include print materials to enhance the tapes, and encourage interactions via voicemail, e-mail, fax, or other means.

Audioconferences via Telephone

Audioconferences that only involve two or three people are relatively easy to set up—many phones have options to "conference," or the phone service may provide a method to place a three-way call. Audioconferences for larger groups of people are more complex and may require speakerphones and telephone bridges.

Speakerphones

Speakerphones have been improved in the past several years, but they still have some limitations. Common speakerphones are called *simplex* message devices. This means they do not allow simultaneous two-way conversations. In other words, the people at both ends of the connection cannot talk at the same time. In some ways, this process is like that of water flowing through a pipe. The water can go in either direction, but it can go in only one direction at any moment.

This flow is in contrast to the standard telephone handset, which is called a *duplex* message device. A standard handset is more like a water system with two pipes—one for water going in each direction. In a standard telephone handset, the earpiece and the microphone are sufficiently separated to prevent faint sounds coming through the earpiece from feeding back into the microphone.

When a person's voice is coming through a speakerphone, however, the standard speakerphone must turn off its microphone. If it is not turned off, the incoming sound will be picked up by the microphone and almost instantly routed directly back to the person originating the message. At the least, this creates a strong echo of the speaker's voice. More likely, it causes a feedback squeal similar to that generated when a microphone is too close to a loudspeaker in a public-address system.

When the distant person pauses, or when someone in a classroom talks loudly, the standard speakerphone switches off its speaker and activates its microphone. At this point, the voice of the distant person is cut off, and the flow reverses so that the distant person can hear what is being said in the classroom. Modern speakerphones are capable of making these simplex changes in direction so quickly that it is usually only a minor distraction.

Telephone Bridges

When more than three locations must be connected in an audioconference, the best solution is the use of a technology called the telephone *bridge*. The bridge is an electronic system that links multiple telephone lines and automatically balances all audio levels. The bridge can be provided through the telephone company or competing long-distance services, or it can be owned and operated by the school system. Unless a bridge is used several times a day, it is usually more economical to rent one.

A telephone bridge does not involve any classroom equipment other than the standard telephone line. The actual bridge system is located at the telephone company or, in the case of a privately owned system, at the school switchboard. Most school systems do not own bridges because of the number of outside telephone lines required. For example, to connect a bridge of 25 students with each in a different location, 25 telephone lines would be required.

A bridge can be either call in or call out. With a call-in bridge, participants in the telephone conference are given the bridge telephone number ahead of time. The participants then call the number at the beginning of the conference. The bridge system automatically connects the calls to the conference. A call-out bridge arrangement requires a person, usually an operator, to dial the telephone numbers of all the locations that will participate in the conference. As each number is reached, it becomes connected to the conference.

Audioconferencing via the Internet

The Internet and web have been used for some time to transfer digitized sound files. In the last couple of years, there has been an expansion of this capability into the digitization and transfer of real-time conversations. Software (given the generic name of Internet telephony software) has the ability to digitize and compress sound on the fly, meaning that it is transmitted almost the instant it is spoken. Examples of telephony software include HearMe, SpeakFreely, Net2Phone, and MaxPhone.

Talking over the Internet allows individuals and schools to bypass standard telephone charges and taxes. The only requirements are an Internet connection, a computer with sound capability, and telephony software (in most cases, both parties must be using the same software). To "call" someone, you generally enter either the person's IP address or his or her e-mail address into the software program. Long-distance communication over the Internet is currently far less expensive than standard long-distance telephone calls. It really is possible to have your students speak directly to students in another country to practice their languages.

Streaming Audio

Streaming audio is another option for merging audio into distance learning. Streaming audio allows audio files to be sent over the Internet in "real-time." That means that you do not have to wait while the file downloads. Instead, a short segment is buffered, and then the audio begins to play.

Streaming audio can be archived or played in (almost) real-time. For example, using a program such as Real SlideShow, a teacher could record audio for a lesson, then save it to a web server. Later, when a student accesses the file, it will automatically stream over the Internet and play. Another option is to use a software system such as HorizonLive, which allows a teacher to directly address a remote audience. As discussed in Chapter 4, the three major players in the streaming audio arena are Apple's QuickTime, RealNetwork's Real, and Microsoft's Windows Media.

Guidelines for Incorporating Audio Technologies

- *Distribute visual materials in advance.* If an audioconference is scheduled, handouts or other visual materials that might be of value during the presentation should be distributed to add to the audio. The materials can be sent via the Internet, regular mail, or fax.

- *Set communication protocols for an audioconference.* Because the participants will not be able to see each other, it is important to agree on protocols to help identify the speakers. Usually, it is advisable to ask all speakers to state their name before making comments. For example, "This is Mary, and I would like to comment about . . ."

- *Encourage interaction.* In an audioconference, instructors should call on specific students, ask students to take turns posing questions, and make sure that one student is not allowed to monopolize the conversation.

- *Record audioconferences on audiotapes or as streaming audio.* It is very easy to record an audioconference. Then, you can either distribute tapes for students who were unable to participate in the conference or set up a web site with audio archives in streaming format.

- *Keep it short.* It may be difficult to maintain students' interest for long periods of time without visuals. Therefore, when using audio technologies for distance learning, make sure the audio segments are short, well-planned, and supplemented with visual materials.

- *Beware of extraneous sounds.* Background noises, electrical interference, and other sounds can be extremely distracting and irritating for distant students. If possible, record audio lessons in a room designed for that purpose.

VIDEO TECHNOLOGIES

The ability to see and hear an instructor offers opportunities for behavior modeling, demonstrations, and instruction of abstract concepts. Video techniques for distance learning are often driven by the transmission media (videotapes, satellites, television cables, computers, and microwave). Each of the media can be described as to the direction of the video and audio signals—one-way video; two-way video; one-way audio; and two-way audio (see Figure 8.1, page 186).

Videotapes

Videotapes offer a popular, easy-to-use format for instructional materials. Almost all students have access to a videotape player in their homes, and they are also common at school. Videotapes can be used for demonstrations or documentaries. It is quite easy to videotape a lecture for a student who cannot attend class.

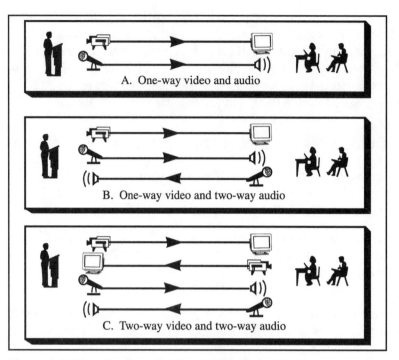

Figure 8.1. Three audio and video configurations.

Videotapes have several advantages for the delivery of distance learning. In addition to easy access to the hardware, the tapes are inexpensive. If a video camcorder is available, videotapes are relatively easy to record (although professional staff and equipment can produce a much better product than an amateur production team). One disadvantage of videotapes is that they are not interactive. In addition, they wear out with continual use and can be costly to send in the mail.

When using videotapes for instruction, record them using the best equipment available. If possible, hire professional videographers and editors to achieve professional quality. (See Chapter 5 for more information about video production.)

Satellite Videoconferencing

Satellite videoconferencing is one of the older, more established techniques for distance learning. Two distinct sets of equipment are needed for satellite systems: an *uplink*, which creates and transmits the signal to the satellite, and a *downlink*, which is necessary to receive and display the signal (see Figure 8.2).

Originating a satellite videoconference can be an expensive and complex undertaking. In most cases, a studio classroom is used, which must be properly wired for lighting, microphones, and cameras. The studio is usually connected to a control room, where one or more technicians control the television cameras and microphones. The resulting television signal is then connected to an uplink transmitter—a large satellite dish that beams the signal to the satellite. Uplink transmitters are expensive and are often shared with other schools or businesses.

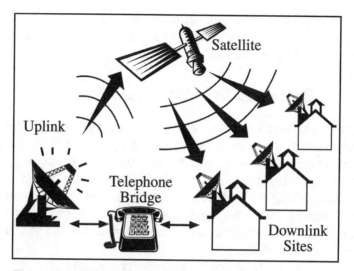

Figure 8.2. Videoconferencing via satellite.

The receiving sites of satellite videoconferences must have satellite downlinks. The most critical part of a downlink is the receiving dish antenna and its associated electronics. These dishes, common even in backyards, select and amplify the desired satellite signals. The signal is then fed into the classrooms, where it is displayed on standard television monitors or projection systems. The videoconferences are generally recorded for subsequent playback.

With regular satellite transmissions, the audio from the sending station is combined with the picture, much as it is in commercial broadcasts. To provide two-way audio with interactions from the remote students back to the teacher, a telephone bridge is usually used.

Because satellite videoconferencing is expensive, it is not cost-effective for most school systems to use uplinks to originate distance-education classes unless the school systems are in a position to market the classes over wide geographic areas. However, several state departments of education and similar entities sponsor satellite educational programs. Also, there are many companies and consortia (such as StarNet and SERC) that sell access to K–12 courses that are delivered through satellite channels.

Microwave Television Conferencing

Satellites are a popular method for enabling video communications over long distances because satellite "footprints" generally cover several states. Microwave transmissions provide a cost-effective method for educational applications of video teleconferencing in local areas. Most microwave systems are designed to transmit video signals to areas that are not more than 20 miles apart.

Microwave frequencies that have been designated by the Federal Communications Commission (FCC) as Instructional Television Fixed Service (ITFS) stations are the most popular systems. When compared with satellite or commercial broadcast television, ITFS stations operate at a low power that makes the transmission equipment more affordable. Reception equipment is also relatively inexpensive, as long as the receiving sites are located within 20 miles of the transmitter and there are no hills or tall buildings to block the signal.

ITFS has become popular with community colleges, universities, and school systems as a method of distributing courses throughout communities. By using pairs of ITFS channels, two-way video teleconferencing can be set up between a main-campus classroom and a branch-campus classroom.

One drawback of microwave ITFS communication involves the limited number of channels available in any one area. Many metropolitan areas already have all available channels in use, so no further expansion of ITFS teleconferencing is possible in these areas.

Cable and Broadcast Television

Cable and public broadcast television have been used to distribute instruction for many years. In addition to the educational networks, such as CNN, TNT Learning, and the Learning Channel, nearly all public cable television systems allow schools to transmit television courses. This type of connection can be used to transmit one-way video and one-way audio to the community at large or between specific schools. For example, if two area high schools do not each have enough students to justify an advanced math course, they might team up to teach a single course delivered through cable television. In one school, the teacher would conduct a regular class; in the other school, the students would watch and listen through a standard cable television channel.

Course distribution through cable television systems is cost-effective. In some cases, only the basic studio classroom equipment is needed if the cable company can provide a direct link to the cable system. In other cases, a microwave link or other connection is needed to send the television signal from the classroom to the front end or origination point for the cable television signals. The cost depends largely on the "partnership" offered by the cable or broadcast system. Even though the broadcast will take place at a scheduled time, students have the option to record the program and play it back at a more convenient time.

As HDTV becomes standard, cable companies will be able to offer hundreds of digital video channels to homes and schools. Many of these channels will be used for commercial entertainment purposes; however, it is expected that a large number of channels will become available for education.

Desktop Videoconferencing

Software is now available that allows videoconferencing directly over the Internet. Presently, the best-known products are NetMeeting (available free of charge from Microsoft) and CUSeeMe, which is marketed by First Virtual Communications. To transmit two-way video, a video camera is required on each workstation. A microphone, speakers (or headset), and an audio card are required for transmitting audio (see Figure 8.3).

Because transmitting video on the Internet is extremely bandwidth-intense, most conferences result in a small 160 x 120-pixel window of "motion" video (about 1/16 of the screen). The size of the image window can be increased, but the resolution is not generally increased. The pixels are simply made bigger.

Depending on the speed of the connection, the motion can range from 1 to about 15 frames per second. In most cases, a regular modem is far too slow to transmit effective video. However, cable modems and DSL connections are making Internet videoconferencing much more feasible. Just remember, the speed of transmission can be affected by many factors, including type of connection (at both ends), congestion on the Internet, and speed of computers.

Because of the transmission issues, Internet videoconferencing generally involves only two people in point-to-point transmissions. However, if you want to conference with more than that (with everyone able to send and receive video), you may need to find a reflector site. A reflector functions like a telephone bridge in that it is an Internet server computer that is running special software. When a group of people "dial in" using the reflector's Internet address, they can see and talk to each other. Multiple little windows open on each workstation, each with an image of one of the other participants.

It is possible to speak to the entire group or privately to individuals. However, for a reflector to be functional, it must have extremely fast connections. Usually a direct LAN connection or a high-speed data line is required.

If better quality is needed for videoconferencing (such as a larger screen size or more frames per second), special videoconferencing boards can be installed into computers to increase the compression of the files before they are transmitted. These boards have the ability to compress and decompress the digitized video, and thus are called *codec* boards (see Chapter 5 for more information on digital video). PictureTel and Vtel are two well-known hardware/software companies that supply desktop video solutions for schools.

A major restriction for desktop videoconferencing is the connection between the computers. Because an Internet connection may be too slow or unstable, schools will often lease a data line (such as ISDN or a T-carrier). See Chapter 7 for more information about leased data lines.

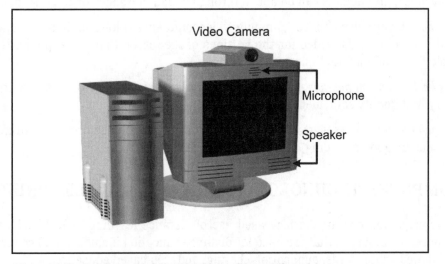

Figure 8.3. Configuration for desktop videoconferencing.

Streaming Video

Streaming video is very similar to streaming audio—a media file is compressed into a format that can be sent over the Internet in small, continuous packets. Using streaming video technology, lectures can be delivered over the Internet in real-time, meaning the students can listen and watch while you lecture, or the streaming video files can be stored on a server for playback later.

An advantage of implementing streaming video for distance learning is that video is well suited to content delivery. It can attract students' attention, enrich demonstrations, and illustrate complex procedures. Especially in web-based courses (which are very text-heavy), video can provide an good alternative for curriculum content.

Streaming technology allows large audio and video files to be played as soon as a small amount of the file has been buffered (usually within a few seconds) on the student's desktop, eliminating the need to download the entire file before playing it. It offers a low-cost, convenient way to deliver video to students—especially if the students have access to a relatively high-bandwidth connection (such as DSL or cable modem). The leaders in streaming video formats are Apple's QuickTime, RealNetwork's Real, and Microsoft's Windows Media. See Chapter 5 for more information about streaming video.

Guidelines for Incorporating Video Technologies

- *Avoid the "talking head."* Talking head refers to simply videotaping the instructor while she or he is talking. To make the video more interesting, try to vary the camera angle, include still images of appropriate graphics, and encourage student interactions.

- *Reduce distraction.* Outside noise and activity can distract from a video presentation.

- *Practice with the cameras and the crew before the lesson.* It is important to plan practice times for the instructor and the camera crew. By working together, they can anticipate each other's needs and provide the best possible instruction.

- *Encourage interactions.* Interactions can be added to video-based delivery in many ways. If the lessons are two-way, questions and other types of interactions can be included. If they are one-way video, interactions can be added through e-mail messages or the telephone.

- *Keep it short.* Many believe that a 15-minute videoconference is long enough (if you want to hold students' attention). Use video for the portions of the lesson that are appropriate; use other technologies to add interactions.

- *Use the best equipment possible.* The old saying "garbage in; garbage out" is very true of video. The very best quality equipment should be used.

- *Ensure quality audio.* Losses in audio quality will be noticed long before losses in video quality. Always ensure good recording, playback, and speaker quality.

COMPUTER TECHNOLOGIES FOR DISTANCE LEARNING

One of the major reasons for the increased use of distance learning in K–12 education is the Internet. Computer technologies that are used for distance education include e-mail communications, Internet chat, shared whiteboards, application sharing, and web-based education.

E-mail Communications

Sending and receiving e-mail messages is a common and inexpensive way for students to communicate with peers and instructors. In some cases, a formal, correspondence-type course can be created via e-mail. In other cases, informal e-mail messages supplement "traditional" classes or enhance more complex distance-learning technologies, such as videoconferencing.

Many faculty members establish bulletin boards or listservs for distance-learning classes to facilitate the interactions among the students. In bulletin boards (also called discussion groups or newsgroups), students can post messages or read messages that others have posted. For example, a literature teacher may ask students to read a novel and post responses to specific issues on the class bulletin board. Students can then read each others' responses and participate in online discussions.

Listservs are e-mail distribution systems that are set up for a purpose or group. For example, you may establish a biology listserv for all the students enrolled in biology. If you want to communicate with all students, you can simply send one e-mail message (addressed to the list), and all students will receive it. Students can also send messages to the list, and they will automatically be distributed to all other members of the listserv.

Internet Chat

Internet chat refers to synchronous, interactive exchanges on the Internet. In *chat mode*, two or more people at remote computers connect to the same "chat room" and type messages. As each types his or her message, the others can see the messages on a shared screen.

The advantages of Internet chat are that it provides immediate feedback (rather than waiting for an answer to an e-mail message), and it is feasible with very low bandwidth. Students can chat with each other about assignments, or instructors can hold virtual office hours to chat with students who have questions. To eliminate the potential for "predators" on the Internet, chat rooms should be confined to students and accessed through passwords.

Shared Whiteboards

Shared whiteboards are another form of collaboration of the Internet. Shared whiteboards consist of graphic programs with basic tools for editing rectangles, patterns, and text, etc. (See Figure 8.4.) First, two people connect via e-mail or a collaborative software program; then, as one opens the whiteboard, it will appear on both screens.

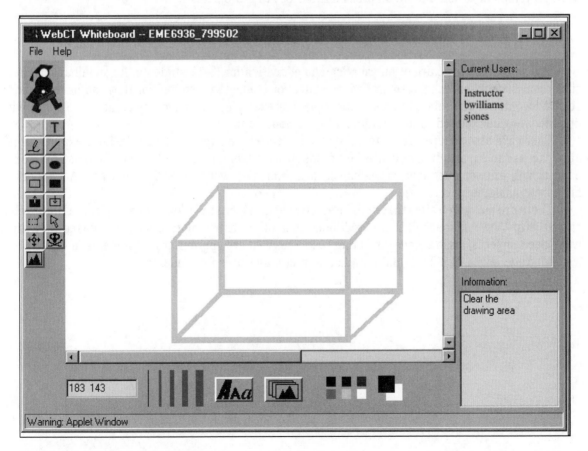

Figure 8.4. Whiteboard in WebCT.

With software that supports shared whiteboards, it is possible to create an image collaboratively (both parties can create or edit on the whiteboard at the same time). It is also possible to paste an image onto the white board, then collaboratively edit it. For example, if a teacher was discussing a geometry problem with a homebound student, she or he could either create the geometric drawing on the whiteboard or "mark" on an image that was pasted into the whiteboard. If the connection is fast enough, the teacher can discuss the graphic with the student at the same time. (If the connection is not fast enough, they can talk on the telephone while viewing the image on the web.)

Application Sharing

Some advanced collaboration software (such as NetMeeting) allows users at remote sites to share applications. For example, an instructor may have PageMaker on his or her computer and be able to display it on a remote student's computer. The student and teacher will both be able to input data and make revisions.

Like shared whiteboards, application sharing is started after two people have connected to a similar software program on the web. After a connection has been made, one of the participants can initiate "sharing." At that point, any program that is on his or her computer can be opened, and it will appear on both screens. Although either participant can input data, only one person can control the mouse or keyboard at a time. Therefore, there is usually a "relinquish mouse control" or similar button to transfer control back and forth between participants. Shared applications are a great way to teach difficult software programs or to collaborate on presentations or other projects.

Informational and Instructional Web Sites

The web offers a wealth of information and education for K–12 students. As an enhancement to classroom instruction, teachers can find web sites for students to explore, or they can have students search for information related to a specific topic. For example, a teacher may create a web page with links to web sites related to the rain forest for a science unit.

There are also several web sites that provide access to experts. These "ask-an-expert" pages allow access to experts in many different fields, from astronauts to zookeepers. In most cases, the experts will answer questions via e-mail in less than two weeks (see Pitsco's Ask An Expert at http://www.askanexpert.com/).

There are many web sites that offer interactive lessons for students. For example, the Blue Web'n site at http://www.kn.pacbell.com/wired/bluewebn/ offers a list of tutorials, web-based activities, web-based projects, lesson plans, and other resources that are appropriate for students in various topics and grade levels. See Table 8.2 for a list of interactive sites for students.

Table 8.2. Instructional Web Sites

Explore Science	http://www.ExploreScience.com/
Eyes on Art	http://www.kn.pacbell.com/wired/art2/
Foreign Languages for Travelers (learn over 80 languages)	http://www.travlang.com/languages/
Gallery of Online Interactive Geometry	http://www.geom.umn.edu/apps/gallery.html
The Heart: An Online Exploration	http://sln2.fi.edu/biosci/heart.html
HTML Tutorial (interactive tutorial about HTML)	http://fcit.coedu.usf.edu/david
Human Anatomy Online & Automotive Learning Online	http://www.innerbody.com/
Stock Market Game	http://www.smg2000.org/frm_rules.html
Japanese Lessons	http://www.japanese-online.com/language/index.htm
MathMol (mathematics and molecules online experiments)	http://www.nyu.edu/pages/mathmol/
Physics 200	http://www.Colorado.EDU/physics/2000
WebQuest Examples	http://edweb.sdsu.edu/webquest/matrix.html

Interactive sites that are designed for K–12 teachers are also on the web. *A Teacher's Guide to the Holocaust* at http://fcit.usf.edu/Holocaust/ provides over 3,000 images, sounds, original plays, student activities, movies, quizzes, and links to relevant Holocaust sites for teachers to use in the classroom (see Figure 8.5, page 194).

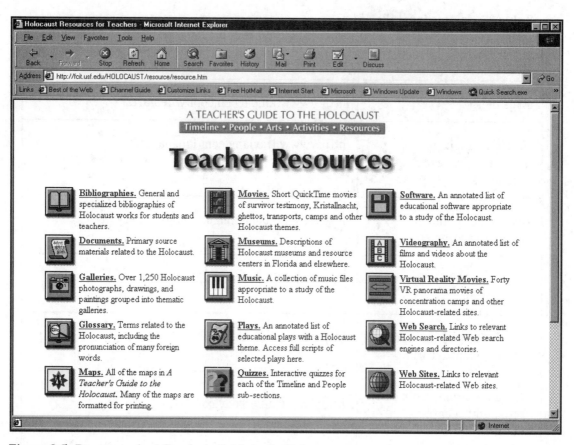

Figure 8.5. Resources in *A Teacher's Guide to the Holocaust.*

Web-Based Courses

Web-based, virtual high school courses (even complete diploma programs) are becoming more common; most involve a combination of technologies, including print, audio, video, and computer. For example, the student will interact with the teachers and other students through a web site that contains bulletin boards, e-mail, chat, etc., and may also receive videotapes or textbooks to supplement the course. Many individual schools and districts are designing their own courses, and there are commercial companies and organizations, such as Class.com, Apex, Florida Virtual School, Keystone National High School, and Virtual High School, that offer courses on a national or international basis.

If teachers want to create an online course, they can use HTML or one of the HTML editors, such as FrontPage, DreamWeaver, or Netscape Composer. Recently, several courseware management tools have also appeared on the market. These programs allow teachers to quickly place syllabi, activities, quizzes, and instruction on the web. They also provide access to bulletin boards, chat rooms, and e-mail (see Figure 8.6). Passwords help to keep student records secure, and students can view their status in the online gradebook at any time.

WebCT, Blackboard, and Learning Space are examples of web course management software. These programs are similar in design and structure, and they are quite easy to use. First, the software must be installed on a web server at a school. Then, the instructor creates an online class by entering the names and initial passwords for the students. Instructional materials are created by adding HTML files or by linking to other web sites. Built-in quiz generators can also be used. When the course is ready, a student can access it from any web browser, sign-in with a password, and view the materials. Students can leave messages for each other or their instructor, and they can participate in online chat sessions. Presentations with streaming audio or video can also be incorporated.

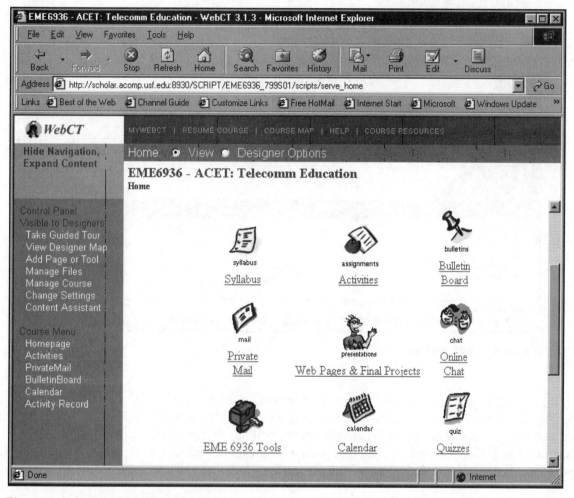

Figure 8.6. Sample WebCT interface.

Synchronous Virtual Classrooms

Course management software (such as WebCT and Blackboard) are designed primarily for asynchronous courses—teachers post instruction and assignments, and students interact via e-mail and bulletin boards. There is another "breed" of software that is designed to aid synchronous virtual classrooms. For example, HorizonLive, Centra, WebEx, and other software systems enable one-way "live" video/audio and two-way interactivity.

For example, Figure 8.7 represents a typical screen in HorizonLive. Note that a small image of the instructor is located in the lower right corner. The top part of the screen is a presentation that is controlled by the instructor, along with streaming audio. While the presentation is taking place, students can send e-mail messages with questions or interact through a chat area.

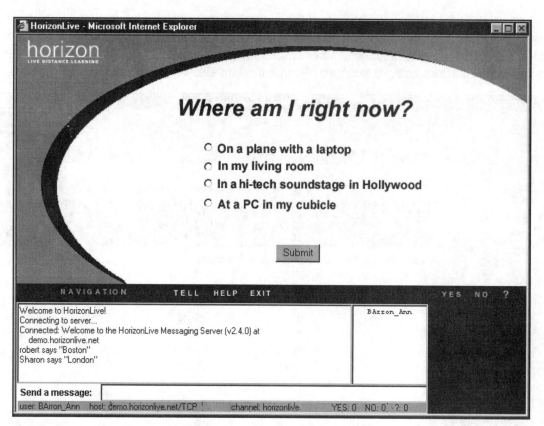

Figure 8.7. HorizonLive interface.

The instructor can also "poll" the students by asking them questions. The students can respond by clicking an answer on the screen (which is immediately tallied and reported to the instructor). Participants can "raise their hands," indicate yes/no polling, demonstrate laughter and applause responses, use public/private text chat, and provide anonymous feedback to the leader and presenters. For students who are unable to "attend" the virtual class, sessions can be recorded for playback later.

Guidelines for Incorporating Computer Technologies

- *Ensure equitable access.* Although it's easy to obtain an e-mail account through Yahoo, Hotmail, and the like, not all students will have a computer at home with Internet access. Never assign a project that requires Internet access unless you are sure that all students will be able to connect.

- *Encourage the use of e-mail for one-to-one communications.* Sometimes a student will seek assistance by e-mail more readily than he or she would in a classroom environment.

- *Establish realistic expectations.* Some students will panic if they don't receive an answer to an e-mail message in thirty minutes. Set the "ground rules" up-front and let the students know how quickly they can expect an answer (teachers deserve a break, too!).

- *Provide adequate structure and guidelines*. The most successful learning activities include deadlines and a structure. Although distance learning is often touted as "any time, any place, any path, any pace," it is unrealistic to let students set their own schedule in most situations. Instead, let them know what the deadlines are, providing as much flexibility as possible.

- *Provide timely feedback to students*. Since the communications in computer-based distance learning are more impersonal than video-based delivery, it is important to provide quick and relevant feedback to students.

- *Encourage collaboration*. If you are teaching several students via a distance, you may have to "require" them to collaborate on projects or post messages to the bulletin board. Be sure to provide sufficient guidelines for the projects and the postings.

- *Ensure sufficient technical support*. Alleviate student frustrations with hardware or software issues. The support may consist of a toll-free number, online help, *FAQs* (frequently asked questions), or a mentor. In some cases, teachers of distance learning courses wear a beeper so that students can reach them in an emergency.

SUMMARY

Distance-learning initiatives in K–12 education offer new options for rural, home-schooled, disenfranchised, and homebound students and others.

Most e-learning courses use a "blended" approach—combining print, audio, video, and computer technologies, in both asynchronous and synchronous formats. The best solution should be determined only after extensive analyses of the content, the audience, the instructor, and the technology. The following factors can serve as keys to the success of your distance-learning initiatives:

- Conduct a complete analysis of the content, audience, instructor, and technology.

- Provide ample time for designing the course and training the instructor.

- Ensure an adequate support structure for the students.

- Include a back-up plan for the technology.

- Give consistent and timely feedback to the students.

- Encourage student-to-student interactions.

GLOSSARY

56Kbps data line. A special telephone line that is designed to transmit computer data at 56Kbps. It will probably be replaced by ISDN lines over the next few years.

analog. Information stored as an electrical signal with a continuous scale. Videotape and audiotape are analog.

asynchronous. Communications between the student and teacher that do not take place simultaneously.

audio bridge. A method used to connect multiple telephone lines for an audioconference.

audioconferencing. Voice-only communications linking two or more sites. In most cases, standard telephone lines and speakerphones are employed.

audiographic conferencing. Voice communications supplemented with the transmission of still images. Pictures, graphs, or sketches can be transmitted during the conference. Standard facsimile (fax) machines are used, or computer-driven systems can be used.

bandwidth. The transmission capacity of a telecommunications system. The greater the bandwidth, the greater the amount of digital information that can be transmitted per second.

baud rate. How many bits a modem can send or receive per second. Derived from the name of Emil Baudot, a nineteenth-century inventor.

bookmarks. A list of sites that can be saved by browser software. The hotlist enables a user to access favorite sites without retyping the URL.

bps (bits-per-second). A measure for bandwidth or speed of modem transmission. Common rates are 28,800 and 56,000.

bridge. A device, often leased through a telephone company, that links three or more telephone lines together for audio teleconferencing. See call-in bridge and call-out bridge.

browser. A software program used to look at various Internet resources. Browsers are either text- or graphics-based.

bulletin board. A computer-based meeting place (and its accompanying software) that allows people to discuss topics of interest, upload and download files, and make announcements.

byte. A set of bits that represents a single character. Usually there are eight bits in a byte.

C-band. Satellite transmissions used in older homes, which requires a large 6 to 8 foot antenna.

call-in bridge. A telephone bridge where the conference is established by having all of the distant sites call in to the bridge telephone number. Long-distance charges are billed to the distant locations.

call-out bridge. A telephone bridge where one location calls all distant sites to connect each site to the teleconference. Any long-distance charges are billed to the one originating location.

capture. To save a file to your computer from a remote system. Capturing data, or saving to disk, allows the user to view or print online data at a later time.

CD-ROM. A small optical disc that can store over 650MB of digital data.

chat mode. Synchronous exchange of text through the Internet.

client. A software program used to contact and obtain data from a server program on another computer; a computer running this software.

closed circuit television. A point-to-point television distribution system installed on a wire-based system. It's used in many schools.

codec (compression-decompression). An electronic device that converts standard television signals into compressed digital signals for transmission. The same device can convert incoming compressed digital signals back into viewable television signals. A codec allows motion images to be transmitted through special telephone lines.

commercial online service provider. A company that provides various online services through a service agreement with the user. Examples are America Online, CompuServe, and Prodigy. Most of these services also provide access to the Internet.

compressed file. A computer file that has been reduced in size through a compression program, such as PKZIP. The user must decompress these files before using.

compression. Digital signal-processing techniques that are used to reduce the amount of information in a video signal. This allows the video signal to be sent through telephone data lines.

connect time. The length of time a user is connected to an online service, such as CompuServe or America Online.

database. A collection of information, usually organized with searchable elements or fields. For example, a library catalog may be searched by author, title, or subject.

dedicated telephone line. A permanent telephone connection between computers. Usually a regular phone line that is not used for anything but data transmission.

desktop videoconference. Multimedia microcomputers are used to display live video images that are transmitted over LANs or digital data lines.

dial-up connection. A temporary, as opposed to dedicated, connection between machines established over a standard phone line.

digital. Information that is stored in bits and bytes. Computer data is digital.

digital data line. A telephone line that is designed to transmit computer data rather than human voices. See 56Kbps data line, ISDN, T1 line, and T3 line.

downlink. A location that receives a video teleconference from a satellite.

download. To transfer a file from a remote computer to your own.

duplex. A process that allows information to flow in both directions at once, like a standard telephone conversation. Contrasts with simplex.

e-mail (electronic mail). Messages that are sent via a computer network, that is, electronically. The messages are stored until the addressee accesses the system and retrieves the message.

fax (facsimile machine). An electronic device that transmits text or graphics material over telephone lines to other locations.

FAQ (frequently asked questions). Files maintained at many Internet sites, especially newsgroups that provide answers to common problems. Intended to bring novices up to speed without posting repetitive questions.

fiber optic. Network cable made from glass. Transmits data at extremely fast rates.

GIF (graphic interchange format). A widely used format for image files.

graphical user interface (GUI) browsers. Mouse/icon-oriented software used to search the web. GUI browsers automatically display the graphics embedded in web pages and usually can be configured to access multimedia features, such as sound. Mosaic and Netscape are two very popular GUI browsers.

graphics tablet. A computer device that converts hand-drawn images into digital information that can be displayed on computer screens.

home page. The introductory page to a web site.

HTML (hypertext markup language). Coding language used to create hypertext documents to be posted on the web. HTML code consists of embedded tags that specify how a block of text should appear, or that specify how the word is linked to another file on the Internet. HTML documents are viewed with a browser, such as Netscape.

HTML editor. A software program that helps to create documents in HTML by automatically embedding the code or tags.

http (hypertext transport protocol). The protocol for moving hypertext files across the Internet; the most important protocol used on the web.

hypermedia. A program that contains links to other media, such as audio, video, or graphics files.

hypertext. Any text that contains links to other documents or files.

Internet. An Internet is a network. The term Internet is usually used to refer to a collection of networks interconnected with routers. What has been commonly called the Internet (with the capital I) is the largest Internet in the world.

ISDN (integrated services digital network). A modern telephone system that allows rapid digital transmission of sound, data, and images.

ISP (Internet service provider). A company or other group that provides access to the Internet through dial-up, SLIP/PPP, or direct connection.

ITFS (instructional television fixed service). A set of microwave frequencies that have been designated for use by educational facilities. Allows line-of-sight television transmissions over ranges of about 20 miles.

JPEG (Joint Photographic Experts Group). A common file format for images.

LAN (local area network). A computer network limited to a building or area of a building.

leased line. A phone line established for exclusive data connections from one location to another.

listserv. A common type of automated mailing list distribution system, developed originally on BITNET, but now common on the Internet. Subscribers receive all messages posted to the list.

microwave. A high-frequency transmission that can be used for television signals or computer data. Microwave transmissions are said to be line of sight, which means that they cannot pass through tall buildings or mountains.

modem (modulator-demodulator). A device that enables a computer to transmit and receive data from another computer through a phone line by converting the data into sound.

MPEG (Motion Picture Experts Group). A digital video file format.

newsgroup. Discussion forum on the Internet.

offline. Literally, not connected. Used to denote time spent preparing information to upload to a remote system or to read information downloaded from a remote system.

online. Communications via a modem or network to a host system; the time the user is actually logged into the host.

packet. A chunk of data sent across a network. In packet switching, the data being transmitted from one computer to another is broken into packets; each packet has the addresses of its origin and where it is going. These chunks mingle in the same lines and are directed and sorted along the way. This system allows more than one person on a line at the same time.

parameters. Values that must be set in a telecommunications software program, including number of stop bits, start bits, and speed.

PPP (point-to-point protocol). A protocol that provides a method for TCP/IP to run over a standard phone line. PPP is newer and faster than SLIP.

protocol. A description of message formats and the rules computers must follow to exchange those messages.

router. A computer or software package that handles the traffic between two or more networks.

server. A computer, or software package, that provides a specific service for client software running on other computers. For example, a web server provides for clients access to the web.

shareware. Software made available free for a limited time. After a trial period, the user is asked to pay a fee to the developer.

simplex. A communication process that allows information to flow in only one direction at a time. Common speakerphones are simplex devices because only one person can speak at a time. It contrasts with duplex.

synchronous. Communications between the student and teacher that take place simultaneously.

T1 line. A special type of telephone line that transmits digital information at a high rate. These lines are much more expensive than regular telephone lines.

T3 line. A telephone line that is capable of transmitting digital information at rates even higher than those of a T1 line.

TCP/IP (transmission control protocol/Internet protocol). The language used by computers to transmit data on the Internet.

telecommunications software. A program that allows a computer to communicate through a modem to another computer. Most telecommunications software can be configured so that dialing and setting of parameters are automatic.

teleconferencing. Electronic techniques that are used to allow three or more people at two or more locations to communicate.

uplink. The site for a video conference from which a signal is sent to a satellite.

upload. The process of sending a file from one computer to another.

URL (uniform resource locator). Addressing scheme used to identify Web sites.

videoconferencing. Transmitting motion video and audio to two or more locations for interactive conferencing.

World Wide Web. The network of hypertext servers, which allows text, graphics, and sound files to be mixed together and accessed through hyperlinks.

whiteboard. A graphic display that can be shared by two or more users on a network.

RESOURCES

American Center for the Study of Distance Education
http://www.ed.psu.edu/acsde/

American Journal of Distance Education
http://www.ed.psu.edu/acsde/ajde/jour.asp

Annenberg/CPB Channel
http://www.learner.org/channel/about.html

Apex Learning
http://www.apexlearning.com/

AT&T Learning Network
http://www.att.com/learningnetwork/

Blackboard
http://www.blackboard.com/

Blue Web'n
http://www.kn.pacbell.com/wired/bluewebn

CallMASTER
http://www.callmaster.com/

Class.com
http://www.class.com/

CNNfyi.com: News for Students; Resources for Teachers
http://www.cnn.com/fyi/

CUSeeMe
http://www.cuseeme.com/

Distance Education at a Glance
http://www.uidaho.edu/evo/distglan.html

Distance Education Clearinghouse
http://www.uwex.edu/disted/denews.htm

Distance Learning: About.com
http://distancelearn.about.com/

Distance Learning Resource Network
http://www.dlrn.org

eSchool News
http://www.eschoolnews.org/

Florida Virtual School
http://www.flvs.net/

Illinois Online Network
http://illinois.online.uillinois.edu

Jonesknowledge.com
http://www.jonesknowledge.com/k12/index.html

Keystone National High School
http://www.keystonehighschool.com/

LearningChannel.org
http://www.learningchannel.org/front.shtml

LearningSpace
http://www.lotus.com/learningspace

MaxPhone
http://www.maxphone.com/index.html

Net2Phone
http://www.net2phone.com/

Net Meeting
http://www.microsoft.com/windows/netmeeting/

NetPhones
http://home.rochester.rr.com/netphones/

No Significant Difference Phenomenon
http://teleeducation.nb.ca/nosignificantdifference/

Online Learning Magazine
http://www.onlinelearningmag.com/

PictureTel
http://www.picturetel.com/home.asp

Pitsco's Ask An Expert
http://www.askanexpert.com/

Satellite Educational Resources Consortium (SERC)
http://www.serc.org

Satlink: Satellite Programming Guide for Educators
http://www.msbanet.org/satlink

SpeechSoft
http://www.speechsoft.com/prodsw_cm.htm

Speak Freely
http://www.fourmilab.ch/speakfree/windows

Star Schools
http://www.ed.gov/prog_info/StarSchools/

TEAMS Distance Learning
http://teams.lacoe.edu

TNT Learning
http://www.learning.turner.com

United States Distance Learning Association
http://www.usdla.org

Virtual High School
http://vhs.concord.org/

VTEL
http://www.vtel.com/

WebCT
http://www.webct.com

World Lecture Hall
http://www.utexas.edu/world/lecture/index.htmll

REFERENCES

Moore, M. G., and M. M. Thompson. 1990. *The effects of distance learning: A summary of the literature.* Research Monograph No. 2. University Park, The Pennsylvania State University, American Center for the Study of Distance Education (ED 330 321).

Verduin, J. R., and T. A. Clark. 1991. *Distance education: The foundations of effective practice.* San Francisco, CA: Jossey-Bass.

9

ASSISTIVE
TECHNOLOGIES
IN THE CLASSROOM

Julie A. Barron, M.S. OTR/L and
Christine M. Hackert CCC/SLP

A Scenario

Sally, a third grade teacher, was a little apprehensive when she learned she was to have a young boy with cerebral palsy in her classroom. Sally knew her student, David, would have support from an occupational therapist and a speech and language pathologist; however, she wondered if he would be able to communicate effectively with the other children. She was also concerned about how she would help him to grow intellectually.

David is an 8-year-old boy with cerebral palsy and impaired vision. He uses an electric wheelchair with a joystick control for mobility and has limited use of both of his arms. He has fair control of his shoulders and elbows, but has difficulty with fine motor control of his hands. David also has a hard time forming words, limiting his ability to communicate with his peers and teachers.

As the semester progresses, Sally is surprised and pleased to learn that, through the use of assistive technologies, David is able to participate in most of the classroom assignments and experience intellectual freedom with his self-expression. David uses a computer equipped with an enlarged QWERTY keyboard and a special pointer stick in his hands to type on the keyboard (without the need for isolated finger movement). Due to his limited vision, he also benefits from a screen enlargement display that allows him to see what he is typing. David can also socialize and communicate his ideas and needs through a Dynamyte using direct selection with his pointer stick.

Although she was originally hesitant about the advantages of the inclusion program (for both David and the other children in her classroom), Sally can see that everyone has benefited. Thanks to a variety of assistive technologies, David no longer feels isolated from his peers, and his classmates have found a new friend!

INTRODUCTION

Advances in technology have led to increased independence for people with disabilities in the past several years. Those who have had difficulty with communication, performing functional activities, self-care activities, and access to resources in school, work, and in the community are now able to perform these tasks with greater independence through the use of assistive technology.

Assistive technology refers to devices and services for increasing participation, independence, and control in persons with disabilities (Assistive Technology Educational Network of Florida 2001). It can be used wherever or whenever it is necessary to increase the functional capabilities of the individual. Some examples of assistive technology include, wheel chairs, walkers, pointing devices, enlarged items, high-tech and lowtech communication devices, pencil grips, adapted eating equipment, equipment to aid in self-care independence, environmental control units, and adapted computers and software. For the purposes of this chapter, we will limit our discussion to high-tech computer peripherals, software, and devices to aid in independence. We will explore a variety of input and output devices that can be instrumental in allowing for increased independence for students with disabilities.

In this chapter we will examine:

- Input devices

- Software to assist with input

- Output devices

- Software to assist with output

- Resources for further information

INPUT DEVICES

Input devices allow the user to tell the computer what to do. By far the most common input devices are the keyboard and the mouse. These and other devices can be manufactured in a variety of forms to address specific disabilities.

Alternate Keyboards

Keyboards differ according to the amount of isolated finger use needed, the arrangement of the keys, the visual acuity required to differentiate the keys, and the placement of the keyboard for ease of access. The extent of a person's disability, the cognitive ability, and the goals a person has for independence determine the input device that he or she will utilize. The following are descriptions of some of the most often used keyboards for people with disabilities.

A common option for alternative keyboard access is through a programmable device that can be customized for specific applications by using overlays. Examples of keyboards with changeable overlays include Intellikeys and Discover Board. With these systems, overlays are placed on a keyboard-like panel that has touch-sensitive cells. Individual or groups of cells are programmed to produce keyboard responses when they are touched (see Figure 9.1 for examples of Alphabet Access, Math Access, and Mouse Access overlays from Intellikeys).

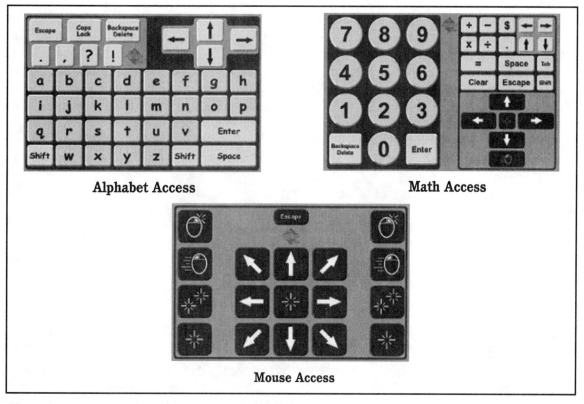

Figure 9.1. Overlay keyboards from Intellikeys.

Another approach is to use keyboards that are small and may have a reduced number of keys. These *minikeyboards* can be used for individuals who have isolated finger use or are capable of using a wand in only small spaces where the use of a standard keyboard would be difficult. When only a few keys are used, keys are often pressed in multiple combinations to produce text. Some of the keyboards can be programmed to produce full words or even phrases with combinations of simultaneous key presses. These minikeyboards vary in brand and use; however, most follow a standard size of 8 x 8 inches. Examples of minikeyboards include the TASH minikeyboard and Unicorn minikeyboard.

Enlarged keyboards can also be purchased, and they generally measure 24 x 18 inches. These keyboards are useful for people with poor finger coordination or those who require an enlarged key target area. An example of an *expanded keyboard* is the Unicorn expanded keyboard and Key Largo.

Split keyboards can place half of the keys on either side of the keyboard or they can be two separate units placed in different locations for the comfort of the user. These keyboards are sometimes referred to as *ergonomically correct keyboards* as they allow for a more natural and less stressed body position. Examples of split keyboards are Microsoft's Natural Keyboard and the MAXIM Adjustable Ergonomic Keyboard.

Joysticks and Trackballs

Joysticks, trackballs, and trackpads (or versa pads) are all alternatives to the mouse that may increase the independent use of computers for people with disabilities. In many cases, a *joystick* can directly replace a mouse; sometimes software drivers need to be modified or replaced. Joysticks can be used with most commercial software that is used with a mouse, requiring different control of the person's arms and hands to provide adequate access. Examples of joysticks include the Penny and Giles Joystick and the Palm Mouse.

A *trackball* has the rotation movement ball placed on the top of device, as opposed to the standard mouse with a rotation ball on the bottom. In other words, instead of moving a mouse around on a flat surface, a large ball may be rotated directly by a person's fingers. Because the trackballs do not move around on the desk, they can allow easier access for students with poor coordination or movement in their arms, but good control of their fingers. Examples of trackballs include the Alps Glidepoint Track Pad, the Kensington Turbo Mouse, the Thumbelina Mini Trackball, and numerous others from Logitech.

Trackpads are similar to trackballs, except a single finger can control the cursor. This input option is very common on laptop and notebook computers. In some cases (such as Macintosh iBooks), a finger is moved over a small flat surface. In others, a small, stationary protrusion (about the size of a pencil eraser) can be manipulated to control the placement of the cursor.

Touch Screens

Computer monitors with touch-sensitive screens can be used when a keyboard or mouse is not practical. The software drivers for touch screens are designed to replace the direct input created by a mouse, so students can access buttons on the screen simply by touching it with their fingers or a pointer. Touch screens can be useful for people who have difficulty understanding the cause-and-effect relationship needed to use direct connection devices. Touch screens can be purchased as special-purpose monitors, or they can be added over an existing computer monitor.

Switches

Switches are simple input devices that are plugged into programmable keyboards or other interface mechanisms. Switches can allow students with limited movement or sensory disabilities to access computers and functional devices, and to control their environment. Individuals with disabilities can use switches with just about any body part, including a hand, finger, foot, head, tongue, eyes, breath, or voice. Switches can be mechanical (requiring pressure input for activation), electromagnetic (using photosensitive or electromyographic sensors), infrared or biopotential (using beams to activate electronic devices in one's environment), or sonic (using ultrasound or voice activation).

Switches can perform many functions and control electronics ranging from toys to computers and environmental control units. Switches can operate in momentary, latching, or proportional modes. *Momentary switches* are pressure released and turn objects on/off until the switch is released. *Latching switches* turn an object on and off until the switch is hit a second time. *Proportional switches* allow for gradual acceleration as needed to start power wheel chairs. Examples of switches include the Gloswitch, Big Red Switch, Ellipse Switch, plate switch, rocker on and off switch, sip and puff switch, tilt switch, twitch switch (activated with any small muscle contraction), Jelly Bean Switch, Light Switch (requiring a person's hand just to pass over the switch), and a voice-activated switch.

Pointing Devices

Simple sticks can be strapped to an arm, held in a mouth, or worn on a head to serve as *pointing devices* to activate keyboards, touch screens, or switches. The pointing device can be held in the palm, or on the side of a student's hand with the use of a "universal cuff" to loop around the hand and hold the stick in place if his or her grip strength is compromised.

More advanced pointing systems include *optical* or *ultrasonic devices* that can be strapped to the head, such as the HeadMaster by the Prentke Romich Company and HeadMouse by Origin Instruments. These devices are for people who have good control over their head position but little or no control over their hands and feet. A sensor on the computer monitor detects head movement and positions the cursor accordingly on the screen. Simple switches controlled by air pressure from the mouth (referred to as a "sip and puff") then make appropriate selections.

Environmental Control Units

Environmental control units (ECU) are used to control (via remote) electrical appliances, telephones, and other items that typically plug into a wall. The goal of the ECU is to increase the user's independence, comfort, safety, convenience, energy, and time. ECUs vary in complexity, ranging from consumer use for people without disabilities (sound-activated devices, remote controls, light dimmers, large push button area lights) to more complex designs engineered specifically for people with disabilities. ECUs designed for people with disabilities can be used for locking and unlocking doors and controlling electric beds. They are also useful for turning on and off lamps, fans, stereos, blenders, coffee makers, pet feeders, and other household devices.

ECUs can use infrared light beams, radio frequency transmissions, ultrasound sound waves, or the house wiring electrical current to activate the desired devices. Price ranges for ECUs range from approximately $10 for over-the-counter simple devices to $6,500 for specialized devices. Common venders of ECUs include AbleNet, Inc., ACS Technologies, Infra-Link, Prentke Romich Company, TASH International, and Toys for Special Children.

SOFTWARE TO ASSIST WITH INPUT

A variety of software programs and settings can function on their own or in combination with other input devices to assist individuals with disabilities with entering information into a computer. Beginning with Windows 95, accessibility options were included on all computers running Windows software (see Figure 9.2, page 210).

A brief overview of these features includes:

- *StickyKeys*. Allows keyboard shortcuts without having to press two keys simultaneously. For example, the Print shortcut (Control, P) can be activated by pressing the keys separately.

- *FilterKeys*. Tells Windows to ignore brief or repeated keystrokes.

- *ToggleKeys*. Sounds a tone when a toggle key (such as Caps Lock) is pressed.

- *Sound Properties*. SoundSentry activates visual signals when a sound occurs. ShowSounds generates captions for sounds.

- *Display Properties*. Displays fonts and colors with high contrast.

- *General Properties*. Sets times or alerts for turning accessibility features on and off.

All of these options allow a person with a disability to access computer programs and hardware with increased accuracy and efficiency.

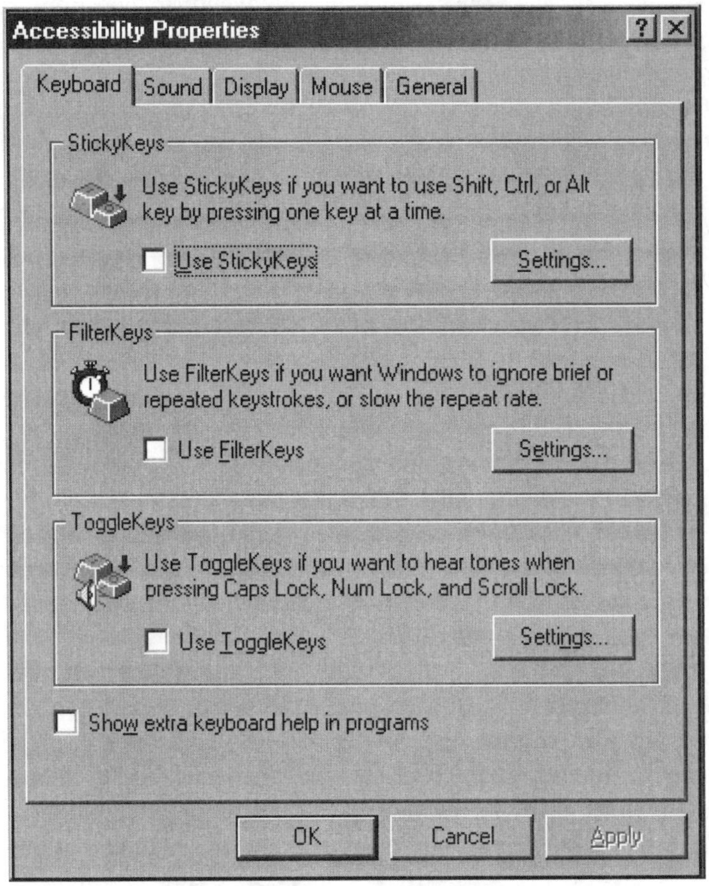

Figure 9.2. Accessibility properties in Windows.

On-Screen Keyboards

One of the most common software techniques for entering information is the *on-screen keyboard*. The software places a standard or modified illustration of a keyboard on a computer monitor (see Figure 9.3).

Figure 9.3. On-screen keyboard available in Windows accessories.

On-screen keyboards are either alternative or standard keyboards presented within the screen of the computer. Because the on-screen keyboards must occupy space on the computer screen, the keyboard usually "sits on top" of the open computer application without getting in the way of it. The on-screen computer keyboard can be accessed by either a direct selection device (e.g., mouse, joystick, or trackball) or by the use of a scanning device.

If a scanning device is used, a single switch can control it. The cursor continually scans across all the keys, and, when the switch is activated, the key is selected. In some cases, the scanners operate by narrowing down first a row, then a group of keys, and finally a single key selection. The speed of the scanning can be adjusted to the needs and reaction time of the individual; however, the overall time required to complete an activity may be greatly increased. An example of an on-screen keyboard is the Ke:nx on: Board.

Voice Recognition

As the power of computers has continued to improve, so has the efficiency of *voice recognition* software. It is now possible to use voice recognition software to issue computer commands, such as "Save file," or to take dictation. As one might expect, voice recognition software still has some limits with words that sound alike, but these programs always have options that allow for spelling individual words when needed. Voice recognition usually requires a period of training to adapt to an individual's voice. To some extent, the individual also adapts to the strengths and weaknesses of the voice recognition software itself. Over a period of time, however, the recognition process can become very efficient. See Chapter 4 for more information about voice recognition systems.

Word Prediction

When individual key presses are difficult and time-consuming for an individual, and voice recognition is not an acceptable alternative, word prediction software and abbreviation expansion can be used to enhance keyboards.

Word prediction software recognizes the first one or two strokes of a word and then displays the most frequently used words or phrases beginning with those letters. If the desired word is not shown in the list after two key presses, then the third letter is entered. In nearly all cases, the desired word appears before the entire word must be typed.

For example, if the student wants to type the word "woman," after typing the "w," the following words might appear: 1) want, 2) what, 3) who, 4) work, 5) will. By typing the next letter, "o", the following list may appear: 1) worry, 2) won't, 3) woman, 4) wok, 5) wood. Finally, by entering the number three, the student will position the word "woman" in the text in three keystrokes versus five, often followed by an automatic space (thus saving a keystroke).

In the cases in which a new word is actually typed, the software enters that word into its database and keeps track of the conditions when it was used. Word-prediction programs can greatly reduce the total key presses required, thus speeding the overall typing rate, and reducing the fatigue of an individual with a disability.

Abbreviation expansion is used to invoke frequently used larger words from the use of only a few keystrokes. This can save the person several keystrokes and thus increase the rate of typing, aid in word finding, and reduce fatigue.

OUTPUT DEVICES

Hardware devices and software exist that help provide computer information to people with disabilities. The extent of a disability determines the type of *output device*. For example, something as basic as a larger monitor can be sufficient to help a mildly vision-impaired person see the characters on the screen. For more severe cases, software can be used to expand small portions of the screen so that just a few characters cover the entire screen at any one time. For people who are blind, text-to-speech systems can almost replace the computer monitor.

Screen Magnification

The most direct way to enlarge information on the computer screen is to use a larger screen. In many cases, simply changing from a 12-inch monitor to an 18-inch monitor is all that is needed to allow visually impaired people to use a computer. This change increases the size of on-screen print by 50 percent and allows for the typical text-based screen of 25 lines with 80 characters per line.

Another option to help visually impaired people use computers is to use screen magnification software. This software allows the text and graphics to be enlarged to a variety of levels (often by 2x to 16x or more). There is a variety of magnification software available, often with a free demonstration disk. Shareware versions are available on the web, and Windows offers magnification options for screen enhancement (under *Programs ... Accessories ... Accessibility*). Figure 9.4 illustrates the options available in the Magnifier Settings for Windows.

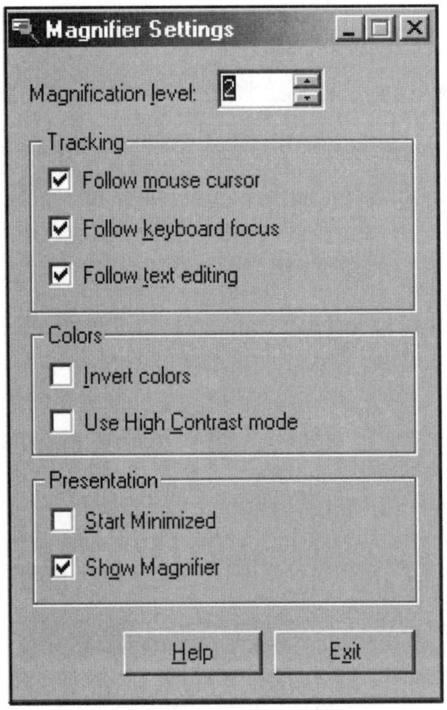

Figure 9.4. Magnifier settings in Windows.

If a student must sit extremely close to a monitor to read the information, antiglare filters can be added to the front of the monitor. The antiglare filters reduce glare, improve contrast, and protect people from ultraviolet rays and other energy emissions. These filters are clear screens that fit over the computer monitor screen.

Refreshable Braille Displays

A *refreshable Braille display* is an electronic, tactile device used to read material from a computer or Braille note taker. Refreshable Braille displays consist of a matrix of movable plastic or metal pins that typically make up from 20 to 80 Braille cells. Each "soft" cell is made up of six to eight pins to display characters as they appear on the computer or Braille note taker. The more advanced Braille displays feature eight-dot Braille, allowing for the position of the cursor in the text to be known, computer coding, and computing advanced math problems.

Electromagnetic solenoids or other devices position the pins in the cells. When the text has been read, the user pushes a button to "refresh" the display and move on to the next line of text. Full size Braille lines are 80 cells in length, which correlates with the number of characters across the width of a typical word processor screen. Braille lines with less than 80 cells will display the text in stages (e.g., a 40-cell line would display it in two stages). The smaller displays are less expensive than the 80 cell lines, making them more affordable to a larger portion of the population. The refreshable Braille display connects to the computer and usually sits under a regular keyboard with the Braille cells closest to the user.

Braille printers—properly called *embossers*—prepare permanent records of computer output by stamping indentations into paper. Some Braille embossers can print line-oriented graphics as well as standard Braille characters. Others are capable of creating double-sided printouts to include printed material and graphics.

Braille displays and Braille embossers normally require translation software that formats standard text for Braille output. In some cases, this software is supplied with the equipment, while in others it must be purchased separately.

SOFTWARE TO ASSIST WITH OUTPUT

There is no clear line between hardware and software with output devices. Most output hardware requires some form of software support. Similarly, most software enhancements require some form of special hardware to support them. The following tools, however, are probably more software than hardware.

Screen Windowing Software

Windowing software allows an individual to select a specific part of the screen to expand or "blow up" to fill the entire screen. A person with a vision disability is then able to examine the details of a portion of the screen. Windowing software is designed to work in the "background" with normal commercial applications, but it is not perfect. Products should always be tested with desired applications before they are purchased.

Text-to-Speech Conversion

Some speech-synthesis systems use *firmware*—programs stored on the sound card—to do the conversion, while other systems such as Write:OutLoud by Don Johnston use software programs. In either case, the quality of the program determines the effectiveness of the conversion. While all text-to-speech programs are designed to convert text files to speech, some also allow real-time screen conversion of text into speech. These programs are a critical component in allowing visually impaired individuals to participate in e-mail and online chat activities of the Internet. (See Chapter 4 for more information on text-to-speech conversation.)

Special Applications Programs

In addition to the creation of hardware and software that handles input and output of information, publishers have been designing programs that address specific learning needs. In particular, individuals with specific learning disabilities have a rapidly increasing assortment of software to help them. Software ranges from early vocabulary development, such as the series by Laureate Learning Systems, to scanning math calculators, such as Big:Calc by Don Johnston, that talk to its users.

SUMMARY

Computers are now tools that can help people with a variety of physical and learning disabilities. Because this is such a rapidly expanding area of computer technology, one of the greatest challenges is to keep up with what is possible. Fortunately, there are excellent support organizations at the national, state, and local levels (as listed in resources and on web sites). A first step is to get in touch with one of these agencies and identify what is available locally. Some of these technologies tend to be expensive—check with your school district or a local organization to investigate opportunities to share resources or get additional support. Also, do not overlook resources on the Internet (see resources listed at the end of this chapter). You will be pleased with the wealth of information available.

GLOSSARY

abbreviation expansion. A type of word prediction software allowing for an abbreviation to be typed, which then is automatically expanded into a commonly used word or phrase. This is designed to increase typing speed, reduce error rate, and decrease the need to type out entire words or phrases.

alternative input device. Optical head pointing, voice scanning, eye tracking, data glove, Morse code, touch tablet, or other devices that permit computer input.

alternative keyboard. A device that replaces or modifies the standard keyboard.

artificial speech. See synthesized speech.

assistive technology. Devices and services for increasing participation, independence, and control of persons with disabilities. (Assistive Technology Educational Network of Florida 2001)

Braille cell. An arrangement of raised dots. Each cell depicts a letter, number, or special character.

Braille input. A Braille-style keyboard or specific keys on a standard keyboard that function in Braille patterns.

Braille output. A device that produces raised-dot Braille on paper. Includes devices that produce paperless, refreshable Braille as output from the computer.

Dynamyte. A multipurpose voice output augmentative communication system designed to aid in communication and serve educational, recreational, or vocational purposes. This is a dynamic display device using either pictures or text from which the user can select.

embosser. A machine for Braille output to raise portions of the paper so the reader can feel the text.

ECU (environmental control units). Devices that are usually connected to computers to enable individuals with mobility impairments to control lights, thermostat, television, radio, and various other appliances.

finger mouse. Finger mice are similar to trackballs, except a single finger can control the cursor.

firmware. Software that is stored in permanent memory rather than on disks.

head stick/head pointer. A simple stick or advanced electronic system that attaches to a person's head. It allows the person to activate keyboards or make selections from the computer screen.

input. The process of giving information or instructions to a computer.

joystick. A manual control lever that can be used as a mouse alternative, or to access devices for greater independence (e.g., environmental control units, power wheel chairs).

keyboard. The part of a computer that looks and acts like a typewriter.

keyboard-enhancement programs. Input devices for people who have difficulty using standard keyboards.

large-print display. Enlarged letters that are displayed on a computer monitor for individuals with visual impairments.

latching switch. A switch or keyboard adaptation designed with a spring-loaded mechanism to close the circuit with one selection and release the circuit upon a second selection. Can be used with switches for environmental control units (lights) or to permit one-handed typing with the selection of the shift key.

mechanical switch. A switch that requires pressure to close the circuit. These are most frequently used for power wheelchairs, environmental control units and computers.

minikeyboard. A small keyboard (usually 8 x 8 inches) designed to be used by individuals with a small work area.

momentary switch. A pressure-released switch that turns objects on and off.

mouth stick/mouth pointer. A simple stick or advanced electronic system that is controlled by a person's mouth. It allows the person to activate keyboards or make selections from the computer screen.

on-screen keyboard. An alternate keyboard displayed on the computer monitor, which can be accessed by direct selection with a touch screen window, through the use of scanning software, or other input devices.

output device. Devices that produce the results of computer activity. Output devices include computer monitors, printers, Braille devices, and speech synthesizers.

pointing device. An extension device that can be used by persons with limited movement to directly select a switch or keyboard through the use of a body part and an extension. Examples include pointers extending from a person's head, hand, elbow, wrist, chin, mouth. Some are infrared.

proportional switch. A switch mode that allows a slow, smooth acceleration of a powered wheelchair, thus preventing an abrupt lurching motion. The device is gradually activated according to the amount of pressure applied to the switch (similar to a gas peddle).

QWERTY keyboard. Keyboards with the standard setup found in most homes and offices with the letters "Q", "W", "E", "R", "T", and "Y" beginning in the top left corner under the numbers.

refreshable Braille. A device that has space for up to 80 Braille cells and for which the dots in each cell are electronically raised and lowered in different combinations to form all the Braille characters.

scanning. Software that causes a cursor to automatically move at an adjustable speed among selected symbols, boxes, or other "hot spots" on a computer screen. A switch or other alternative input device is then used to make a selection.

sip and puff switch. A switch accessed through a straw. Varying sipping air in or puffing it out allows for directional movement of wheelchairs, or activation of two toys or devices through a single switch.

speech recognition system. Software that allows an individual's voice to be recognized by the computer.

speech synthesis. Artificial speech that is generated by computers. For example, a computer can "read" web pages and produce spoken e-mail output.

speech synthesizer. An output device that enables a computer to speak.

split keyboard. An alternative keyboard that can place half of the keys on either side of the keyboard or in two separate units at different locations for the comfort of the user.

switch. Devices that allow individuals to operate electric or electronic objects. A switch can be operated by hand, foot, puff of air, or a variety of other methods, depending upon the needs of the user and the configuration of the switch.

touch screen. An alternate interface for the computer, in which the screen is touched to activate and manipulate software programs.

trackball. An alternate input device, similar to a mouse, in which the ball is located on the top of a stationary device and manipulated by the person's hand or fingers to move the cursor across the screen.

trackpad "versa pad." An alternate input device usually used with laptop computers, in which a small touch area replaces a mouse to move the cursor and select items on the screen.

universal cuff. An adapted grasp device that a person with limited hand function uses to hold a variety of items to increase independence. This device wraps around the person's hand and has a small pocket on the palm side where the items are placed (e.g., pencil, spoon, crayon, pointer, toothbrush, comb).

voice recognition. Technology that uses a person's voice to access a computer, device, or environmental control unit and make commands to operate software and hardware.

windowing software. Windowing software allows an individual to select a specific part of the screen to expand or "blow up" to fill the entire screen.

word prediction. Software that allows the computer to anticipate the next word choice to reduce the number of keystrokes. Word prediction software can be customized over time to be responsive to each user.

RESOURCES

Alternate Keyboards

Contoured Keyboards
http://www.tifaq.com/keyboards/contoured-keyboards.html

Discover Board by Don Johnston
http://www.donjohnston.com

Fixed-Split Keyboards
http://www.tifaq.com/keyboards.html

Intellikeys by Intellitools
http://www.intellitools.com

Key Largo by Don Johnston
http://www.donjohnston.com

Kinesis keyboards
http://www.kinesis-ergo.com

MAXIM Adjustable Ergonomic Keyboard
http://www.kinesis-ergo.com/max-spec.htm

Microsoft Natural Keyboard
http://www.microsoft.com/products/

TASH Minikeyboard by TASH
http://www.wmich.edu/metl/hardware/tash.html

Unicorn Expanded Keyboard by Don Johnston
http://www.donjohnston.com

Unicorn Minikeyboard by Don Johnston
http://www.donjohnston.com

Joysticks and Trackballs

Alps Glidepoint Track Pad by Alps
http://www3.alps.co.jp/us/

Kensington Turbo Mouse Trackball
http://www.kensington.com/

Logitech
http://www.logitech.com/

Palm Mouse by Fujitsu Takamisawa America Inc.
http://www.fujitsu.takamisawa.com

Penny and Giles Joystick
http://www.pgcontrols.com/

Thumbelina Mini Trackball by Infogrip
http://www.infogrip.com

Switches

Big Red Switch by AbleNet
http://www.ablenetinc.com

Ellipse Switch by Don Johnston
http://www.donjohnston.com

Gloswitch
http://www.orcca.com/Switches.htm

Jelly Bean Switch by Ablenet
http://www.ablenetinc.com

Light Switch by Linda Burkhart
http://lburkhart.com/

Plate Switch by Toys for Special Children
http://specialchildren.miningco.coom

Rocker Switches
http://www.pronic.com.tw

Tilt Switch by Toys for Special Children
http://www.enablingdevices.com

Sip and Puff Switch by Toys for Special Children
http://www.enablingdevices.com

Twitch Switch by Toys for Special Children
http://www.enablingdevices.com

Pointing Devices

HeadMaster by Prentke Romich
http://www.prentrom.com

HeadMouse by Origin Instruments
http://www.orin.com

Vendors

AbleNet
http://www.ablenetinc.com

ACS Technologies
http://acssd.com/

Don Johnston
http://www.donjohnston.com

Enabling Devices
http://www.enablingdevices.com

Infogrip
http://www.infogrip.com

Infra-Link
http://www.minot.com/~ndipat
/products/fact/ecu/tphone.htm

Laureate Learning Systems
http://www.LaureateLearning.com

Toys for Special Children
http://www.enablingdevices.com

Web Sites

American Council of the Blind
http://www.acb.org/

Americans with Disabilities Act
http://www.ppspublishers.com

American Occupational Therapy Association (AOTA)
http://www.aota.org

American Speech-Language-Hearing Association (ASHA)
http://www.asha.org

Assistive Technology On-Line
http://www.asel.udel.edu/

Carroll Center for the Blind Computer Access
http://www.carroll.org

Closing the Gap
http://www.closingthegap.com

Directory of Sources for Input Technologies
http://www.billbuxton.com
InputSources.html

Don Johnston
http://www.donjohnston.com

Equal Access to Software and Information
http://www.rit.edu:80/~easi/

Mayer~Johnson
http://www.mayer~johnson.com

National Braille Press
http://www.nbp.org

National Easter Seals Society
http://www.easterseals.org

National Organization on Disability (NOD)
http://www.nod.org

Technical Aids and Systems for the Handicapped, Inc. (TASH)
http://www.tashinc.com

Trace Research and Development Center on Communication Control and Computer Access
http://www.trace.wisc.edu

University of Illinois—Project PURSUIT
http://www.rehab.uiuc.edu/

University of Waterloo Electronic Library Disability Issues
http://www.lib.uwaterloo.ca/discipline /Disability_Issues/index.htm

Western New York Disabilities Forum
http://freenet.buffalo.edu/~wnydf/

REFERENCES AND RECOMMENDED READING

Alliance for Technology Access. 2000. *Computer and web resources for people with disabilities: A guide to exploring today's assistive technology*, 3d ed. Alameda, CA: Hunter House.

Angelo, J. 1997. *Assistive technology for rehabilitation therapists.* Philadelphia: F. A. Davis.

Flippo, K. F., K. J. Inge, and J. M. Barcus. 1995. *Assistive technology: A resource for school, work, and community.* Baltimore: Paul H. Brookes.

Golden, D. 1998. *Assistive technology in special education policy and practice.* Reston, VA: Council of Administrators of Special Education (CASE) and The Technology and Media (TAM) Division of The Council for Exceptional Children.

Mann, W. C., and J. P. Lane. 1995. *Assistive technology for persons with disabilities*, 2d ed. Bethesda, MD: American Occupational Therapy Association.

INDEX